PAST SOCIETIES

Sidestone Press

PAST SOCIETIES

Human Development in Landscapes

edited by
JOHANNES MÜLLER AND ANDREA RICCI

Published by Sidestone Press, Leiden
www.sidestone.com

Lay-out & cover design: Sidestone Press
Photograph cover: Stone mound (*ovoo*) near Ugii Lake in Central Mongolia
(photo: Birte Ahrens).

Final editing and proof reading: Eileen Küçükkaraca, Kiel
Image editing: Tine Pape, Kiel

ISBN 978-90-8890-924-5 (softcover)
ISBN 978-90-8890-925-2 (hardcover)
ISBN 978-90-8890-926-9 (PDF e-book)

Published with funding of the Deutsche Forschungsgemeinschaft (DFG, German Research Foundation) under Germany's Excellence Initiative GSC 208 – 39071778 and Germany's Excellence Strategy – EXC 2150 ROOTS – 390870439.

Contents

Preface of the editors

Past Societies: Human Development in Landscapes

The understanding of the history of human development is deeply connected with the reconstruction of the interactions between human beings and both the perceived and physical environment where they lived. In order to study the interwoven social, environmental, and cultural phenomena together with processes of past societies, a broad interdisciplinary conceptual approach is necessary, combining the results of the natural and life sciences with studies in the humanities.

Emerging from this premise of human-environmental dynamics, the Graduate School "Human Development in Landscapes" (GSHDL) at Kiel University was initiated by scholars and scientists who recognized the need to apply a truly interdisciplinary approach that combines models of past climatic and environmental conditions with investigations of societal aspects and their reciprocal influence in order to reconstruct human-environmental histories. The GSHDL concept merged research from molecular biology and archaeology, geoinformatics and art history, geophysics and isotope research, ancient languages and palaeoecology, written/oral traditions and palaeoclimate to study and understand this interactive development. The dynamics of human development – and thus of landscape and living space – are captured by a complex interplay of diverse factors (*e.g.* biological traits of social groups, conditions of the natural environment, social constants and their material representations) covered by the joint disciplinary research. This is exemplified by numerous projects in the natural sciences that have and continue to tackle archaeological problems and, at the same time, by cultural and archaeological studies that provide crucial directions for scientific investigations. Moreover, the research initiative GSHDL provided new impulses for innovative graduate training with an emphasis on interdisciplinary research involving both the Arts and Humanities and Natural Sciences.

A workshop retreat in April 2008 officially kicked off the activities of the Graduate School "Human Development in Landscapes" at Kiel University. Over the subsequent 12 years, more than 200 researchers continually explored and reconstructed how human communities reciprocally shaped their surrounding environments, and vice versa.

Research spanned from the Palaeolithic to contemporary issues of human-environmental interaction, and ranged from Northern Europe to Oceania and from Siberia to South America. Thanks to the success of this initiative, the study of socio-environmental-cultural dynamics increasingly became a core research area at Kiel University. Truly integrative interdisciplinary work on these topics concerning the past has since become a 'trademark' of Kiel University. This work has now successfully culminated in the establishment of the Cluster of Excellence ROOTS – Social, Environmental and Cultural Connectivity in Past Societies – in January 2019. ROOTS builds on the experience and the expertise developed over the years in the GSHDL, now bringing together a group of researchers who investigate archaeological and historical 'laboratories' under the basic assumption that humans and environments have deeply shaped each other, creating long-term socio-environmental connectivities, which resulted in a range of changes, challenges, and crises under diverse economic, ecological, and social conditions.

The present book is the second of two edited volumes of the GSHDL initiative. It provides an overview of the research conducted by the GSHDL community over the last 12 years. The first volume appeared in 2018 and covered crucial topics of the overall research agenda of the Graduate School. The second volume builds on that work to present the results of the investigations that doctoral candidates and post-doctoral researchers conducted in the framework of the GSHDL on questions specifically relating to human-environment-social interactions.

Two rounds of generous funding by the DFG in the scheme of the German Excellence Initiative made the long-term sustainability and realisation of the research efforts of the GSHDL possible. The completion of this volume would have not been possible without this DFG support. In addition, we would like to thank Eileen Küçükkaraca for her careful scientific editorial guidance and Tine Pape for her high graphical skills. Their consistent efforts were crucial for the realisation of this volume. This book is dedicated to all members of the vibrant community of the GSHDL in appreciation for their engagement in the creation of a highly stimulating and successful research environment.

Kiel, December 2019
Johannes Müller
Andrea Ricci

Introduction

Concepts of Human Developments in Landscapes for Past Societies

Johannes Müller and Andrea Ricci

Past Societies presents the efforts of alumni researchers of the Kiel Graduate School "Human Development in Landscapes" (GSHDL) to tackle questions regarding socio-environmental interactions in past societies and environments. The sixteen contributions provide a partial synthesis of the multi-faceted theories, concepts and practices on the study of past landscapes, conducted over the last 12 years in the framework of the GSHDL initiative. Different theoretical and practical attempts, methodological approaches, as well as case studies on different regions and periods are illustrated under the common lens of the concept of landscapes. As both products and arenas of human-environmental dynamics, landscapes are the underlying "glue" that is applied to interlink a wide scope of research endeavours on past human-environmental interactions. The contributions of this volume often argue that only interdisciplinary approaches can support similar ventures.

The contributions in this volume are organised following a rough chronological order. **Aikaterini Glykou** investigates the Late Mesolithic-Early Neolithic transition in Northern Europe on the basis of the analysis of pottery and faunal remains originating from Scandinavian and Northern German sites. Her study indicates that this transition was continuous and gradual. Aikaterini, who is currently based at the Archaeological Research Laboratory of Stockholm University, has expanded her research, which now includes stable isotope analysis to explore the impact of environmental change in prehistoric animal and human populations.

The study of pottery is also central in the investigation that **Julia Menne** completed on the megalithic Funnel Beaker culture tombs in Northwestern Germany. In particular, her study unveils the complexity of sociocultural links and communication networks in the Emsland District as emerging from funerary contexts. Active in different projects at Kiel University, Julia is now based at Hamburg University, where she continues her research into the Neolithic of Central Europe with the additional support of archaeometrical analyses.

In her contribution, **Welmoed Out** illustrates innovative phytolith-based methods for the identification of leaves of various cereal crops retrieved in archaeological contexts. The application of these methods can significantly impact studies on the development of prehistoric agricultural societies and their relationships with the environment. Following her post-doctoral work at the GSHDL, Welmoed joined the Moesgaard Museum in Denmark, where she continues to research past plant-people interactions and the Neolithisation process.

The joint contribution by **Hermann Gorbahn** and **Markus Reindel** of the DAI also investigates the transition from foraging to agriculture, here based in the Andean foothills of Southern Peru. Dated to 5800-5000 cal BP, the Preceramic site of Pernil Alto is the main focus of the study. The excavations that were conducted at this site in cooperation with the German Archaeological Institute (DAI) documented one of the earliest villages of the region, providing data to reconstruct the emergence of early complex societies in the Central Andes. Currently, Hermann is a research coordinator of the CRC 1266 "Scales of Transformation" at Kiel University, whereas Markus is a senior researcher at the Americas division of the Commission for the Archaeology of Non-European Cultures (KAAK) of the DAI, from where he has been directing numerous projects to study past landscape and settlements in the Americas.

Ralph Großmann´s investigation focuses on the 3rd millennium BC of Central Europe. His study of grave goods and decoration patterns on vessels unveils that the so-called Corded Ware and Bell Beaker phenomena shared material cultural and symbols as part of dense exchange networks. Since his PhD, Ralph´s research interests have included the study and measurement of social inequalities in past societies.

In his investigation, **Andrea Ricci** illustrates that the longevity of settlement choices along the Euphrates River in modern Syria and Turkey led to the formation of tell sites during the 5th and the 3rd millennia BC. This nucleation on tell phenomenon left a profound signature on the landscape of the region which is still visible nowadays. Andrea is currently one of the two scientific coordinators of the Cluster of Excellence ROOTS, and he has been continuing research on the formation of cultural landscapes in Southwest Asia.

In her paper, **Silvia Balatti** discusses the methodological challenges as well as the significance of writing a history of the "silent" people of the Zagros Mountains of Iran during the 1st millennium BC. In particular, she illustrates how a truly interdisciplinary approach can enrich historical debates in order to reconstruct the life of those communities who left no written documents. Silvia is an Assistant Professor at the Institute of Classical Studies, where she has been expanding her research into the history of the eastern Mediterranean area.

Manuel Fernández-Götz reconstructs the transformations of the communities who lived in the Middle Rhine-Moselle region during the Iron Age and the Early Roman Period. Specifically, his contribution highlights the emergence of different identities and power relations. Manuel is currently reader at Edinburgh University, where he has been continuing his research on the archaeology of identities and conflict archaeology, in particular during the Iron Age in Europe.

In her paper, **Anne Liewert** analyses the impact of the environment on societies as presented in the Hippocratic Corpus and she discusses that this large collection of medical works represents one of the earliest examples of the study of human-environmental interactions. Currently, Anne is head of the Special Collections at the University and State Library of Düsseldorf.

In their study on human-environmental relationships in southern Latium (Italy) between the 4th century BC and the 4th century AD, **Michael Teichmann** and **Hans-Rudolf Bork** emphasise the need for a truly interdisciplinary approach to reconstruct past human adaptation processes and use of the landscape. Since his time at Kiel University, Michael has held numerous positions at various institutions, where he has continued his research on the ancient Roman world. As a founding member of the GSHDL, Hans-Rudolf continues to conduct countless geoarchaeological projects from Europe to Eastern Island.

Magdalena Wieckowska-Lüth and **Dieter Bischop** introduce a highly detailed palynological study of the infilling of a Roman Iron Age well excavated at Bremen-Kirchhuchting. This study enables them to reconstruct the environmental conditions that surrounded this archaeological archive as well as to discuss the potential of methodological advancements by combining analyses of pollen grains with diverse non-pollen polymorphs (NPPs) studies. Magdalena continues to work at Kiel University, where she has been expanding her research into the reconstruction of vegetation and settlement histories. Based at the State Archaeological Office of Bremen, Dieter conducts research on the Roman Iron Age and the Middle Ages for the cities of Bremen and Bremerhaven.

By illustrating the transformation of human-environmental interactions at Döberitzer Heide during the Early Middle Ages, **Donat Wehner** contributes to the theoretical and methodological debate on this topic. After his research work at Kiel University, Donat currently conducts research at the State Office for Heritage Management and Archaeology of Saxony-Anhalt in Halle (Saale).

Philipp Grassel presents a study on late Hanseatic seafaring in the North Sea. By investigating archaeological archives, which are little known and often hard to detect, he assesses the potential of maritime-archaeological investigations for a reconstruction of the history of Hanseatic trade. Philipp is currently conducting maritime and limnic archaeological investigations at the German Maritime Museum, Bremerhaven.

In her study, **Maren Biederbick** identifies and reconstructs power relationships in 16th century Europe by analysing the material presence of devices in complex symbolic scripts as well as in mobile and architectural items. By linking the historical and artistic records, this approach provides new insights on the politics and identity of the period. Currently, Maren is based at the German Medicine History Museum in Ingolstadt, Germany.

Christoph Nübel's contribution discusses First World War warscapes, providing an original perspective on how soldiers experienced these landscapes, both in terms of physical and perceived spaces. Christoph continues to conduct research on contemporary military history at the Center for Military History and Social Sciences of the German Armed Forces.

Artur Ribeiro and **Gustav Wollentz** complete this volume with a discussion on the use and management of heritage in the aftermath of armed conflicts. Artur is currently based at Kiel University, where he is conducting investigations on the impact of climate in the development of prehistoric societies as well as expanding his research interests in archaeological theory. Gustav is currently working as a project leader at the Nordic Centre of Heritage Learning and Creativity, Sweden.

With their diverse research agendas and advanced methodological approaches, the contributions to this alumni volume of the Graduate School "Human Development in Landscapes" provide you with a compact introduction outlining the in-depth perspectives and inputs concerned with the theories, concepts and practices for the study of past landscapes.

Transitions during Neolithisation Processes in Southern Scandinavia

New Insights from Faunal Remains and Pottery from the Site Neustadt LA 156 in Northern Germany

Aikaterini Glykou

Abstract

This paper explores the transition from the Late Mesolithic to the Early Neolithic in Southern Scandinavia and Northern Germany by focusing on two key elements: pottery and faunal remains. A typological and technological comparative analysis of pointed-based pottery and funnel beakers showed that the two pottery inventories belonged to one pottery tradition and that funnel beakers evolved from their pointed-based precursors by development in the manufacture. Spatial analysis of pottery, radiocarbon dating and correspondence analysis support the existence of a short time period when pointed-based pots and funnel beakers were used in parallel. While funnel beakers already become a substantial part of subsistence before 4000 cal BC, it was not until after 3900 cal BC that domesticated animals increased in frequencies and marked the onset of an economic change. Consequently, the transition to the Neolithic was continuous and gradual and was based on the chronology of the Funnel Beaker type 0. A new date for the transition to the Neolithic in Northern Germany, around 3900 cal BC, is proposed.

Introduction

This paper focuses on the Mesolithic-Neolithic transition in Southern Scandinavia and Northern Germany and presents the results of my PhD thesis based on two key aspects

in: Müller, J. and Ricci, A. 2020 (eds.), *Past Societies: Human Development in Landscapes*. Sidestone Press: Leiden, 13-26.

of material culture and economy: pottery and faunal remains. Traditionally, pointed-based pottery in Southern Scandinavia and Northern Germany is assigned to the Late Mesolithic Ertebølle culture, while the funnel beakers and the first presence of domesticated animals, sheep, goat and cattle are assigned to the Neolithic Funnel Beaker culture. While there is general consensus that hunter-gatherers of the Ertebølle culture had contacts and interacted with Neolithic cultures in Central Europe for more than 1000 years as shown by imported objects, such as amphibolite axes (Klassen 2004; Hartz *et al.* 2007), the development and the date of the transition to the Neolithic have been strongly debated (*e.g.* Klassen 2004; Fisher and Kristiansen 2002; Fischer 2002; Koch 1998). Based on radiocarbon dating of charred food deposits from Funnel Beaker pottery and the first appearance of domestic animals, the transition to the Neolithic in Northern Germany is dated to 4100 cal BC and has been described as a stepwise autochthonous development with a shift in the economy from wild animals to domesticated animals and the appearance of Funnel Beaker pottery (Hartz 2004; Hartz and Lübke 2006; Hartz *et al.* 2007).

The current paper aims to clarify the question if pointed-based and earliest Funnel Beaker pottery represent different ceramic traditions and to clarify when the presence of domesticated animals can be linked with an economic change.

Material and Methods

The study material of the completed PhD thesis originates from the submerged site of Neustadt, situated in the Bay of Lübeck on the German Baltic coast (Fig. 1).

The site was excavated in 2000-2006 by S. Hartz, Archäologisches Landesamt Schleswig-Holstein (Hartz 2004). During the excavations, thousands of pottery sherds, faunal remains, plant and macro fossil remains as well as flint artefacts were recovered. For the aims of the study, two categories of material were analysed by the author: pottery and faunal remains (except fish). The combination of both of these materials was expected to improve our understanding regarding the development and transformation of human subsistence strategies in Southern Scandinavia during the transition to agriculture. At present, the site lies 3 to 5 m below sea level due to a sea level rise over the last seven millennia. The excavated area is a coastal dump of cultural debris, where finds were deposited in a 0.20-0.50 m deep mud layer beneath a thick sand layer with excellent preservation conditions (Glykou *et al.* 2014; Hartz 2004). A stratigraphic division into different chronological phases was not possible. Therefore, all materials were evaluated as one entire unit.

Pottery analysis

The pottery was registered in the NoNeK registration system (Nordmitteleuropäische Neolithische Keramik; Mischka 2011). Statistical analyses were performed by using the statistical programme SPSS (Statistical Package for the Social Sciences). For the correspondence analysis, the programme WinBASP (Bonn Archaeological Software Package) was used. The ArcMap 9.x (Fa. ESRI) GIS-Software was used for the spatial analyses of pottery.

Figure 1. Map of the location of the site Neustadt and selected contemporaneous sites of the Late Ertebølle culture in Northern Germany and Denmark (map: Glykou 2016).

Faunal analysis

The identification of mammal bone fragments and the determination of species were carried out at the Archaeological State Museum Schloss-Gottorf in Northern Germany by using the vertebrate reference collection of the Archaeological-Zoological Working Group (AZA).

The quantification of frequencies was based on NISP (Number of Identified Specimens) and MNI (Minimal Number of Individuals) (Glykou 2016, 73; Binford 1981; Lyman 2008). Age estimation at the time of death was obtained by using epiphyseal fusion data (for specices-related literature see Glykou 2016). Cut marks, tooth marks, intentional breakages and other modifications were registered and quantified. The position and variety of butchering and cutting marks were recorded on drawings and quantified. This helps to identify and qualify killing and butchering patterns and thus to evaluate and differentiate processing patterns (skinning, filleting and scraping, dismembering; Binford 1981; Lyman 1987; 1992; Trolle-Lassen 1992).

Complementary analyses

The project was complemented by a series of up-to-date scientific methods and analyses, which gave the investigation a multidisciplinary character. Lipid-residue analysis of charred food crusts and pottery matrix from Ertebølle pointed-based and Funnel Beaker pottery were carried out within the project 'Pottery Use among late Foragers and early Farmers in the Baltic' (Craig *et al.* 2011; Heron *et al.* 2013). Pollen analysis of sediments was implemented in two sediment cores (Hartz *et al.* 2011; Glykou 2016, 45ff.) and macro fossil analysis was conducted on one sediment core (Rickert 2007). aDNA was extracted from aurochs/cattle bones to answer questions about the presence of domesticated cattle in Neustadt (Scheu and Burger 2008).

Results

Chronology of the site and spatial analysis of pottery

The coastal site of Neustadt was used for over 600 years according to a series of ^{14}C dates without reservoir effect falling between ca. 4400 and 3800 cal BC (Glykou 2016). This corresponds to the transition from the Late Mesolithic to the Early Neolithic. The spatial analysis of 270 pottery sherds, belonging to 84 pots, showed that the majority of the pottery sherds were found as concentrated deposits, while some others were located within small distances. This is in accordance with the results from the analysis of macrobotanical remains (Glykou 2016, 47) and pollen (Hartz *et al.* 2011), which showed that sedimentation was not disturbed and the area underwent several periods of alternating drought and flood due to successive changes in sea levels. This resulted in restricted soil accumulation. Additionally, the area served partly as a refuse zone (shallow water zone) and partly as an activity zone (on shore zone), *e.g.*, for the setting up of fishing nets, processing hunted prey, flint knapping, *etc.* Human activity might have also contributed to a further compression of the already thin cultural layers.

Faunal remains

The faunal remains consist of 12,693 bones of which 3874 bone fragments from mammals, birds and amphibians have been identified to a species level. These bones derive from 26 species of wild mammals (Tab. 1), 37% of which belong to marine mammals, mainly seals (Glykou 2016; 2014).

Domesticated animals are represented by three species: cattle is represented by 11 bones (0.3%), and sheep/goat by 12 bones (0.3%). An evaluation of diverse modifications observed on the bones, such as butchering, cutting and filleting marks, or lesions caused by hunting weapons, showed that the majority of the bones derived from animals hunted and processed by humans within proximity of the site (Glykou 2016, 347-351; 2013).

According to aDNA analysis data, three bones carried mitochondrial DNA of domesticated cattle from the Near East (Glykou 2016, 57-58; Scheu 2018; Bollongino

SPECIES	NISP	% NISP	MNI	% MNI
Hedgehog *Erinaceus europaeus*	20	0.5	3	2.3
Fox *Vulpes vulpes*	6	0.2	1	0.8
Dog *Canis lupus f. familiaris*	234	6.0	5	3.8
Wolf *Canis lupus*	7	0.2	1	0.8
Wolf/dog *Canis lupus/Canis lupus* f. familiaris	3	0.1	1	0.8
Wildcat *Felis silvestris*	12	0.3	2	1.5
Lynx *Felis lynx*	3	0.1	1	0.8
Biber *Castor fiber*	24	0.6	5	3.8
Otter *Lutra lutra*	68	1.8	3	2.3
Pine marten *Martes martes*	19	0.5	4	3.1
Badger *Meles meles*	7	0.2	1	0.8
Polecat *Mustela putorius*	3	0.1	1	0.8
Roe deer *Capreolus capreolus*	242	6.2	9	6.9
Red deer *Cervus elaphus*	798	20.6	13	9.9
Elk *Alces alces*	54	1.4	3	2.3
Wild boar *Sus scrofa*	521	13.4	14	10.7
Auerochs/Cattle *Bos sp.*	182	4.7	3	2.3
Aurochs *Bos primigenius*	176	4.5	13	9.9
Wild horse *Equus ferus*	1	0.0	1	0.8
Brown bear *Ursus arctos*	1	0.0	1	0.8
Seals Phocidae (indet.)	913	23.6		
Harp seal *Phoca groenlandica*	243	6.3	18	13.7
Grey seal *Halichoerus gryphus*	116	3.0	7	5.3
Ringed seal *Phoca hispida*	20	0.5	2	1.5
Common dolphin *Delfinus delfis*	3	0.1	1	0.8
Harbour porpoise *Phocoena phocoena*	137	3.5	6	4.6
Bank vole *Clethrionomys glareolus*	3	0.1	1	0.8
Yellow-necked mouse *Apodemus flavicolis*	1	0.0	1	0.8
Water vole *Arvicola terrestris*	33	0.9	6	4.6
Field vole *Microtus agrestis*	1	0.0	1	0.8
Sheep/goat *Ovis/Capra*	12	0.3	2	1.5
Cattle *Bos primigenius f. taurus*	11	0.3	1	0.8
Total	3874		131	

Table 1. Identified species (mammals) in the faunal assemblage of Neustadt. Absolute and relative frequencies in terms of NISP and MNI (Glykou 2016).

Sample	Age BP	cal BC 1 sigma	cal BC 2 sigma	Site	Specimens	Species	DNA
KIA-30590	5235±31	4226-3968	4051-3981	Neustadt LA 156	*Humerus*	cattle	Scheu and Burger 2008 in Glykou 2016
KIA-28210	5231±25	4222-3971	4044-3990	Rosenhof LA 58	*Scapula*	cattle	Scheu *et al.* 2008
KIA-39767	5055±28	3952-3787	3942-3798	Neustadt LA 156	*Talus*	cattle	Scheu and Burger 2008 in Glykou 2016
KIA-29092	5010±34	3943-3705	3912-3713	Neustadt LA 156	*Metatarsus*	cattle	Scheu and Burger 2008 in Glykou 2016

Table 2. Radiocarbon dates of cattle bones from Neustadt and Rosenhof. KIA-30590 and KIA-28210 represent the oldest evidence of cattle within the context of the Ertebølle culture also verified by aDNA analysis (modified, Glykou 2016, 58).

et al. 2006; Edwards *et al.* 2004). All three cattle bones were radiocarbon dated, one before 4000 cal BC (KIA-30590) – the oldest dated domesticated cattle within an Ertebølle context so far – and two after 3900 cal BC (KIA-29092, KIA-397679; Tab. 2).

Pottery

From 7509 pottery sherds and fragments, 3646 meet the criteria for a characterisation as pottery sherds (Glykou 2016, 65). The pottery assemblage consists of pointed-based pots (66.7%), lamps (1.7%), three different types of funnel beakers (type 0, I and II after Koch 1998), and flasks and lugged jars (altogether 5.3%). Part of the material remained unclassified (Glykou 2016, 79, table 77). Regarding manufacturing, two steps are worth mentioning: tempering and forming. Both pointed-based pots and funnel beakers are tempered by using the same raw materials – but in different proportions. The pointed-based pottery was primarily tempered with coarse crashed granite with red feldspar, while funnel beakers were tempered with rounded sand grains combined in most cases with crashed granite with red feldspar (Glykou 2016, 163-165). Moreover, both were manufactured using the coiling technique (Glykou 2010, 2011, 2012). The H-, U- and N-techniques were used for the pointed-based pots, while the funnel beakers were made exclusively with the N-technique.

Discussion

The significance of domesticated animals, cattle, sheep and goat for the Neolithisation process of the region can be addressed by distinguishing between two questions: when did domesticated animals first appear in Southern Scandinavia and when can their presence be linked to an established productive economy?

The first appearance of cattle in Southern Scandinavia has long been debated (*e.g.* Price and Noe-Nygaard 2009a, 560, fig. 28.1; 2009b). The main reason is the difficulty to morphologically distinguish between male cattle and female aurochs because of a pronounced sexual dimorphism between the indigenous male and female Central European aurochs (Fig. 2; Rowley-Conwy 1995, 116ff.; 2003, 101ff.).

Thus, based on radiocarbon dated aurochs bones that were wrongly assigned to domesticated cattle, the earliest appearance of domesticated cattle was dated during the first half of the 5th millennium BC within the Ertebølle culture context (*e.g.* in Rosenhof, Ostholstein, cf. Scheu *et al.* 2008). Meanwhile, analysis of mithochondrial

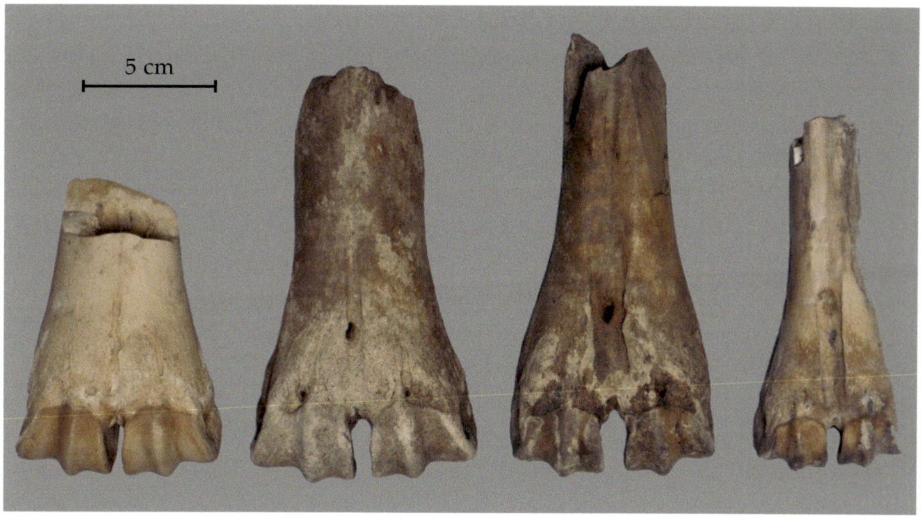

Figure 2. Metapodial bones from aurochs and cattle (first from the right) showing the size difference among the different individuals. The metatarsus from cattle has been radiocarbon dated (KIA-29092) (after Glykou 2016).

DNA from cattle/aurochs bones proved that most of these bones belonged to female aurochs (Scheu *et al.* 2008; Edwards *et al.* 2007; Bollongino *et al.* 2006). A combination of radiocarbon dates and aDNA analysis is therefore crucial for the debate on the earliest appearance of cattle in Southern Scandinavia. Until now, only two cases with a combined use of these analyses have provided evidence for the presence of domesticated cattle before 4000 cal BC – in Rosenhof and Neustadt (Tab. 2; Glykou 2016; Scheu *et al.* 2008, 1262).

Even if the presence of domesticated cattle seems to become more frequent around 4000 cal BC, as other dated bones from Wangels (AAR-4998; Hartz 2004, 64), Åkonge in Åmose (Fischer 1987, 258-259; 1993, 58ff.) and Skumparberget close to Stockholm (Price and Noe-Nygaard 2009b) show, it is not until after 3900 cal BC that the frequencies increase throughout entire Southern Scandinavia and Northern Germany (Price and Noe-Nygaard 2009a, 560, fig. 28.1). Similarly, sheep and goat appear frequently within the context of the Ertebølle culture, but in extremely low numbers before 4000 cal BC (Glykou 2016; Hartz and Lübke 2004).

The question that emerges is whether the scarce but consistent appearance of domesticated animals within the Ertebølle culture context can be linked to a Neolithic economy. Both the relative frequencies and MNI of domesticated animals (Tab. 1) in Neustadt are extremely low and, according to Zvelebil's availability model about the Neolithisation process, a representation of domesticated animals in a percentage lower than 5% (Zvelebil 2008) is not significant for an economic change. Furthermore, the observation that two out of 11 bones were dated after 3900 cal BC corroborates the assumption that domesticated animals did not have an economic significance until 3900 cal BC (Price and Noe-Nygaard 2009a; 2009b). There is evidence for this after 3900 cal BC based on radiocarbon dates and high frequencies of bones from domesticated animals, *e.g.*, from Wangels (Heinrich 2000).

In contrast, Funnel Beaker pottery was already introduced in several different forms before 4000 cal BC, as was shown by the radiocarbon dates and seriation, indicating that the new pottery forms were a substantial part of everyday life. This implies that the new pottery forms, especially during the earliest phase of their appearance, were not necessarily linked to a shift in the economy.

The results of technological and typological analysis support that pointed-based pots and funnel beakers belong to the same pottery tradition. A comparable study of the manufacturing techniques has revealed pronounced technological similarities between the H-, U- and N-techniques. However, the N-technique differs from the other techniques in three aspects: tempering material, thickness and fragmentation. Pots built with the U- and H-techniques very often lack a good junction between the coils, which makes them extremely fragile. In contrast, the N-technique requires that the coils are obliquely set on top of each other, while subsequent smoothing of the surface, which occurs in opposite directions, upwards inside/downwards outside, provides better junction between the coils and produces thin-walled vessels. Consequently, the N-technique facilitates the construction of considerably less fragile pots between the coils as opposed to the U- and H-techniques. Furthermore, the combined use of sand and crushed granite as tempering material for the funnel beakers, which are exclusively formed in N-technique, optimises their function as cooking pots by reducing porosity and increasing resistance to thermal shock during cooking. Thus, the use of the N-technique and a change in the proportions of tempering material show an optimisation of the manufacturing process. Due to the fact that the N-technique had already been used for the manufacturing of a small amount of pointed-based pottery and it is the only common technique between pointed-based pots and funnel beakers (see also Hulthén 1977, 34), it can be regarded as a technological improvement in the process of production generated by the H- and U-techniques. Thus, all manufacturing techniques can be seen as part of the same ceramic tradition. Radiocarbon dating of different coiling techniques derived from charcoal in the ceramic matrix showed that while the U- and H- techniques predate the N-technique, all three techniques were used in parallel from approximately 4200-4000 cal BC as was also confirmed by the correspondence analysis (Glykou 2016, 157, tab. 10).

In addition to these technological aspects, the presence of the Funnel Beaker type 0 in Neustadt (Glykou 2016, 142) enhances the notion of an autochthonous development of Funnel Beaker pottery. This form is considered as an intermediate step between the pointed-based pots and funnel beakers, as it combines the S-shaped profile of the former and the rounded bottom and manufacturing technique of the latter (Koch 1998, 172; Koch Nielsen 1987). This form has always been found in association with pointed-based pots in Jutland (Andersen 2008; 71; 1991, fig. 21.2; 1993, fig. 32; Koch 1998, 83, fig. 53), Zealand (Koch 1998, 311; Fischer 1993, 63) and Scania (Jennbert 1994, 38ff.; Klassen and Jonsson 1999, 23, 26). The Funnel Beaker type 0 dates between 4000-3800 cal BC according to radiocarbon dates from Norsminde, Bjørnsholm, Åkonge and Neustadt (KIA-39768, Glykou 2016, 56, 204; Andersen 2008; Koch 1998, 81-86) and the presence of this type has been assigned to a short transitional phase (Koch 1998, 172). While this coexistence has been previously interpreted as a result of disturbed stratigraphy, re-evaluation of the stratigraphy of three kitchen middens in Norsminde, Bjørnsholm and Krabbesholm clarified the continuous occupation of the sites from the Late Mesolithic to the Early Neolithic. Furthermore, it verified the existence of a thin culture layer dated between 4000-3800 cal BC in which culture elements from both cultures were found (Andersen 2008). This is supported by the current results on the spatial analysis of pottery, radiocarbon dating and correspondence analysis, which provided evidence that pointed-based pots and funnel beakers co-existed for a short time period. This notion of a gradual transition from the terminal Mesolithic to the Neolithic is supported by other aspects of material culture, *e.g.*, unchanged flint industry remains (Hartz *et al.* 2007). Furthermore, a continuation of the Mesolithic economy has been observed in all transitional sites, where wild resources continued to be exploited together with the newly introduced domesticated animals, while there is no observed change during the earliest Neolithic in the use of plant species (Saul *et al.* 2012; 2013; Schmölcke 2004). Lipid residue analysis data of pottery from such transitional sites showed a continuation of the Mesolithic cooking tradition (Craig *et al.* 2011; Saul *et al.* 2014). The present study supports the idea of a rather gradual transition, where new cultural elements are incorporated into the Late Mesolithic cultural environment. The main element is the transfer of new knowledge as shown in the example of pottery technology. Thus, the transition to the Neolithic in this region can be regarded as a transformation of already existing traditions.

Conclusions

Based on typological and technological comparative analysis (Glykou 2016, 357-358), the study presented here provided strong evidence that the Late Mesolithic Ertebølle pointed-based pots and the earliest funnel beakers of the Early Neolithic Funnel Beaker culture belonged to the same tradition. It seems that funnel beakers evolved from their pointed-based precursors by development/improvement in manufacturing techniques, while the differentiation in forms was due to external influences. The spatial analysis of pottery together with radiocarbon dating and seriation showed that both pointed-based pots and funnel beakers were used in parallel for a short time period between approximately 4100-4000 cal BC. After 4000 cal BC, the pointed-based pots disappear and the archaeological assemblage consists exclusively of funnel beakers. While Funnel Beaker pottery gradually becomes a substantial part of the subsistence before 4000 cal BC, domesticated cattle, sheep and goat start to appear on a regular basis both in terms of relative frequencies and number of individuals, and can thus first be seen as a substantial part of the Neolithic economy after 3900 cal BC in Neustadt and other contemporaneous sites in Southern Scandinavia. Based on this and the chronology of the Funnel Beaker type 0, a new date for the transition to the Neolithic in Northern Germany, namely 3900 cal BC, is proposed.

Acknowledgments

I would like to thank the Graduate School "Human Development in Landscapes" for financing my PhD thesis and all the complementary scientific analysis that was carried out within my thesis, and also for the great opportunities I had to obtain insights into other disciplines and to interact within a multi-cultural and multi-scientific environment. Especially, I would like to thank my supervisors Professor Johannes Müller,

Institute of Prehistoric and Protohistoric Archaeology, and Professor emeritus Dirk Heinrich, Zoological Institute, both Kiel University, for intellectual stimulation and fruitful discussions during the years of my PhD. My special gratitude goes to Sönke Hartz who offered me invaluable advice, stimulating discussions and help throughout the PhD and for providing me with the uncalibrated radiocarbon date of the cattle from Rosenhof. I would like to thank Vasiliki Papakosta for revising the English and for commenting on this paper. I would also like to thank Helge Erlenkeuser for his valuable comments on this paper which helped me to improve it.

References

Andersen, S.H. 1991. Norsminde. A "Køkkenmøding" with Late Mesolithic and Early Neolithic Occupation. *Journal of Danish Archaeology* 8, 13-40.

Andersen S.H. 1993. Bjørnsholm. A stratified Køkkenmøding on the Central Limfjord, North Jutland. *Journal of Danish Archaeology* 10, 59-96.

Andersen, S.H. 2008. The Mesolithic-Neolithic transition in Western Denmark seen from a kitchen midden perspective. A survey, in: Fokkens, H., Coles, B., van Gijn, A., Kleijne, J., Slappendel, C.G. (eds.), *Between Foraging and Farming: an Extended Broad Spectrum of Papers Presented to Leendert Louwe Kooijmans*. Analecta Praehistorica Leidensia 40. Leiden: Leiden University, 67-74.

Binford, L.R. 1981. *Bones: Ancient Men and Modern Myths*. Academic Press Studies in Archaeology 5. New York: Academic Press.

Bollongino, R., Edwards, C.J., Burger, J., Alt, K.W., Bradley, D.G. 2006. Early history of European domestic cattle as revealed by ancient DNA. *Biology Letters* 2, 155-159.

Craig, O.E., Steele, V.J., Fischer, A., Hartz, S., Koch, E., Glykou, A., Andersen, S.H., Saul, H., Donohoe, P., Jones, D.M., Heron, C.P. 2011. Ancient lipids reveal continuity in culinary practices across the transition to agriculture in Northern Europe. *Proceedings of the National Academy of Sciences (PNAS)* 108/44, 17910-17915. doi:10.1073/pnas.1107202108.

Edwards, C.J., Bollongino, R., Scheu, A., Chamberlain, A., Tresset, A., Vigne, J.-D., Baird, J.F., Larson, G., Ho, S.Y.W., Heupink, T.H., Shapiro, B., Freeman, A.R., Thomas, M.G., Arbogast, R.M., Arndt, B., Bartosiewicz, L., Benecke, N., Budja, M., Chaix, L., Choyke, A.M., Coqueugniot, E., Döhle, H.-J., Göldner, H., Hartz, S., Helmer, D., Herzig, B., Hongo, H., Mashkour, M., Özdogan, M., Pucher, E., Roth, G., Schade-Lindig, S., Schmölcke, U., Schulting, R.J., Stephan, E., Uerpmann, H.-P., Vörös, I., Voytek, B., Bradley, D.G., Burger, J. 2007. Mitochondrial DNA analysis shows a Near Eastern Neolithic origin for domestic cattle and no indication of domestication of European aurochs. *Proceedings B of the Royal Society* 274/1616, 1377-1385. http://dx.doi.org/10.1098/rspb.2007.0020 or via http://www.journals.royalsoc.ac.uk.

Fischer, A. 1987. Recent Excavations and Discoveries, Kongemose A and L. *Journal of Danish Archaeology* 5, 258-259.

Fischer, A. 1993. Mesolithic inland settlement, in: Hvass, S. and Storgaard, B. (eds.), *Digging into the Past. 25 Years of Archaeology in Denmark*. Aarhus: Aarhus Univ.-Forl., 58-63.

Fischer, A. 2002. Food for Feasting? An evaluation of explanations of the neolithisation of Denmark and southern Sweden, in: Fischer, A. and Kristiansen, K. (eds.), *The Neolithisation of Denmark – 150 Years of Debate*. Sheffield: Collis, 341-393.

Fischer, A. and Kristiansen, K. 2002 (eds.), *The Neolithisation of Denmark – 150 Years of Debate*. Sheffield: Collis.

Glykou, A. 2010. Technological and typological analysis of Ertebølle and early Funnel Beaker pottery from Neustadt LA 156 and contemporary sites in northern Germany, in: Vanmontfort, B., Louwe Koojimans, L., Amkreutz, L., Verhart, L. (eds.), *Pots, Farmers and Foragers: Pottery traditions and social interaction in the earliest Neolithic of the lower Rhine Area*. Archaeological Studies Leiden University 20. Amsterdam: Leiden University Press, 177-188.

Glykou, A. 2011. Neustadt LA 156: A submarine site from the Late Mesolithic-Ertebølle and earliest Neolithic-Funnel Beaker in Northern Germany – first results of the typological and technological analysis of the ceramics. *Bericht der Römisch-Germanischen Kommission* 89, 277-286.

Glykou, A. 2012. Pointed-based pottery: An experimental approach to the manufacturing of the pottery of the late Mesolithic in Northern Germany. *The Old Potter's Almanac* 17/1, 10-15.

Glykou, A. 2013. Seal hunting at the Baltic Sea coast – a case study from the Late Mesolithic and earliest Neolithic Neustadt in Holstein, Germany, in: Grimm, O. and Schmölcke, U. (eds.), *Hunting in Northern Europe until 1500 AD – Old Traditions and Regional Developments, Continental Sources and Continental Influences*. Schriften des Archäologischen Landesmuseums 7. Neumünster: Wachholtz, 101-111.

Glykou, A. 2014. Late Mesolithic-Early Neolithic Sealers: a case study on the exploitation of marine resources during the Mesolithic-Neolithic transition in the southwestern Baltic Sea. *Internet Archaeology* 37, University of York. http://dx.doi.org/10.11141/ia.37.7.

Glykou, A. 2016. *Neustadt LA 156. Ein submariner Fundplatz des späten Mesolithikums und frühesten Neolithikums in Schleswig-Holstein. Untersuchungen zur Subsistenzstrategie der letzten Jäger, Sammler und Fischer an der norddeutschen Ostseeküste*. Untersuchungen und Materialien zur Steinzeit in Schleswig-Holstein 7. Kiel/Hamburg: Wachholtz.

Glykou, A., Goldhammer, J., Hartz, S. 2014. Versunkene Steinzeit – Taucharchäologische Untersuchungen an der schleswig-holsteinischen Ostseeküste, in: Huber, S. and Kleingärtner, S. (eds.), *Gestrandet, Versenkt, Versunken – Faszination Unterwasserarchäologie*. Neumünster/Hamburg: Wachholtz, 76-97.

Hartz, S. 2004. Aktuelle Forschungen zur Chronologie und Siedlungsweise der Ertebølle- und frühesten Trichterbecherkultur in Schleswig-Holstein. *Bodendenkmalpflege in Mecklenburg-Vorpommern* 52, 61-81.

Hartz, S. and Lübke, H. 2004. Zur chronostratigraphischen Gliederung der Ertebølle-Kultur und frühesten Trichterbecherkultur in der südlichen Mecklenburger Bucht. *Bodendenkmalpflege in Mecklenburg-Vorpommern* 52, 119-142.

Hartz, S. and Lübke, H. 2006. New Evidence for a Chronostratigrafic Division of the Ertebølle Culture and the Earliest Funnel Beaker Culture on the Southern Mecklenburg Bay, in: Kind, C.-J. (ed.), *After the Ice Age – Settlements, subsist-*

ence and social development in the Mesolithic of Central Europe. Proceedings of the International Conference, 9th-12th September 2003, Rottenburg/Neckar, Baden-Württemberg, Germany. Stuttgart: Theiss, 59-74.

Hartz, S., Lübke, H., Terberger, T. 2007. From fish and seal to sheep and cattle: new research into the process of neolithisation in northern Germany, in: Whittle, A. and Cummings, V. (eds.), *Going Over: The Mesolithic-Neolithic Transition in North-West Europe*. Proceedings of the British Academy 144. Oxford: Oxford University Press, 567-594.

Hartz, S., Kalis, A.J., Klassen, L., Meurers-Balke, J. 2011. Neue Ausgrabungen zur Ertebøllekultur in Ostholstein und der Fund von vier stratifizierten durchlochten donauländischen Äxten, in: Meurers-Balke, J. and Schön, W. (eds.), *Liber Amicorum: Vergangene Zeiten. Gedenkschrift für Jürgen Hoika*. Archäologische Berichte 22. Deutsche Gesellschaft für Ur- und Frühgeschichte. Bonn: Habelt, 25-61.

Heinrich, D. 1977/98. Die Tierknochen des frühneolithischen Wohnplatzes Wangels LA 505. Ein Vorbericht. *Offa* 54/55, 43-48.

Heron, C., Andersen, S., Fischer, A., Glykou, A., Hartz, S., Saul, H., Steele, V., Craig, O. 2013. Illuminating the Late Mesolithic: residue analysis of 'blubber' lamps from Northern Europe. *Antiquity* 87, 178-188.

Hulthén, B. 1977. *On Ceramic Technology During the Scanian Neolithic and Bronze Age*. Theses and Papers in North-European Archaeology 6. Stockholm: Akademilitteratur.

Jennbert, K. 1994. Getreide als Geschenk. Ertebøllekultur und frühneolithische Trichterbecherkultur, in: Hoika, J. and Meurers-Balke, J. (eds.), *Beiträge zur frühneolithischen Trichterbecherkultur im westlichen Ostseegebiet*. 1. Internationales Trichterbechersymposium in Schleswig, 4-7 März 1985. Untersuchungen und Materialien in Schleswig-Holstein 1. Neumünster: Wachholtz, 155-164.

Klassen, L. 2004. *Jade und Kupfer. Untersuchungen zum Neolithisierungsprozess im westlichen Ostseeraum unter besonderer Berücksichtigung der Kulturentwicklung Europas 5500-3500 BC*. Jutland Archaeological Society Publications, Moesgård Museum 47. Aarhus: Aarhus University Press.

Klassen, L. and Jonsson, E. 1999. A Unique Shafthole Axe from Recent Excavations in the Järavallen Beach Ridge. *Lund Archaeological Review*, 21-39.

Koch, E. 1998. *Neolithic bog pots from Zealand, Møn, Lolland and Falster*. Nordiske Fortidsminder B16. Copenhagen: Det Kongelige Nordiske Oldskriftselskab.

Koch Nielsen, E. 1987. Ertebølle and Funnel Beaker Pots as Tools. On Traces of Production Techniques and Use. *Acta Archaeologica* 57, 107-120.

Lyman, R.L. 1987. Archaeofaunas and Butchery Studies: A Taphonomic Perspective. *Advances in Archaeological Method and Theory* 10, 249-337.

Lyman, R.L. 1992. Prehistoric Seal and Sea-Lion Butchering on the Southern Northwest Coast. *American Antiquity* 57/2, 246-261.

Lyman, R.L. 2008. *Quantitative paleozoology*. Cambridge: Cambridge University Press. http://dx.doi.org/10.1017/CBO9780511813863.

Mischka, D. 2011. NoNeK – Ein Aufnahmesystem für Steinzeitliche Keramik Nordmitteleuropas. *Bericht der Römisch-Germanischen Kommission* 89, 47-58.

Price, T.D. and Noe-Nygaard, N. 2009a. Domestic Cattle and the Early Neolithic in Southern Scandinavia, in: Crombe, P., Van Strydonck, M., Sergant, J., Boudin, M., Bats, M. (eds.), *Chronology and Evolution of Mesolithic Northwest Europe*. Newcastle upon Tyne: Cambridge Scholars, 557-571.

Price, T.D. and Noe-Nygaard, N. 2009b. Early Domestic Cattle in Southern Scandinavia, in: Finlay, N. (ed.), *From Bann Flakes to Bushmills: Papers in Honour of Prof. Peter Woodman*. Oxford: Oxbow Books, 198-210.

Rickert, B.-H. 2007. *Ergebnisse botanischer Makrorestanalysen an Proben des Fundplatzes Neustadt LA 156*. Unpublished report.

Rowley-Conwy, P. 1995. Wild or Domestic? On the evidence for the Earliest Domestic Cattle and Pigs in South Scandinavia and Iberia. *International Journal of Osteoarchaeology* 5, 115-126.

Rowley-Conwy, P. 2003. Early Domestic Animals in Europe: Imported or Locally domesticated?, in: Ammerman, A. and Biagi, P. (eds.), *The Widening Harvest: The Neolithic Transition in Europe: Looking Back, Looking Forward.* Boston, Massachusetts: Archaeological Institute of America, 99-117.

Saul, H., Wilson, J., Heron, C.P., Glykou, A., Hartz, S., Craig, O.E. 2012. A Systematic Approach to the Recovery and Identification of Starches from Carbonised Deposits on Ceramic Vessels. *Journal of Archaeological Science* 12/39, 3483-3492.

Saul, H., Madella, M., Fisher, A., Glykou, A., Hartz, S., Craig, O.E. 2013. Phytoliths in Pottery Reveal the Use of Spice in European Prehistoric Cuisine. *PLoS ONE* 8/8: e70583. doi:10.1371/ journal.pone.0070583.

Saul, H., Glykou, A., Craig, O. 2014. Stewing on a Theme of Cuisine. Biomolecular and Interpretive Approaches to Culinary Changes at the Transition to Agriculture, in: Whittle, A. and Bickle, P. (eds.), *Early Farmers. The View from Archaeology and Science.* Proceedings of the British Academy 198. Oxford: Oxford University Press, 197-213.

Scheu, A. 2018. Neolithic animal domestication as seen from ancient DNA. *Quaternary International* 496, 102-107. https://doi.org/10.1016/j.quaint.2017.02.009.

Scheu, A. and Burger, J. 2008. *aDNA-Analyse von fünf bovinen Überresten des Siedlungsplatzes Neustadt LA 156 (Lkr. Ostholstein).* Unpublished report.

Scheu, A., Hartz, S., Schmölcke, U., Tresset, A., Burger, J., Bollongino, R. 2008. Ancient DNA provides no evidence for independent domestication of cattle in Mesolithic Rosenhof, Northern Germany. *Journal of Archaeological Science* 35, 1257-1264.

Schmölcke, U. 2004. Neue archäozoologische Untersuchungen zur Mecklenburger Bucht und zum Jasmunder Boden. *Bodendenkmalpflege in Mecklenburg-Vorpommern* 52, 145-153.

Trolle-Lassen, T. 1992. Butchering of Red Deer (Cervus elaphus L.) – A Case Study from the Late Mesolithic Settlement of Tybrind Vig, Denmark. *Journal of Danish Archaeology* 9, 7-37.

Zvelebil, M. 2008. Innovating Hunter-Gatherers: The Mesolithic in the Baltic, in: Bailey, G. and Spikins, P. (eds.), *Mesolithic Europe*. Cambridge: Cambridge University Press, 18-59.

Author address

Aikaterini Glykou
Archaeological Research Laboratory
Department of Archaeology and Classical Studies
Stockholm University
SE-10691 Stockholm, Sweden
aikaterini.glykou@arklab.su.se

About the author

Aikaterini Glykou studied archaeology in Athens, Greece and after participating in several excavations in Greece, she continued with her PhD studies at Kiel University. During her PhD, she specialised in Stone Age archaeology and zooarchaeology. Since 2013, she has been employed as a researcher at the Archaeological Research Laboratory, Stockholm University, where she applies stable isotope analysis to explore the impact of environmental change in prehistoric animal and human populations by reconstructing palaeodiet and mobility patterns.

Interaction and Networks in the Neolithic Funnel Beaker Culture

Julia Menne

Abstract

The study presented here deals with the ceramic grave goods recovered from a selection of megalithic tombs associated with the Funnel Beaker culture (more precisely with the TRB West Group) in Northwestern Germany. The main focus of this particular study was on the sociocultural and economic links between the individual funerary communities as represented by stylistic changes in terms of the diversity of the deposited vessels. Based on its high density of megalithic tombs, the Emsland District, which is one of the regional groups within the TRB West Group, was chosen as the study area. The small groups throughout the region were examined for potential connections between the individual burial sites. As part of this study, it has been possible for the first time to obtain proof of the existence of a dense system of communication networks within the TRB West Group in this region.

Introduction

The following study, based on a high density of megalithic tombs, deals with the ceramic grave goods recovered from several megalithic tombs associated with the Funnel Beaker culture (TRB West Group) in Northwestern Germany. Today, more than 60 of over 130 known monuments are preserved (Sprockhoff 1975) (Fig. 1).

These sites have been known for a long time. Since the beginning of the 20th century, scientific interest increased and first compilations of these megalithic sites were published. This led to excavations and several publications of the sites between the 1950s and the 1970s. These investigations dealt with first data collections and arrangements of finds. As a consequence, after an interruption of the investigation of megalithic graves for decades, the aim of the presented study was a revision of the old excavation material. In particular, the ceramic assemblages, including technical and material analyses, were investigated extensively by statistic and geochemical methods. These focus

in: Müller, J. and Ricci, A. 2020 (eds.), *Past Societies: Human Development in Landscapes*.
Sidestone Press: Leiden, 27-36.

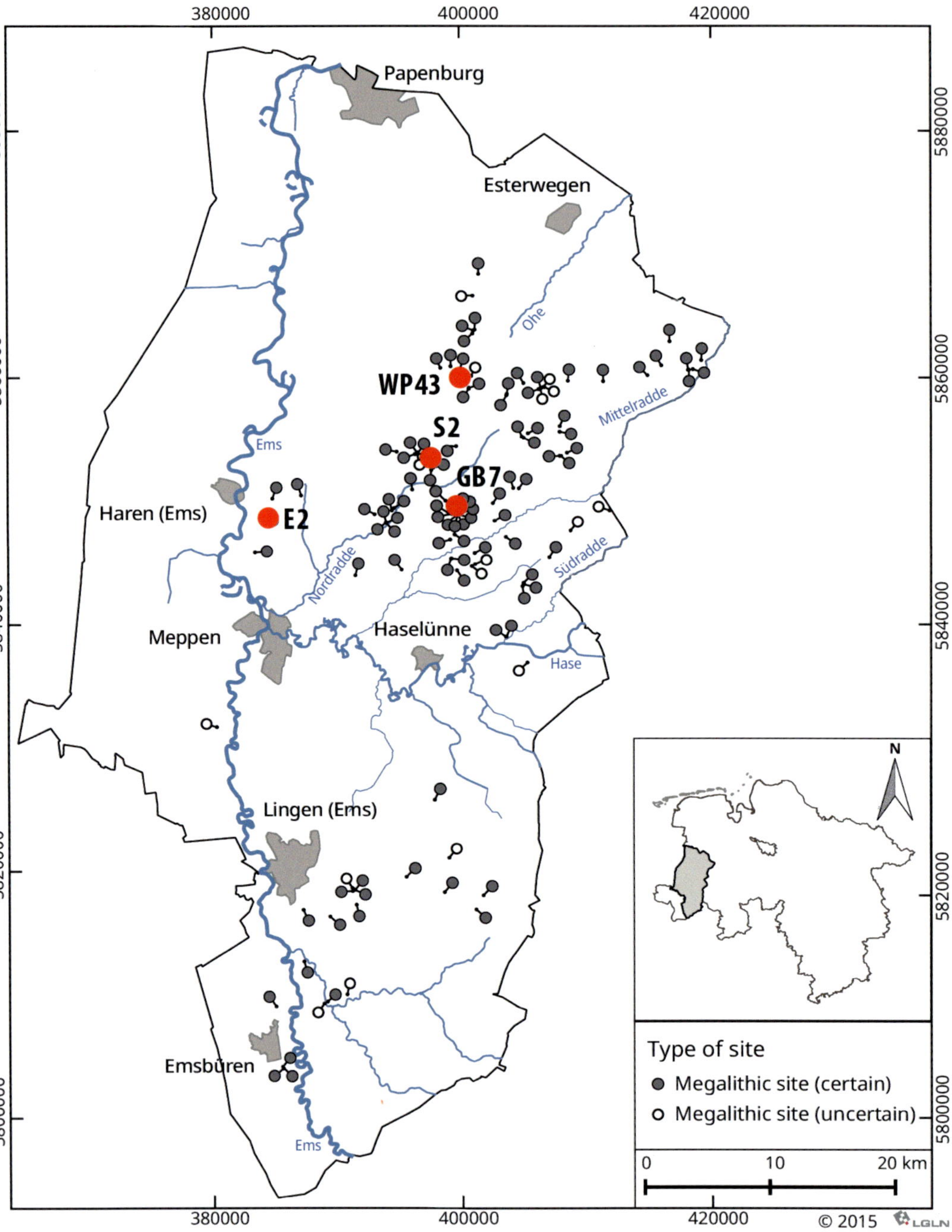

Figure 1. Distribution map of megalithic sites in the area of research (Emsland District, Lower Saxony) (map: J. Menne).

on interdisciplinary approaches for the study of past human-environmental dynamics in the research area (*e.g.* Lorenz 2018).

The main emphasis of this work focused on the sociocultural and economic links between the individual funerary communities as represented by stylistic changes in terms of the diversity of the deposited vessels. The high density of megalithic tombs in this area made a broad investigation of several megalithic groups possible. The small groupings throughout the region were examined for potential connections between the individual burial sites. As part of this study, it has been possible for the first time to obtain proof of the existence of a dense system of communication networks within the TRB West Group in this region.

Material and Methods

The pottery assemblages studied here were recovered from Emmeln 2 on the River Ems, from Groß Berßen 7, Werpeloh 43 and Sögel 2 in the Hümmling area, and also included finds from surface collections at megalithic tombs in the Emsland District (Fig. 2).

The sites were investigated by E. Schlicht in the 1950s and 1960s and some of the results were subsequently published (Schlicht 1953; 1968; 1972; 1982). The funerary constructions had been completely removed in some cases so that only the artefacts from inside the chambers could be recovered. The reassessment of the ceramic finds from these tombs now allows us to directly compare them with each other.

The finds were catalogued and classified using the modular NoNeK system (Nordmitteleuropäische Neolithische Keramik = North Central European Neolithic pottery; https://www.uf.phil.fau.de/abteilungen/juengere-urgeschichte/projekte-der-juengeren-urgeschichte/nonek-nordmitteleuropaeische-neolithische-keramik/) (NoNeK 2006). It allows researchers to compare finds from different sites, categories and chronological periods. The system was slightly modified for the purposes of this study, which allowed us to compile a detailed description of each vessel unit comprising up to 60 features. A total of 2068 vessel units from 12 sites consisting of 8522 individual sherds weighing 110 kg were part of the study. Despite the high degree of fragmentation, it was possible to identify the exact type for two thirds of the vessels.

Figure 2. Emmeln 2. Excavation situation in 1953/54 with a view into the former chamber (photo: estate E. Schlicht, EHB).

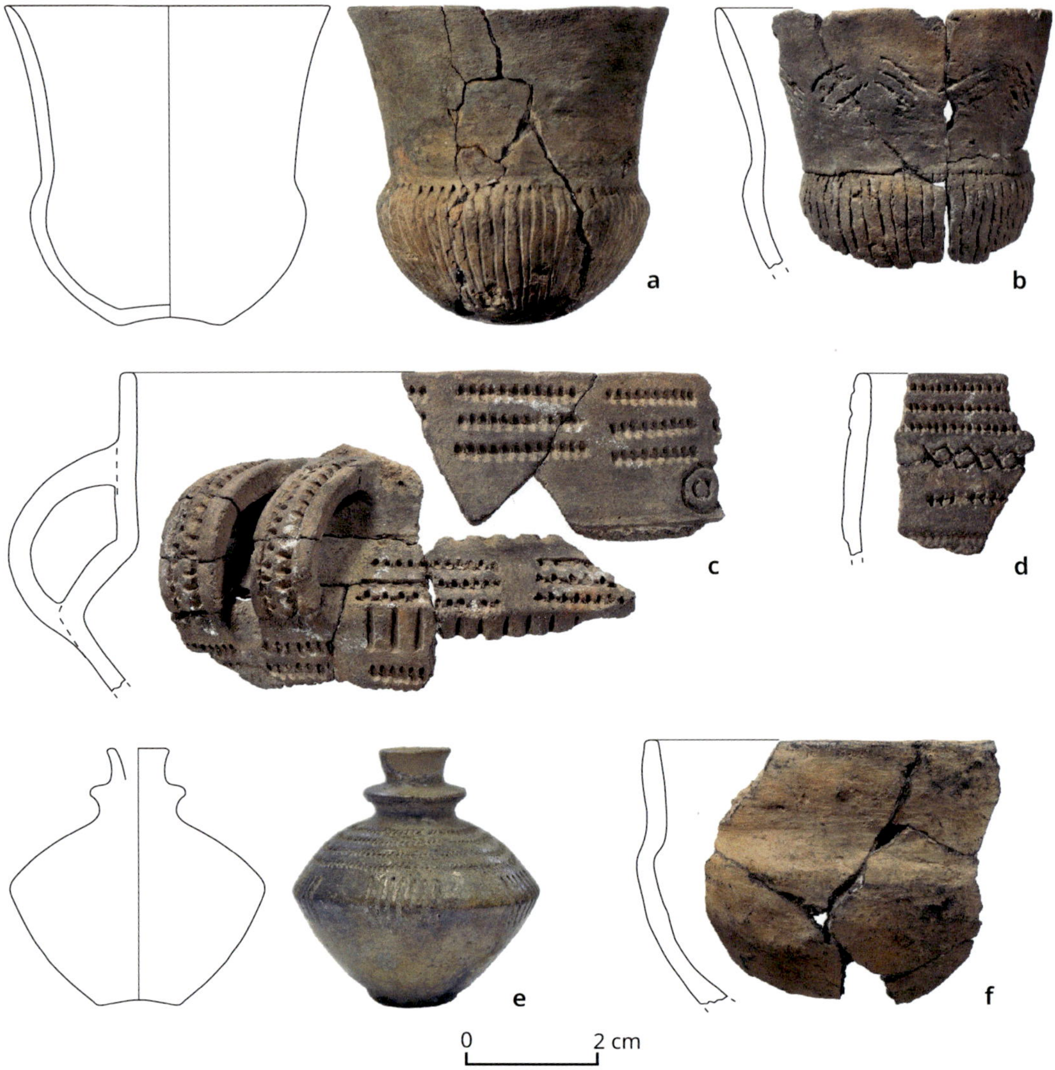

Figure 3. TRB-pottery – Funnel Beaker collared flasks and cylinder-necked vessels from the megalithic sites Emmeln 2, Sögel and Groß Berßen 7: (a-d) Emmeln 2; (e) Sögel; (f) Groß Berßen 7 (plate: J. Menne).

The surfaces of the TRB pottery were highly decorated and 155 patterns were defined. The individual patterns were combined to form numerous more complex pattern sets. By virtue of the craftsmanship and arrangement of the individual patterns, each vessel is unique (Fig. 3-4).

Descriptive statistical methods were used for this purpose, including data sample, cross-tables and chi-squared tests, and tests for normal distribution at different scale levels, based on metric and non-metric variables. Emmeln 2, Groß Berßen 7 and Werpeloh 43 were selected for this next step because of their verified contexts and the large numbers of finds (Menne 2012a; 2012b; 2014).

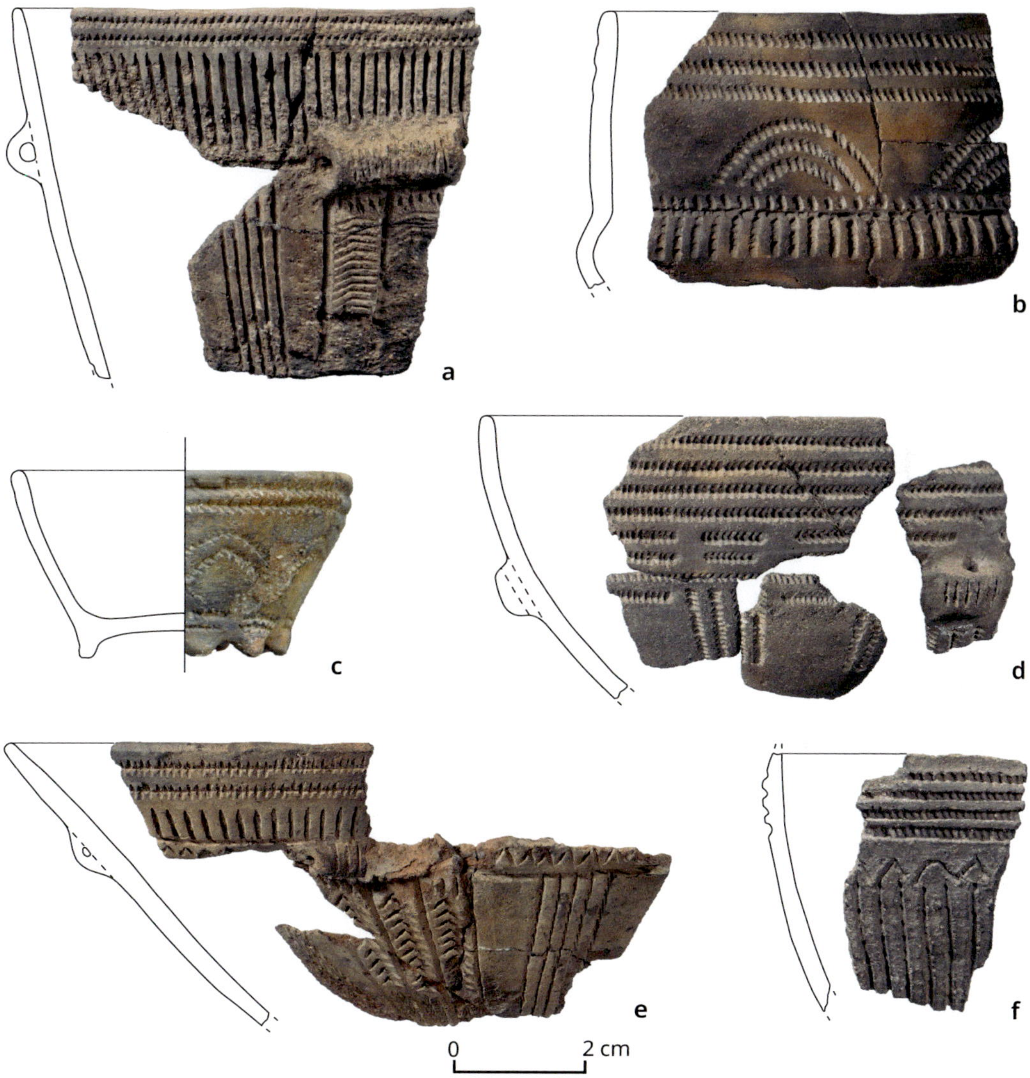

Figure 4. Bowls and pails from the excavation of Emmeln 2 and Groß Berßen 7: (a, e) Groß Berßen 7; (b-d, f) Emmeln 2 (plate: J. Menne).

Additionally, material analyses by means of petrographic thin sections and portable energy-dispersive X-ray fluorescence spectrometry (P-ED-XRF) were conducted to determine the differences in the use of the raw material sources between the megalithic sites. This enables us to draw conclusions on the pottery production for each site. It clearly shows that local raw material sources with similar chemical compositions were exploited for pottery production. The pottery was therefore produced locally and the possibility that pottery was imported, for instance, via exchange contacts or kinship relations can be excluded.

Results

The quantitative overall study of the material was followed by an analysis of the individual assemblages. Comparisons between the sites showed that the production techniques, vessel shapes and decorations were largely similar. This was carried out by qualitative analysis, including correspondence analysis and network analysis, visualised by GIS (Fig. 5).

The conclusion could therefore be drawn that the funerary pottery from the megalithic tombs in the Hümmling region defined a homogenous area with uniform funerary rites. This was clearly borne out by the repeated deposition of the same ratios of bowls, collared flasks, and funnel-necked or cylinder-necked vessels.

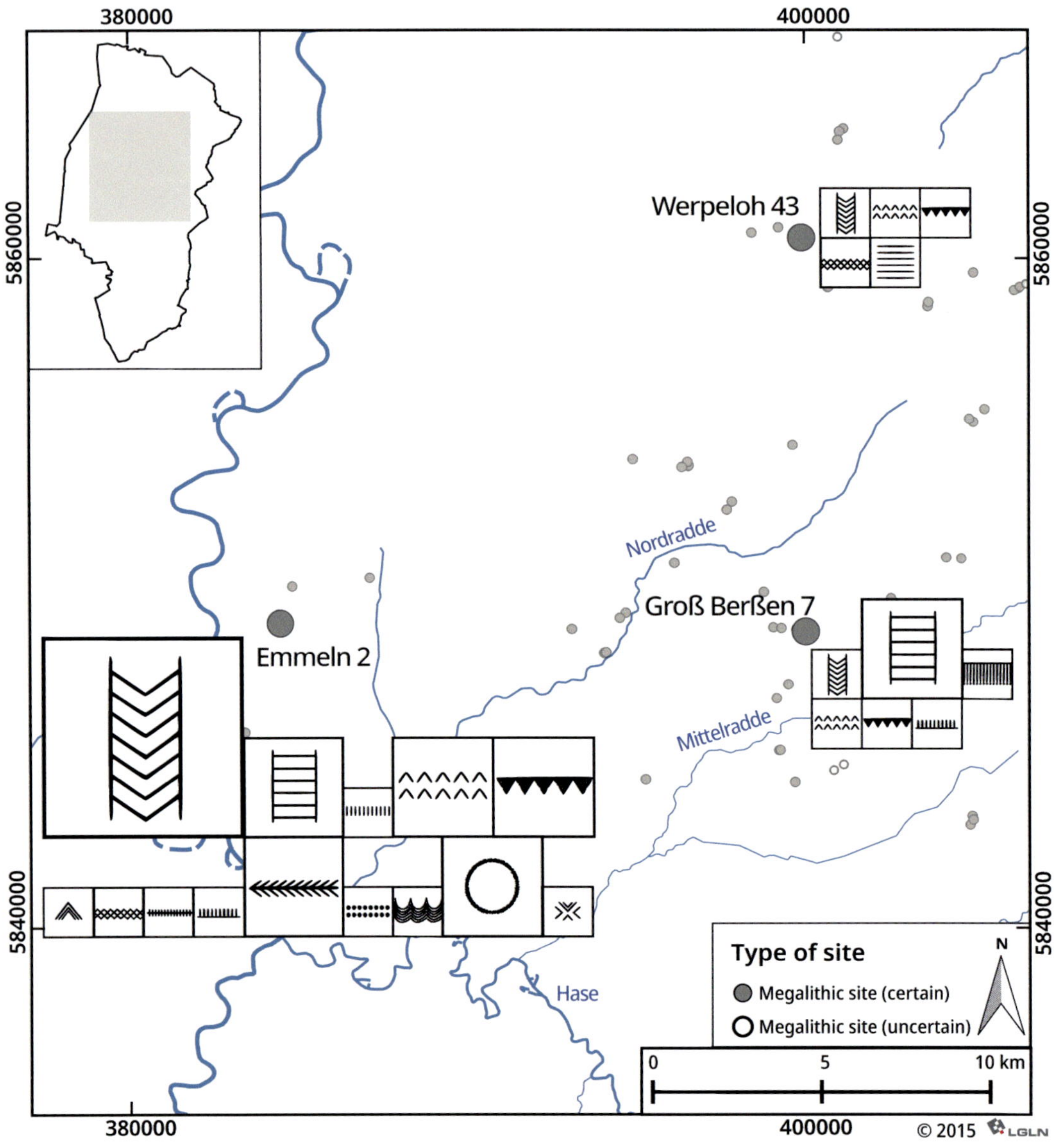

Figure 5. Distribution of stylistic patterns for the sites Emmeln 2, Groß Berßen 7 and Werpeloh 43 (map: J. Menne).

The same uniformity was also visible in the use of decorative patterns on the vessels. So-called "standard pattern types" occurred at every site and were employed by all potters with the same regularity. Bands, garlands, circles, lozenges, zig-zags and triangle garlands, in comparison, allowed us to differentiate between the individual sites. Each funerary community expressed itself by choosing site-specific pattern types to decorate its pottery. These were then combined with the standard pattern types, thus creating an individual formal vocabulary which differentiated each assemblage from its counterparts. The individual funerary communities also had an apparent influence on each other, which can be seen in the distribution of pattern types within the study area. Emmeln 2 appears to have been an innovative driving force behind various stylistic expressions in the region. The tomb was located at the geographical and typological interface between the Hümmling and Drente areas, which acted as a gateway for the transfer of decorative motifs between both regions. The greater the distance between two sites, the more dissimilar the vessel surface decorations became (Fig. 5). Observations about the existence of trading routes and potters' workshops in the Neolithic, concentrating on the distribution of different pottery styles, were made some time ago by the excavator E. Schlicht (Schlicht 1962a; 1962b; 1971).

For an absolute chronological view in order to indicate the period of grave use, radiocarbon dating of charcoal and bone from the inside the chambers was carried out. The results coincide with the typological dates of the pottery. The deposits in the excavated tombs at Emmeln 2, Groß Berßen 7 and Werpeloh 43 were made between 3500/3400 cal BC and 2800/2700 cal BC. Typochronologically, this corresponds to a Funnel Beaker period use in horizons 2 to 6/7 after Brindley (1986b) (cf. Bakker 1979). Deposits began to decline in number from around 3350 BC onwards and this coincided with a general change in the climate of Central and North Central Europe and certain social changes associated with it.

Discussion

In order to put the homogeneity of the study area into context with microregions of the TRB West Group, megalithic tombs from the adjacent site of Ostenwalde 1 (Fansa 1978) and from neighbouring regions were also examined. They included assemblages of funerary pottery from the Oldenburg region (Fansa 1980; 1982), the Netherlands (Brindley 1986a; Brindley and Lanting 1992) and northern Westphalia (Knöll 1983). This part of the study showed that vessel shape ratios in these regions followed a similar principle. The distribution of decorative motifs again relied on the use of standard pattern types.

There was an obvious gradual change and development in the formal and decorative pottery vocabulary, which could be seen in the different microregions within the TRB West Group. Each of these microregions had its own identity as expressed by the formal vocabulary of its funerary pottery which, however, was based on the overall regional formal vocabulary of the TRB West Group. Social and cultural areas apparent within territorial and environmental boundaries were thus influenced by contrasting identities. The ritual landscape as defined by the construction of megalithic tombs and by the associated funerary rites can be viewed as a process of adaptation and standardisation in which patterns of contact are reflected within a dense network of social relationships. The internal coherence of the TRB West Group was not only manifested just by way of the funerary architecture but also by the relationships between the individual deposits. The statistical analysis of the material from Emmeln 2, Groß Berßen 7, Werpeloh 43 and Sögel 2 allowed us to postulate the existence of close communication networks between the individual TRB West Group sites.

However, based on the data currently available, the supra-regional study has only allowed us to identify tendencies. Detailed comparisons with neighbouring regions will only be possible if the corresponding data become available for those areas.

Conclusion

As part of this study, it has been possible for the first time to obtain proof of the existence of a dense system of communication networks within the TRB West Group in the region of Northwestern Germany. Based on the quantitative distribution of the pottery in the individual megalithic tombs, it has also been possible to reconstruct periods of use that continued for the entire duration of the TRB period occupation of the sites. The qualitative analysis of the finds yielded evidence of a dense cultural web of funerary communities. The Hümmling region was thus an extraordinarily densely occupied archaeological region within Northwestern German Neolithic research (Menne 2018).

References

Bakker, J.A. 1979. *The TRB West Group. Studies in the chronology and geography of the makers of hunebeds and Tiefstich pottery*. Cingula 5. Amsterdam: Universiteit van Amsterdam.

Brindley, A.L. 1986a. Hunebed G2. Excavation and Finds. *Palaeohistoria* 28, 27-92.

Brindley, A.L. 1986b. The typochronology of TRB West Group pottery. *Palaeohistoria* 28, 93-132.

Brindley, A.L. and Lanting, J.N. 1992. A Re-Assessment of the Hunebedden O1, D30 and D40. Structures and finds. *Palaeohistoria* 33/34, 97-140.

Fansa, M. 1978. Die Keramik der Trichterbecherkultur aus dem Megalithgrab I von Ostenwalde, Kreis Aschendorf-Hümmling. Ein Versuch zur Klassifikation und Dokumentation steinzeitlicher Keramik. *Neue Ausgrabungen und Forschungen in Niedersachsen* 12, 33-77.

Fansa, M. 1980. Die Trichterbecherkeramik aus dem oldenburgischen Raum. Töpferwerkstatt oder Einzelproduktion? *Nachrichten aus Niedersachsens Urgeschichte* 49, 99-118.

Fansa, M. 1982. *Die Keramik der Trichterbecherkultur aus den Megalith- und Flachgräbern des oldenburgischen Raumes*. Göttinger Schriften zur Vor- und Frühgeschichte 20. Neumünster: Karl Wachholtz Verlag.

Knöll, H. 1983. *Die Megalithgräber von Lengerich-Wechte (Kreis Steinfurt)*. Bodenaltertümer Westfalens 21. Münster: Aschendorff.

Lorenz, L. 2018. *Kommunikationsstrukturen mittelneolithischer Gesellschaften im nordmitteleuropäischen Tiefland*. Frühe Monumentalität und soziale Differenzierung 14. Bonn: Habelt.

Menne, J. 2012a. Megalithgräber im Emsland. Der Hümmling im Fokus geografischer Informationssysteme, in: Hinz, M. and Müller, J. (eds.), *Siedlung, Grabenwerk, Großsteingrab. Studien zu Gesellschaft, Wirtschaft und Umwelt der Trichterbechergruppen im nördlichen Mitteleuropa*. Frühe Monumentalität und soziale Differenzierung 2. Bonn: Habelt, 337-346.

Menne, J. 2012b. Das vergessene Großsteingrab von Werpeloh. Neue Untersuchungen zu den Megalithgräbern im Hümmling. *Jahrbuch des Emsländischen Heimatbundes* 58, 69-78.

Menne, J. 2014. Studies on the Funnel Beaker West Group: A European Comparison, in: Müller, J. (ed.), *Exploring Landscapes: The Reconstruction of Social Space – Landschaft erforschen: Sozialen Raum rekonstruieren*. Bonn: Habelt, 98-99.

Menne, J. 2018. *Keramik aus Megalithgräbern in Nordwestdeutschland. Interaktionen und Netzwerke der Trichterbecherwestgruppe*. Frühe Monumentalität und soziale Differenzierung 16. Bonn: Habelt.

NoNeK 2006. Nordmitteleuropäische Neolithische Keramik = North Central European Neolithic pottery. https://www.uf.phil.fau.de/abteilungen/juengere-urgeschichte/projekte-der-juengeren-urgeschichte/nonek-nordmitteleuropaeische-neolithische-keramik/.

Schlicht, E. 1953. Die Untersuchung der urgeschichtlichen Fundstellen auf dem Emmelner Berg bei Haren. *Jahrbuch des Emsländischen Heimatvereins* 1, 83-89.

Schlicht, E. 1962a. Handelsverbindungen vor 4000 Jahren. *Emsland-Jahrbuch* 3/4, 17-23.

Schlicht, E. 1962b. Von alten Verkehrswegen – die Hünengräberstraße des Hümmlings. *Jahrbuch des Emsländischen Heimatbundes* 9, 74-85.

Schlicht, E. 1968. *Die Funde aus dem Megalithgrab 2 von Emmeln, Kreis Meppen. Studien zur Keramik der Trichterbecherkultur im Gebiet zwischen Weser und Zuidersee.* Göttinger Schriften zur Vor- und Frühgeschichte 9. Neumünster: Wachholtz.

Schlicht, E. 1971. Töpferwerkstätten in Niedersachsen vor 4500 Jahren. *Die Kunde* N.F. 22, 14-26.

Schlicht, E. 1972. *Das Megalithgrab 7 von Gross Berssen, Kreis Meppen. Studien zur Keramik der Trichterbecherkultur im Gebiet zwischen Weser und Zuidersee.* Göttinger Schriften zur Vor- und Frühgeschichte 12. Neumünster: Wachholtz.

Schlicht, E. 1982. Meine Ausgrabungen im Rahmen der Emslanderschließung. *Jahrbuch des Emsländischen Heimatbundes* 28, 25-37.

Sprockhoff, E. 1975. *Atlas der Megalithgräber Deutschlands. Teil 3: Niedersachsen – Westfalen*. Bonn: Habelt.

Author address

Julia Menne
Institute of Pre- and Protohistoric Archaeology
University of Hamburg
Edmund-Siemers-Allee 1
20146 Hamburg, Germany
julia.menne@uni-hamburg.de

About the author

The author studied Pre- and Protohistoric Archaeology, Medieval and Post Medieval Archaeology, and Heritage Sciences at the University of Bamberg (Magistra Artium 2011) and subsequently researched at the Altertumskommission für Westfalen in Münster. From 2013 onwards, she worked on her PhD at the Graduate School "Human Development in Landscapes", Kiel University, and received her doctorate in 2017 for her thesis entitled *Keramik aus Megalithgräbern in Nordwestdeutschland. Interaktionen und Netzwerke der Trichterbecherwestgruppe* (Menne 2018) from the Institute for Pre- and Protohistoric Archaeology, Kiel University. In 2017/18, she was awarded a travel grant from the German Archaeological Institute (DAI) and was active in various research projects at Kiel University (GS, SFB 1266 and SPP 1400). She is currently working at the University of Hamburg.

Development of Identification Criteria of Non-Dietary Cereal Crop Products by Phytolith Analysis to Study Prehistoric Agricultural Societies

Welmoed A. Out

Abstract

While identification criteria based on pollen, macro-remains (such as fruits) or chaff phytoliths, all originating from the flowering parts of plants, are available for various cereal crops that are of major economic importance in the world, identification criteria for the leaves of these crops, based on remains that can be recovered from the archaeological record, are very scarce. The development of relevant identification criteria can improve the visibility and understanding of crop by-products consisting of leaves in the archaeological record. This contribution provides an overview of a line of research concerning the development of phytolith-based identification criteria to distinguish between leaf phytoliths of broomcorn millet, foxtail millet, pearl millet and sorghum – four crops that have been of significant importance since prehistory.

Introduction

"Development of identification criteria of non-dietary cereal crop products by phytolith analysis to study prehistoric agricultural societies" was a postdoc project supported by the Graduate School "Human Development in Landscapes" within the framework of new proxy development. This project started as an IEF Marie Curie fellowship in cooperation with M. Madella at the research group 'Complexity and Socio-Ecological Dynamics (CaSES)', Institución Milà y Fontanals, National Research Council Spain (CSIC), in Barcelona, and was afterwards expanded in Kiel (2013-2015). Funding by the Graduate School allowed for further data collection, statistical analysis in cooperation with M.

in: Müller, J. and Ricci, A. 2020 (eds.), *Past Societies: Human Development in Landscapes*. Sidestone Press: Leiden, 37-50.

Hasler from the Faculty of Agricultural and Nutritional Sciences, Kiel University, and publication and dispersal of the results. This paper presents an overview of the outcomes.

Although non-agricultural plant resources receive increasing attention, archaeobotany applied to agricultural societies has focused mostly on understanding crop domestication and cultivation practices, *i.e.* on food production. However, many cereals supply not only food products but also so-called secondary products, such as straw, hay and chaff, derived from culms, leaves and inflorescences. Both ethnographical and archaeological studies have demonstrated that these secondary products always played a fundamental role, supplying fuel, animal fodder and components for construction material (*e.g.* Grubben and Partohardjono 1996; Miller 1984; Ryan 2011).

Non-dietary, secondary crop products are created during harvest and crop processing (Hillman 1984). Crop processing concerns the separation of edible grains from non-edible secondary products and arable weeds. The technical, organisational, temporal and spatial details of these processes depend on the crops' morphology as well as on socio-economic aspects of communities and societies. The study of secondary crop products in archaeological sites can, therefore, not only provide a more thorough understanding of both dietary and non-dietary functions of crop plants but will also lead to better knowledge of prehistoric crop processing, thus revealing the underlying socio-economical aspects of past societies (*e.g.* Fuller and Stevens 2009).

Due to a bias in current research approaches, secondary crop products are regularly overlooked in archaeobotanical studies. Effectively, the study of archaeobotanical assemblages is routinely based on plant macroremains, primarily seeds and fruits. Therefore, plant parts that do not relate to inflorescences with small chances to get carbonised and/or that are particularly sensitive to mechanical destruction after carbonisation (soft tissues such as leaves) tend to be underrepresented in the archaeobotanical record in most parts of the world, being only incidentally recovered and/or recognised at archaeological sites. From these depositional and taphonomical peculiarities, the necessity thus arises to develop a distinct approach to study the full spectrum of archaeobotanical evidence of crop plants and crop plant utilisation.

Phytoliths, microscopic bodies formed in living plants and consisting of hydrated opal silica (SiO_2), offer a good alternative research method to solve the problems on the preservation of secondary crop products. The main advantages of this proxy are preservation independent of fire, long preservation in most sedimentary environments, ubiquity in the archaeological deposits, good taxonomic relevance and good plant tissue/organ relevance (Piperno 2006). These unique characteristics enable the retrieval of phytoliths from many types of archaeological sites and contexts. As phytoliths are formed mostly at intracellular spaces, they have the anatomical characteristics of the original plant cells and tissues. Although phytoliths are rarely unique for a single species, this allows the distinction of both plant taxa and plant parts. The grass family, which includes all cereal crops and is therefore of high economic importance, is particularly suitable for the application of phytolith analysis, because grasses produce abundant numbers of phytoliths in different anatomical locations. Apart from inflorescence cells, particularly grass leaves are known for taxonomically diagnostic phytoliths (Ellis 1987). However, while the potential of phytoliths within the framework of archaeobotany and secondary crop products is indeed recognised (Harvey and Fuller 2005; Madella 2001), it has not been developed to its full potential yet. In order to fill this gap, this project aimed to investigate:

1) whether bilobate and cross-shaped phytoliths from leaf veins (Fig. 1) allow for taxonomic identification of broomcorn millet – P. miliaceum (L.) – and foxtail millet – S. *italica* (L.) P. beauv. – by phytolith morphometry. The studied taxa co-occur in regions of Asia and Europe since prehistory and are regularly found at archaeological sites in Eurasia (Bakels 2013; Hunt *et al.* 2008; Motuzaite-Matuzeviciute *et al.* 2013; Stevens *et al.* 2016).
2) whether bilobate and cross-shaped phytoliths from leaves allow for taxonomic identification of sorghum – *Sorghum bicolor* ssp. *bicolor* (L.) Moench – and pearl millet – *Pennisetum glaucum* (L.) R. Br. – by phytolith morphometry. These taxa are two important crop plants that regularly co-occur at archaeological sites in Africa and on the Indian subcontinent.
3) whether bilobate and cross-shaped phytoliths from leaves allow for taxonomic distinction between the four above-mentioned taxa.
4) whether bilobate and cross-shaped phytoliths from leaves show differences within species.
5) whether the comparison of short cell assemblages from leaves of broomcorn and foxtail millet allows for distinction between the two taxa.

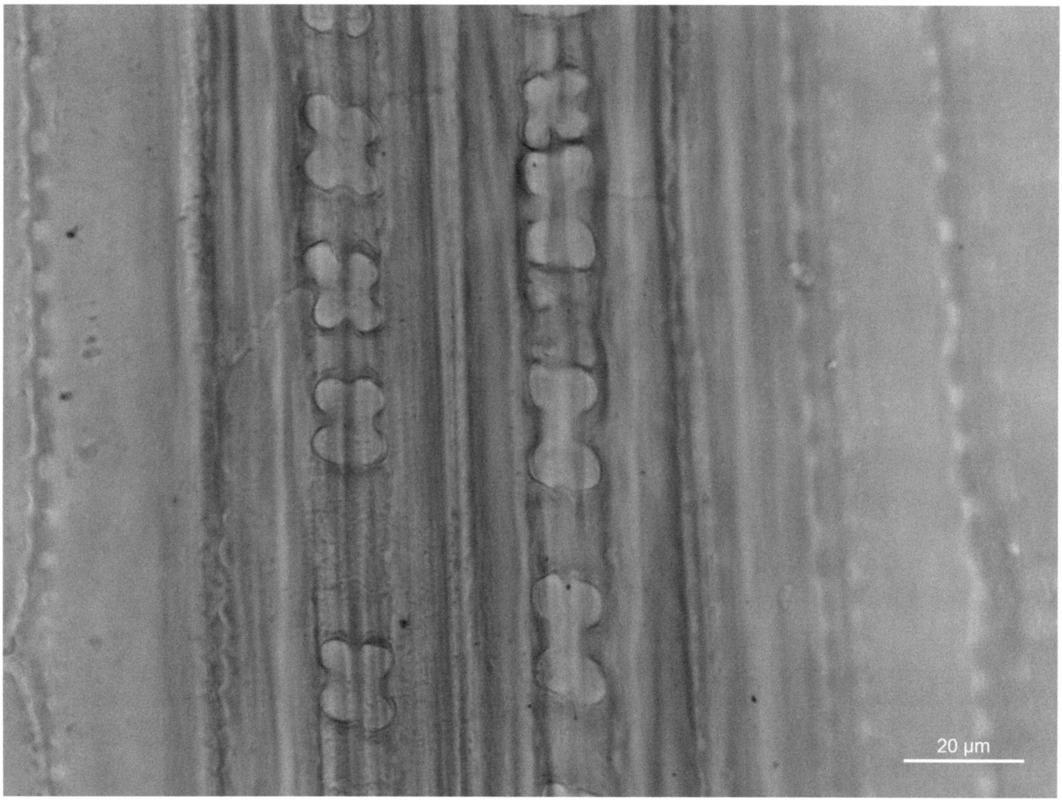

Figure 1. A leaf fragment of broomcorn millet mounted in water, showing bilobate and cross-shape short cell phytoliths (photo: W. Out).

Methods

The project was based on the following methodology, inspired by studies by Ball *et al.* (*e.g.* 1999):

1) The creation and collection of a reference collection of various plant parts of 12 modern-day cereal species, focusing on taxa that are of major economic importance in Asia, Africa and Europe.
2) A systematic sampling protocol, aiming at the analysis of 2 samples per leaf, 2 leaves per plant, 2 plants per population and 5 populations per species, whenever possible originating from and/or grown in different parts in the world. In this way, it was possible to investigate intra-species variation and take possible genetic and environmental variation into consideration.
3) Wet-oxidation of plant tissue.
4) Dry-ashing of plant tissue.
5) Collection of microphotographs of bilobate and cross-shaped phytoliths (hereafter called bilobates) from leaves.
6) Morphometric analysis of the phytoliths by means of partially newly developed software (further explained below).
7) Statistical analysis consisting of the definition of an appropriate statistical mixed model (Laird and Ware 1982; Verbeke and Molenberghs 2000), analysis of variances, multiple contrast tests and stepwise discriminant analysis, carried out in SPPS and R. The results of the various analyses generally provide similar results. This contribution will focus on the discriminant analysis' outcomes.

Results

Development of new software to collect morphometric measurements of phytoliths

Phytolith analysis is based on the classification of phytolith morphotypes with the aim to assign them anatomically and taxonomically. Morphotypes can further be classified by typology, based on differences in specific parts of the morphotype. Bilobate phytoliths can, for example, be grouped into bilobates with flat, convex or concave lobes, or short or long shanks. This approach may, however, not be sufficient to differentiate between taxa, and can moreover suffer from inter-observer variation: where is the clear-cut border between the various types, and are types classified in the same way by different specialists? These challenges, particularly relevant when aiming to distinguish between closely related species, can be overcome by applying morphometry, the collection of measurements of size and shape. One way to collect morphometric data, working towards automatic image analysis, is by semi-automatic image analysis.

As part of this project, a new, user-friendly method for phytolith morphometry based on image analysis by means of open-source software (FIJI) was developed (Out *et al.* 2014). Existing software elements designed for morphometry were combined into two new tools. The macro "Draw a mask" enables the isolation of a phytolith – or any other object – from a photograph by creating a digital mask of it. To do so, the software helps the user to select a photograph, to set the scale for a series of images, to zoom in,

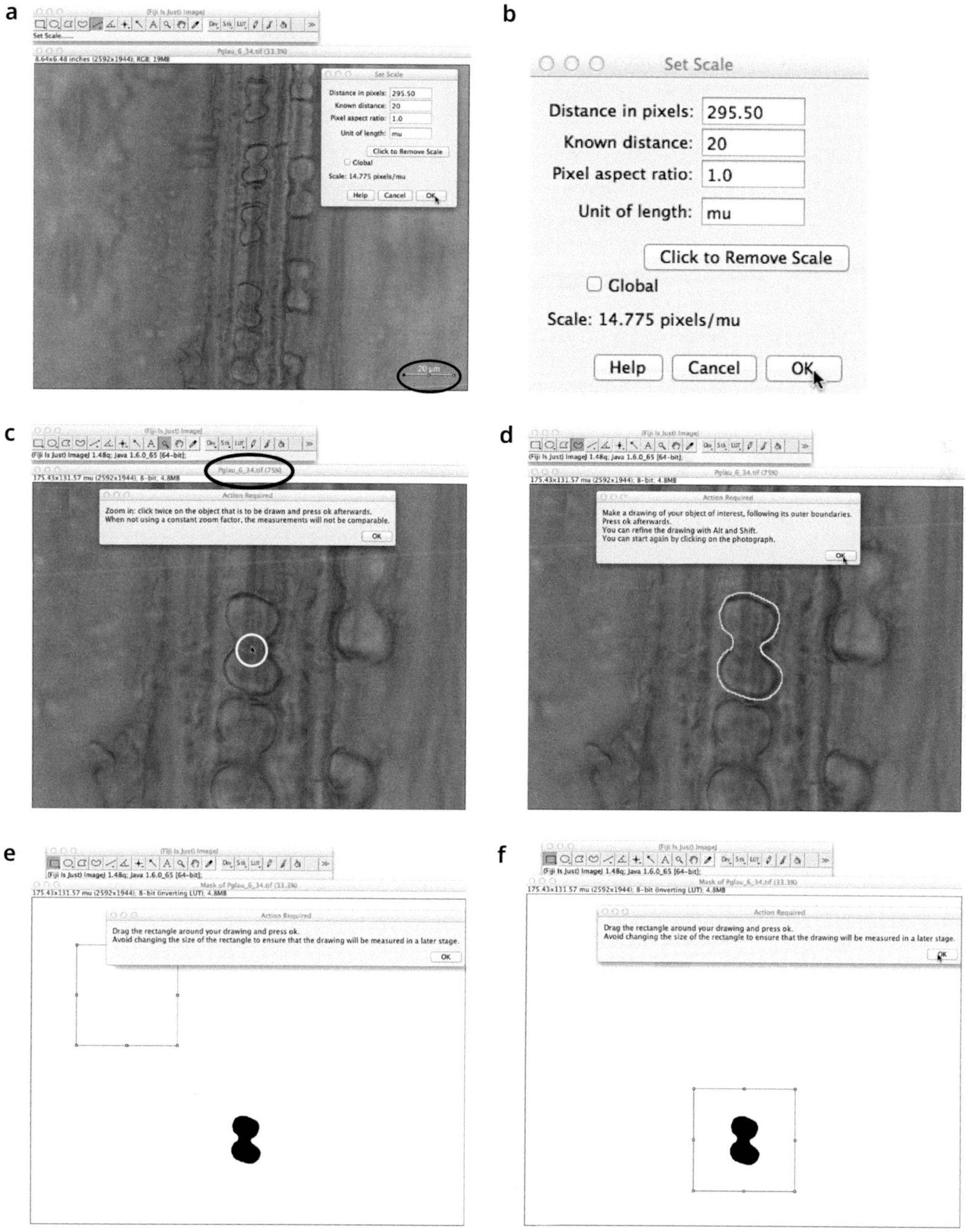

Figure 2. Screen shots of a selection of steps of the macro "Draw a mask" (figure from Out et al. 2014, copyright Microscopy Society of America, reprinted with permission): (a and b) Set scale. Black ellipse: the user draws a straight line along the scale bar beforehand once to set the scale for multiple images; (c) Zoom in. White circle and black ellipse: the user clicks with the cursor on the area of interest in order to zoom in. In the upper part of the window frame, the scale of the photograph is provided; (d) Make a drawing of the object of interest. The user draws a closed line; (e) The closed line is automatically transformed into a black mask of the object of interest. The background is neutralised and becomes white; (f) Drag the rectangle around the mask. Those parts of the photo that are located outside the rectangle and that do not contain relevant information are removed.

Type	Label	Description	Unit
Size	ArBBox	Feret*Breadth, area of the Bounding Box along the Feret diameter, which is not necessarily the minimal bounding box.	μm^2
Size	Area	The area inside the polygon defined by the Perimeter.	μm^2
Size	Area Equivalent Diameter	Area Equivalent Diameter = sqrt((4/π)*Area).	µm
Size	Breadth	The largest axis perpendicular to the Feret (not necessarily colinear).	µm
Size	Convex Hull	Convex Hull or Convex polygon calculated from pixel centres. Perimeter calculated in a different way.	µm
Size	Concavity	Convex Area-Area.	μm^2
	Convex Area	Area of the Convex Hull polygon (= Area/Solidity). Area calculated in a different way.	μm^2
Size	Curve length	The arc length of the centerline curve between the points with the largest separation.	µm
	Curve width	Maximum width perpendicular to medial axis.	µm
Size	Equivalent Ellipse Area	(π*Feret*Breadth)/4, this is the area of an ellipse with the same long and short axes as the particle.	μm^2
Size	Feret	Largest axis length = the longest distance between 2 points in the perimeter.	µm
Size	MaxR	Radius of the enclosing circle centred at the centre of mass. Centre of mass: the brightness-weighted average of the x and y coordinates of all pixels in the image or selection.	µm
Size	MBCRadius	Radius of the Minimal Bounding Circle.	µm
Size	MinR	Radius of the inscribed circle centred at the centre of mass.	µm
Size	Perimeter	The length of the outside boundary of the selection, calculated from the centres of the boundary pixels.	µm
Size	Perimeter Equivalent Diameter	Area/π.	
Shape	Aspect ratio	Feret/Breadth.	
Shape	Circularity	4*π*Area/Perimeter^2, sometimes called Form Factor, distinguishes between perfect round circles and dentated circles.	
Shape	Compactness	Sqrt((4/π)*Area)/Feret or alternatively ArEquivD/Feret.	
Shape	Convexity	Convex Hull/Perimeter, it is 1 for a perfectly convex shape, diminishes if there are surface indentations.	
Shape	Modification Ratio	(2*MinR)/Feret.	
Shape	Rectangularity	Area/ArBBox, this approaches 0 for cross-like objects, 0.5 for squares, π/4=0.79 for circles and approaches 1 for long rectangles.	
Shape	RFactor	Convex Hull/(Feret*π).	
Shape	Roundness	4*Area/(π*Feret^2), it is 1 for a perfect circle and diminishes with elongation of the feature.	
Shape	Shape	Perimeter^2/Area.	
Shape	Solidity	Area/Convex Area, it is 1 for a perfectly convex shape, diminishes if there are surface indentations.	
Shape	Sphericity	MinR/MaxR.	

Table 1. The measured morphometric variables of size and shape. To make the variables more concrete, the relation between the variables and phytolith shape is visualised in Out et al. (2014) (table: also see Out and Madella 2016a; Out and Madella 2017).

to establish the contours of the phytolith by digitally drawing its outer borders, and to crop those parts of the photograph that do not contain relevant information (Fig. 2). The resulting mask is saved automatically. The macro "Measure masks" subsequently facilitates the selection of an earlier created folder with masks and the measurement of all masks in this folder at once, automatically collecting 27 commonly used variables of size and shape (Tab. 1). The resulting data are again saved automatically. Written explanations, step-by-step screen shots and technical instructions facilitate quick adoption of the software. This method allows for a systematic, uniform collection of data, and is not only useful for phytolith analysis but may also be useful for other fields that make use of morphometry.

Within the framework of the International Committee for Phytolith Morphometrics of the International Phytolith Society, it was possible to contribute to the development of recommendations towards the standardisation of morphometric phytolith analysis. The resulting paper (Ball *et al.* 2016) discusses the role of morphometric analysis in phytolith studies and provides recommendations for the application of phytolith morphometry, criteria for data collection and publication, definitions for basic measurements and software for computer-assisted image analysis. Similar to the paper by Out *et al.* (2014), this paper presents software and instructions for semi-automatic phytolith morphometry. The use of this software and resulting morphometry standardisation will allow for compatibility of data produced by different researchers and laboratories, and substantially improve the possibilities for data sharing.

Comparison of phytoliths from leaves of broomcorn millet, foxtail millet, pearl millet and sorghum

First, phytolith morphometry was applied to compare bilobate phytoliths from broomcorn and foxtail millet. Using morphometric data of 27 morphometric parameters from 4000 phytoliths (2 x 2000) originating from 10 populations, 20 plants, 40 leaves and 80 samples, it was possible to develop a discriminant function that distinguishes between bilobates of the two taxa (see the distribution of the discriminant function scores in Fig. 3a). This function shows that, on average, broomcorn bilobates are less elongated, less roundish and more irregular in shape than foxtail bilobates. As a result, 88% of the phytoliths from modern plant material could be correctly identified, with slightly better chances for correct identification of foxtail millet (93.2%) than of broomcorn millet (82.9%). 83.5% of the bilobate phytoliths from a modern plant sample to which the method was applied were correctly identified as well (Out and Madella 2016a).

Second, as a complementary method in addition to the morphometric identification, it was investigated whether the short cell assemblages from leaves of broomcorn and foxtail millets differ from each other. While differences in short cell types were not observed during the non-quantitative exploration of wet-oxidised samples of leaf fragments (Out and Madella 2016a), quantitative analysis of ashed samples that provide primarily disarticulated phytolith cells does suggest the presence of unique morphotypes. The "*intercostal morphotype*" particularly occurs in broomcorn millet, but not equally in all populations, while a trapeziform morphotype seems to occur particularly in foxtail millet. Based on the classification of 80 samples from 10 populations, 20 plants and 40 leaves, with ca. 300 short cells per sample analysed, it was possible to develop a discriminant function that distinguishes between the leaf short cells of the

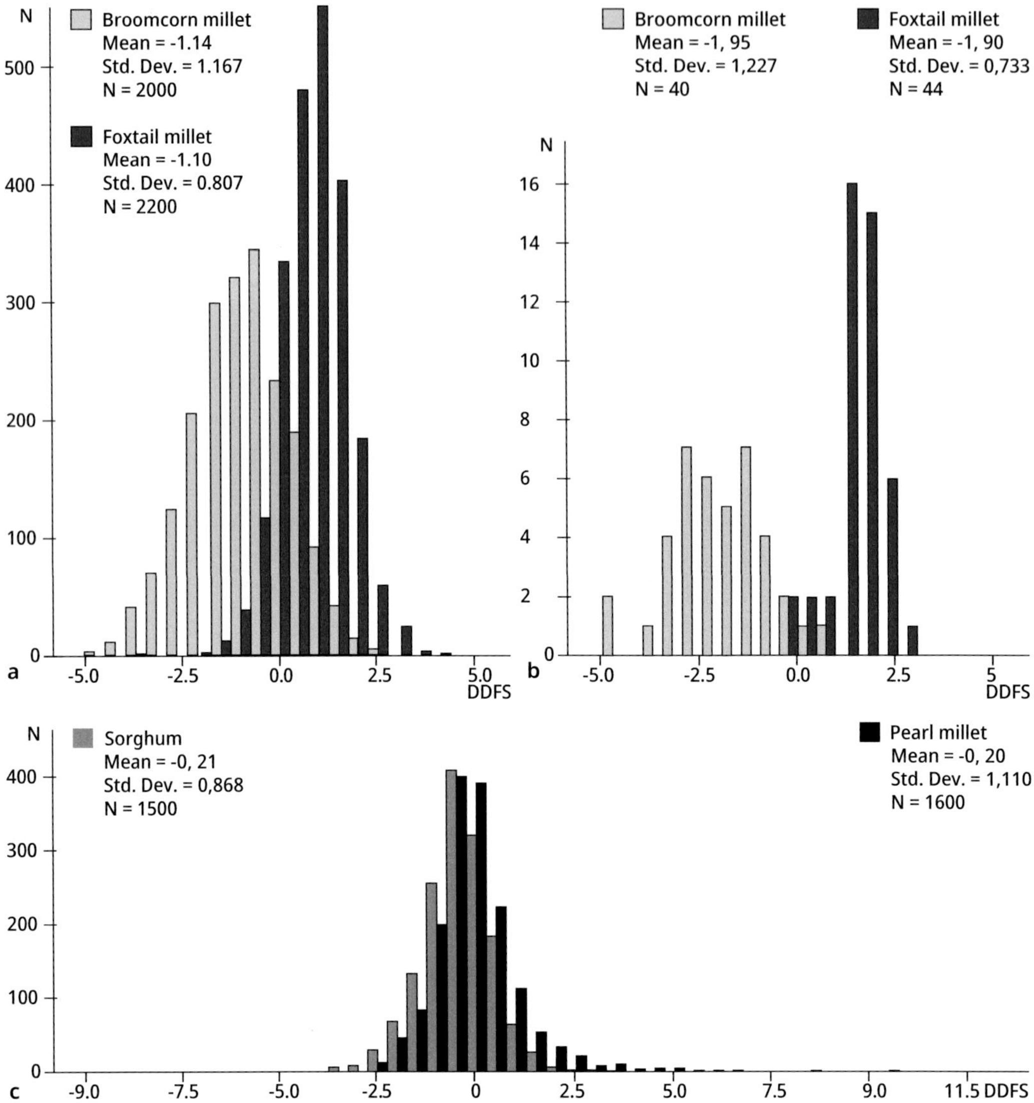

Figure 3. Distribution of the discriminant function scores (DDFS) of the various data. The less overlap between the taxa, the more powerful the discriminant function, and the better the possibility to distinguish between the taxa: (a) DDFS of morphometric data of broomcorn millet and foxtail millet; (b) DDFS of the short cell proportions of broomcorn millet and foxtail millet; (c) DDFS of the morphometric data of sorghum and pearl millet (graphs: W. Out and L. Hilmar, Moesgaard Museum).

two taxa (Fig. 3b). This discriminant function allows for correct identification of 94% of the samples used for the criteria's development, which is 45% more than when samples are randomly assigned to one of the two taxa (which would result in 50% correct identification). Furthermore, the discriminant function's validity was tested by applying it to four samples from a foxtail millet population that had not been used for the development of the discriminant function. This test population was identified completely correct (Out and Madella 2019).

Third, phytolith morphometry was applied to compare bilobates and cross-shaped phytoliths from pearl millet and sorghum. In this case, the use of morphometric data of the 27 morphometric parameters from altogether 3100 phytoliths (1600 and 1500 respectively) from 10 populations, 18 plants, 31 leaves and 62 samples did not allow the development of a discriminant function that successfully classifies bilobates of the two taxa. The results show that 60% of the phytoliths of the modern plant material could be correctly identified, but this is only 10% better than when phytoliths are assigned to one of the two groups randomly (Fig. 3c; Out and Madella 2017).

Fourth, the bilobates and crosses from all four taxa together were compared morphometrically by multiple group discriminant analysis. Again, using morphometric data of 27 parameters, now from 7100 phytoliths (4000 + 3100), it was possible to develop discriminant functions that can successfully distinguish between pearl millet/sorghum, broomcorn millet and foxtail millet, although the chances to successfully distinguish broomcorn millet and foxtail millet are better than the chances to successfully distinguish pearl millet/sorghum (Out and Madella 2017).

Within species-variation in broomcorn millet, foxtail millet, pearl millet and sorghum

The development of phytolith-based identification criteria is a time-consuming challenge because of population-related variation in plants, the large variation of cells occurring within individual taxa and similarity of plant cells between taxa. As a result, the development of identification criteria, based on multiple or single accessions per species, focusses much on the study of inter-taxa variation (distinction between two or more taxa), while there is only restricted effort spent on exploring intra-taxa variation (how much variation is there within a single taxon). Intra-taxon variation is, however, highly relevant, since phytoliths, representing plant cells, are subject to natural variation. This is especially important when identification criteria concern taxa with a worldwide distribution area.

The experimental set-up of the above-presented studies allowed for the analysis of intra-species variation (Fig. 4). The morphometric analyses showed that concerning broomcorn millet, one population grown in Korea significantly differs from the other four populations. For foxtail millet, one population grown in England stands out. For pearl millet, one population grown in Japan stands out. The analysis of short cell types in broomcorn millet and foxtail millet showed strong differences between populations of both taxa. The observed within-species variance is not fully understood, but at least the morphometric variation could well be related to environmental variation. This implies that there is a need for careful application and interpretation of taxonomic identification criteria and ideally the collection of data from additional reference material grown outside Europe.

Discussion

This contribution presents an overview of various studies focusing on the development of leaf phytolith identification criteria as a way to identify both taxa and crop by-products. Two different methods enable the distinction between leaves of broomcorn and foxtail millet, while one of the methods additionally allows a differentiation of these

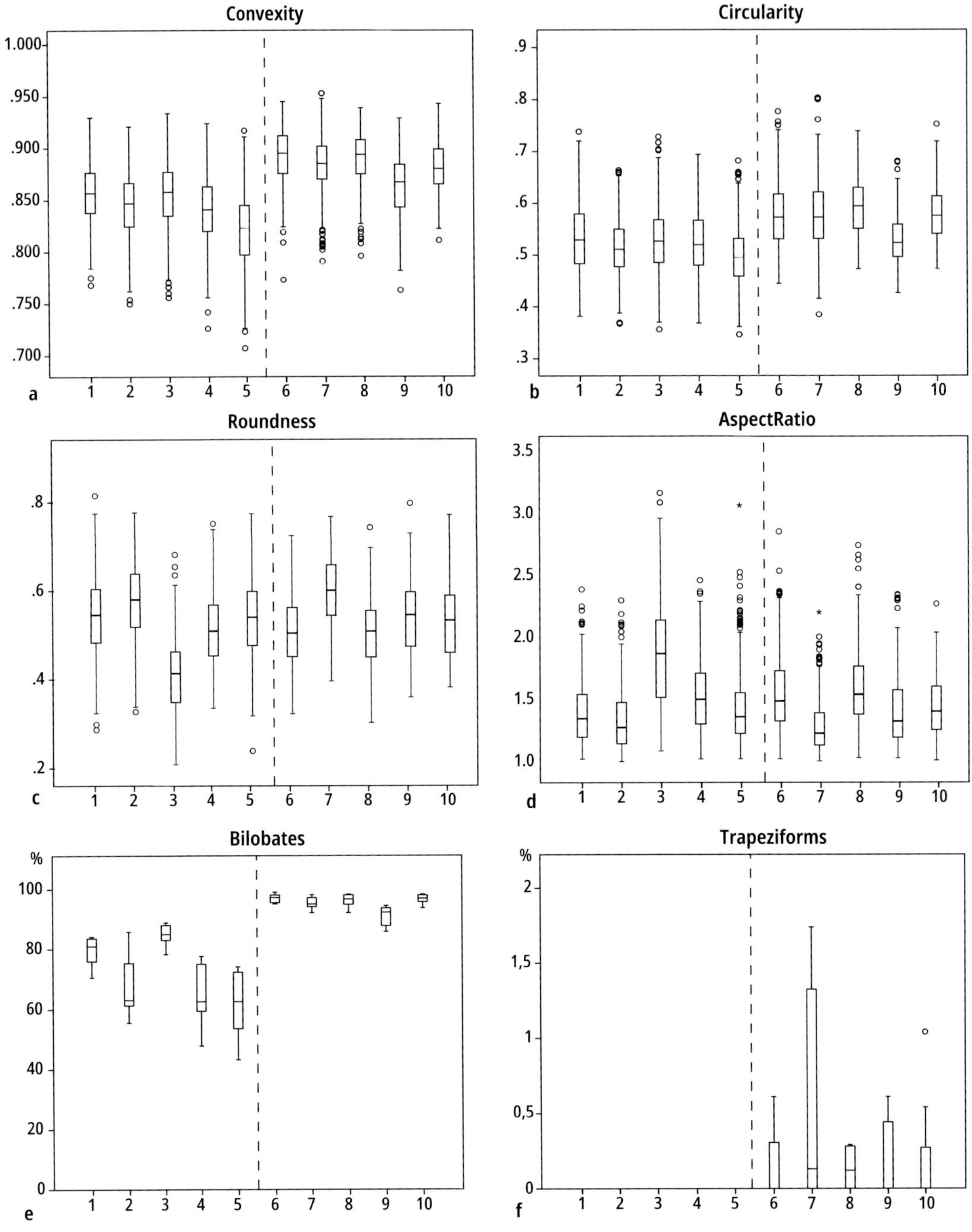

Figure 4. Box plots showing the variation between populations concerning: (a-b) bilobate morphometrics of the variables' convexity and circularity of broomcorn millet (left of the dashed line) and foxtail millet (right of the dashed line); (c-d) bilobate morphometrics of the variables roundness and aspect ratio of pearl millet (l) and sorghum (r), and (e-f) short cell percentages of bilobates and trapeziform phytoliths of broomcorn millet (l) and foxtail millet (r) (graphs: W. Out and L. Hilmar, Moesgaard Museum; for graph 4a see Out and Madella 2016a).

two taxa from pearl millet and sorghum for those sites where combinations of these crops can be expected, particularly in South Asia, Eastern Asia and Africa. An important condition for all identification criteria is, however, that analyses should always be based on populations of phytoliths (see the original papers for further recommendations concerning the minimum sample size). Another practical recommendation is to submit measurements of reference collections both graphically and in tables. Graphs enable users to quickly visually understand differences and similarities between the various taxa, while raw data (tables) allow for further analysis.

It is expected that the developed identification criteria can contribute to reveal crop resources and particularly crop by-products in archaeological sites in regions where these crops were used in the past. The outcome of this better identification of plant materials has the potential to significantly influence the understanding of prehistoric agricultural societies in Europe and Asia, the role of crop plants in socio-economic changes, such as sedentism and the development of urban societies, and the evidence of past human communities' impact on/adjustment to environmental change over time.

The current state of the art generates a clear agenda for future research. On a methodological level, it is of primary importance to investigate the inter-user variation, to see whether morphometric results obtained by one researcher or institute can be compared with those from others. This is relevant for morphometry applied to phytoliths and other archaeobotanical or archaeological remains. Concerning the development and application of the presented identification criteria, there is a clear need to compare bilobates of the studied taxa with those from other taxa, particularly those taxa that have been used as crops or famine food in East Asia and South Asia, and additionally those that occur as weeds in fields of the studied taxa. Until then, application of the identification criteria is particularly recommendable for sites where the presence of one of the relevant taxa has been tested by means of other plant remains such as the charred grains. Moreover, not only bilobates but also other morphotypes may be relevant for taxonomic identification. In addition to the comparison between taxa, it may additionally be equally relevant to compare bilobates of leaves with bilobates of other plant parts within taxa, even though leaf phytolith assemblages can, in principle, be recognised based on their unique assemblage of phytolith morphotypes (cf. Out and Madella 2016b). Finally, an important next step will be to apply the developed identification criteria to archaeological contexts. This will require attention from archaeologists and archaeobotanists to collect and distinguish relevant samples. While all these recommendations together concern a quantity of work that can easily span a lifetime, all efforts are steps forward through which phytoliths can provide new glimpses into the past.

Acknowledgements

These studies were funded by an Intra-European Fellowship of the Marie Curie Actions program (PHYTORES, ID 273610, 2011-2013) and the Graduate School "Human Development in Landscapes" (2013-2015) and made possible by all the people and institutes providing reference material. The author is especially grateful to colleagues of the Graduate School "Human Development in Landscapes" and the Institute of Prehistoric and Protohistoric Archaeology, Kiel University for the excellent work environment.

References

Bakels, C.C. 2013. Foxtail Millet (*Setaria italica* [L.] P. Beauv.) in Western Central Europe, in: von Carnap-Bornheim, C., Dörfler, W., Kirleis, W., Müller, J., Müller, U. (eds.), Von Sylt bis Kastanas. Festschrift für Helmut Johannes Kroll zum 65. Geburtstag. *Offa* 69/70 Neumünster: Wachholtz, 139-145.

Ball, T.B., Gardner, J.S., Anderson, N. 1999. Identifying inflorescence phytoliths from selected species of wheat (*Triticum monococcum*, *T. dicoccon*, *T. dicoccoides*, and *T. aestivum*) and barley (*Hordeum vulgare* and *H. spontaneum*) (Gramineae). *American Journal of Botany* 86, 1615-1623.

Ball, T.B., Davis, A.L., Evett, R., Ladwig, J.L., Tromp, M., Out, W.A., Portillo, M. 2016. Morphometric analysis of phytoliths: recommendations towards standardization from the International Committee for Phytolith Morphometrics. *Journal of Archaeological Science* 68, 106-111.

Ellis, R.P. 1987. A review of comparative leaf blade anatomy in the systematics of the Poaceae: the past twenty-five years, in: Soderstrom, T.R. (ed.), *Grass systematics and evolution*. Washington DC: Smithsonian Institution Press, 3-10.

Fuller, D.Q. and Stevens, C. 2009. Agriculture and the development of complex societies: an archaeobotanical agenda, in: Fairbairn, A.S. and Weiss, E. (eds.), *From foragers to farmers: Papers in honour of Gordon C. Hillman*. Oxford: Oxbow Books, 37-57.

Grubben, G.J.H. and Partohardjono, S. 1996 (eds.), *Plant resources of South-East Asia 10. Cereals*. Leiden: Backhuys Publishers.

Harvey, E.L. and Fuller, D.Q. 2005. Investigating crop processing using phytoliths analysis: the example of rice and millets. *Journal of Archaeological Science* 32, 739-752.

Hillman, G.C. 1984. Interpretation of archaeological plant remains: the applications of ethnographic models from Turkey, in: van Zeist, W. and Casparie, W.A. (eds.), *Plants and ancient man*. Rotterdam: Balkema, 1-41.

Hunt, H.V., Vander Linden, M., Liu, X., Motuzaite-Matuzeviciute, G., Colledge, S., Jones, M.K. 2008. Millets across Eurasia: chronology and context of early records of the genera *Panicum* and *Setaria* from archaeological sites in the Old World. *Vegetation History and Archaeobotany* 17/Suppl. 1, 5-18.

Laird, N.M. and Ware, J.H. 1982. Random-effects models for longitudinal data. *Biometrics* 38/4, 963-974.

Madella, M. 2001. Understanding archaeological structures by means of phytolith analysis: A test from the Iron Age site of Kilise Tepe – Turkey, in: Meunier, J.D., Colin, F., Faure-Denard, L. (eds.), *Phytoliths: applications in earth science and human history*. Lisse: Balkema, 173-182.

Miller, N. 1984. The use of dung as fuel: an ethnographic example and an archaeological application. *Paléorient* 10/2, 71-79.

Motuzaite-Matuzeviciute, G., Staff, R., Hunt, H., Liu, X., Jones, M. 2013. The early chronology of broomcorn millet (*Panicum miliaceum*) in Europe. *Antiquity* 87/338, 1073-1085.

Out, W.A. and Madella, M. 2016a. Morphometric distinction between bilobate phytoliths from *Panicum miliaceum* and *Setaria italica* leaves. *Archaeological and Anthropological Sciences* 8/3, 505-521.

Out, W.A. and Madella, M. 2016b. The identification of non-dietary crop products from *Eleusine coracana* (L.) Gaertn. ssp. *coracana*, *Pennisetum glaucum* (L.) R. Br. and *Sorghum bicolor* (L.) Moench by phytolith analysis, in: Thanheiser, U. (ed.), *News from the past: Progress in African archaeobotany*. Proceedings 7th International Workshop for African Archaeobotany. Advances in Archaeobotany 2. Groningen: Barkhuis Publishing, 83-94.

Out, W.A. and Madella, M. 2017. Towards improved detection and identification of crop by-products: morphometric analysis of bilobate leaf phytoliths of *Pennisetum glaucum* and *Sorghum bicolor*. *Quaternary International* 434B, 1-14.

Out, W.A. and Madella, M. 2019. Towards identification of millet crop by-products by phytolith analysis: a comparison of short cell assemblages of *Panicum miliaceum* and *Setaria italica* leaves, in: Eichhorn, E. and Höhn, A. (eds.), *Trees, grasses and crops. People and plants in Sub-Saharan Africa and Beyond*. Frankfurt Archaeological Studies 3. Bonn: Habelt, 287-306.

Out, W.A., Pertusa Grau, J., Madella, M. 2014. A new method for morphometric analysis of opal phytoliths from plants. *Microscopy and Microanalysis* 20/06, 1-12.

Piperno, D.R. 2006. *Phytoliths: a comprehensive guide for archaeologists and paleoecologists*. Lanham: AltaMira Press.

Ryan, P. 2011. Plants as material culture in the Near Eastern Neolithic: perspectives from the silica skeleton artifactual remains at Çatalhöyük. *Journal of Anthropological Archaeology* 30, 292-305.

Stevens, C., Murphy, C., Roberts, R., Lucas, L., Silvia, F., Fuller, D.Q. 2016. Between China and South Asia: A Middle Asian corridor of crop dispersal and agricultural innovation in the Bronze Age. *The Holocene* 26/10, 1541-1555.

Verbeke, G. and Molenberghs, G. 2000. *Linear mixed models for longitudinal data*. New York: Springer New York.

Author address

Welmoed A. Out
Moesgaard Museum
Department of Archaeological Science and Conservation
Moesgaard Allé 20
8270 Højbjerg, Denmark
wo@moesgaardmuseum.dk

About the author

Welmoed Out studied Biology in the Netherlands. Her PhD (2009, Leiden University) was concerned with vegetation and plant exploitation in Dutch wetlands from 6000 to 3500 BC. She subsequently worked in a Marie Curie-project on Integrated Archaeobotanical Research at Sheffield University, in project-based archaeology for the companies ADC and ARC in the Netherlands, as a Marie Curie-fellow at the IMF-CISC in Barcelona, and as a post-doc at Kiel University. She is now working as an archaeobotanist at Moesgaard Museum in Denmark. Her research interests concern plant-people interactions, neolithisation and the methodological development and application of archaeobotanical research.

Early Agriculture in Southern Peru

Hermann Gorbahn and Markus Reindel

Abstract

The Preceramic site of Pernil Alto is located on the desertic Andean foothills of Southern Peru. It dates to 5800-5000 cal BP and with that to the end of the Middle Preceramic Period of the Central Andes. It was possible to detect the transition from foraging to agriculture starting at around 5300 cal BP in the permanent village of Pernil Alto. With these results, early village agriculture is evident in Southern Peru, which in turn contributes to an overall understanding of the emergence of the first complex societies in the Central Andes.

Introduction

The Central Andes are one of the few areas in which sedentary life and food-producing economies emerged independently, in a multifaceted and non-evolutionary manner. Given the size of the area, which includes a high variety of ecological zones, these processes were very complex. All processes that finally led to the emergence of early complex societies within the Central Peruvian Coast region, at around 5000 cal BP (Makowski 2006; Shady Solís and Leyva 2003; Shady Solís 2010; Shady Solís *et al.* 2014), were located in the entire northern area of South America (cf. Piperno and Pearsall 1998) making it a "non-centre" of domestication and early settled life (cf. Harlan 1971). Even though there is detailed information about first complex societies introducing monumental architecture at numerous sites (Fuchs 2009; Haas and Creamer 2004; Haas *et al.* 2004; Shady Solís 1999; Shady Solís 2000), the preceding cultural, social, and economic developments are hitherto not completely understood. The mentioned societies practiced a jointed agricultural-marine economy, which integrated the exploitation of the rich marine resources at the coast and agriculture in the coastal hinterland (Shady Solís 2006a; Shady Solís 2006b). The emergence of these monumental societies on the Central Peruvian coast dates to the Late Preceramic

in: Müller, J. and Ricci, A. 2020 (eds.), *Past Societies: Human Development in Landscapes*.
Sidestone Press: Leiden, 51-68.

Figure 1. The site of Pernil Alto during fieldwork in 2010 (view direction: west; photo: Proyecto Palpa).

Period[1] (5000-3800/3500 BP), but previous required developments – including the emergence of sedentism, villages, exploitation of marine resources, and agriculture – took place in the preceding Middle Preceramic Period (8000-5000 BP) in the Central Andes. Whereas early sedentary villages with a marine based subsistence are known from the Peruvian and Ecuadorian coast (Benfer 2008; Benfer 1999; Benfer 1990; Bird and Hyslop 1985; Dillehay *et al.* 2012a; Dillehay *et al.* 2012b; Donnan 1964; Engel 1988; Sandweiss 1996; Stothert 1985), the development of agriculture as a subsistence strategy is hitherto poorly understood. There are strong indications for early agriculture beginning maybe as early as 7500 BP, but more securely from 5600 BP onwards (Dillehay *et al.* 2005; Dillehay 2011), originating in Northern Peru in the area of the Nanchoc/Jequetepeque Valley. However, most of this evidence is indirect, based on the presence of plant-species, and which, thus far, has not been connected to village- or hamlet-like settlements that have been studied in detail.

The site of Pernil Alto was discovered in the Andean foothills in Southern Peru within the "Andean Transect" project of the German Archaeological Institute in 2001 (Fig. 1).

1 The Preceramic Period is synonymic to the Archaic Period and refers to the time from the beginning of the Holocene to the introduction of ceramics.

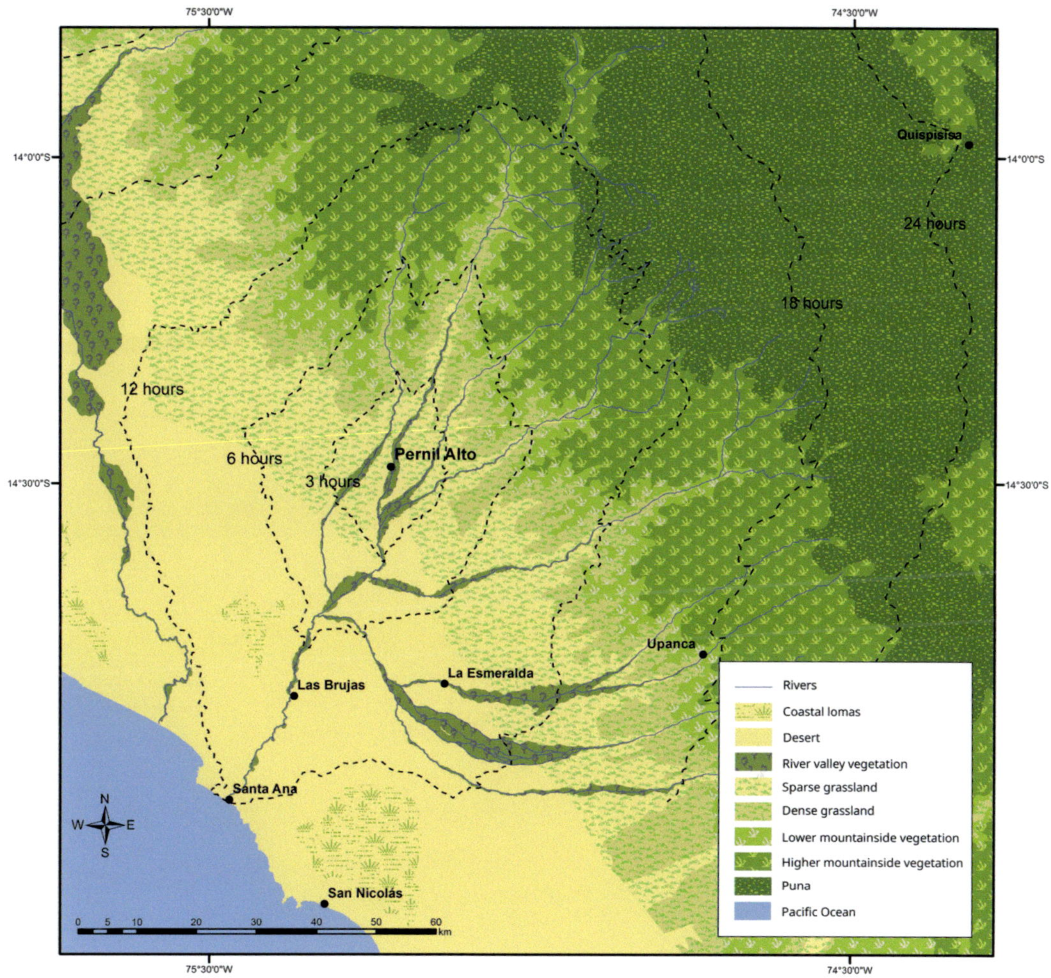

Figure 2. Pernil Alto in the mid-Holocene landscape. The reconstruction of the ecological zones is based on the literature mentioned in the text. All mapped sites are Preceramic. The dotted lines indicate walking distances from Pernil Alto. The highland begins more or less with the puna vegetation (after: Gorbahn 2013, fig. 8; Reindel and Gorbahn 2016, fig. 5; Reindel and Gorbahn 2018, fig. 5).

Its investigation has contributed to the research agenda with new information, thus providing a better understanding of the highly complex process of the emergence of agriculture and sedentism in the Central Andes. The preceramic remains of Pernil Alto date to 5800-5000 cal BP, that is, to the end of the Middle Preceramic Period, which directly precedes the emergence of the first complex societies at the Central Peruvian coast. The preceramic remains were excavated from 2005-2009 and were analysed shortly thereafter. The research aimed at understanding the prevailing subsistence economy, the internal structure, and the possible mobility form of the people of Pernil Alto. Other aspects were also studied, but have been excluded from this paper.

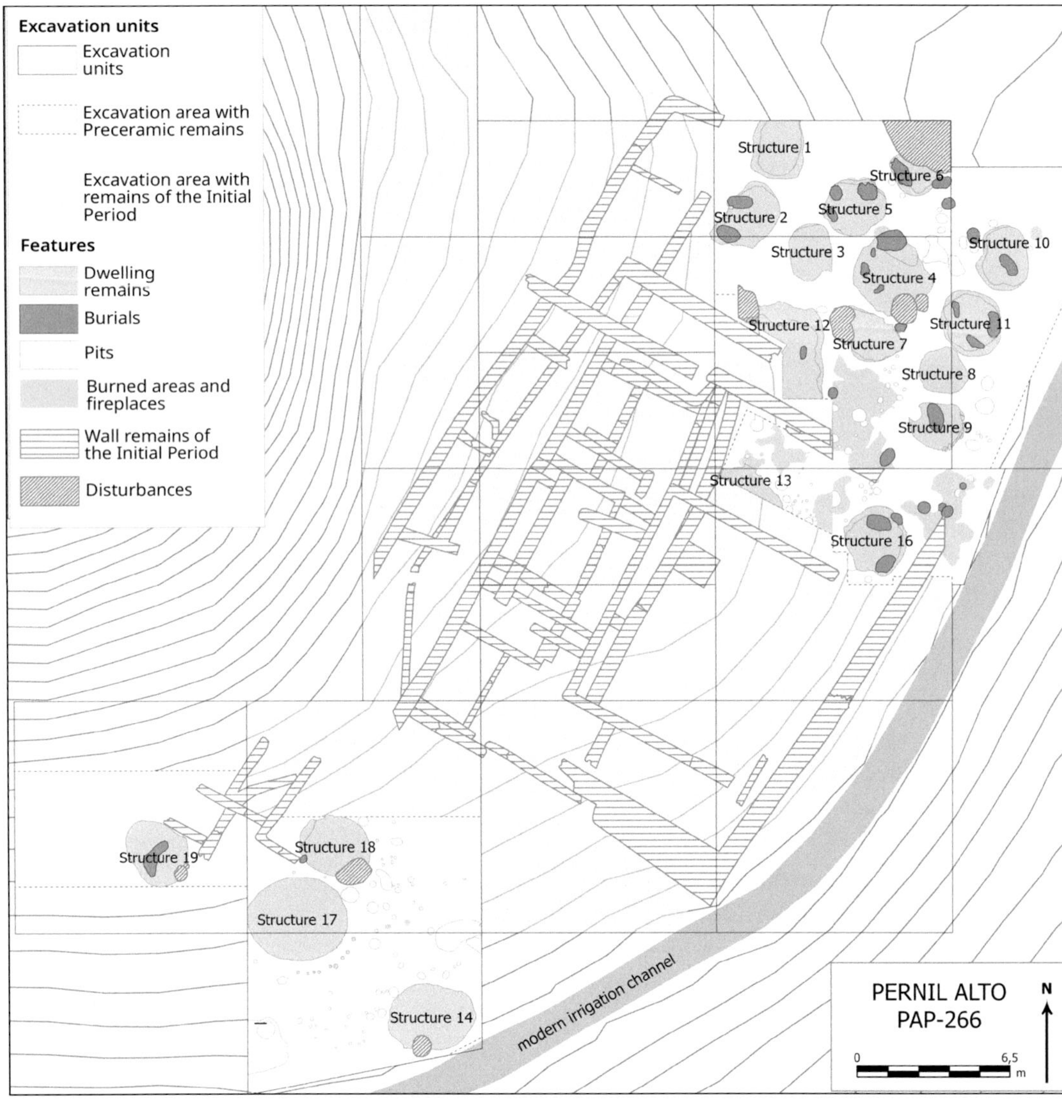

Figure 3. Plan of Pernil Alto indicating the most important remains of the Initial and the Preceramic Periods (after: Reindel and Gorbahn 2018, fig. 7).

Material and Methods

Pernil Alto is located in the Rio Grande Basin in Southern Peru in the district of Palpa. It is situated on the desertic Andean foothills at an altitude of 400 m on a small spur 10 m above the fertile river valley bottom of the Rio Grande. Following the river upstream, the Andean highlands are about 50 km away. Downstream, the Pacific coast is located at a distance of about 60 km (see Fig. 2).

The first archaeological research at this site focused on a settlement from the Initial Period (3500-2800 cal BP) (Reindel and Isla 2006). Below this settlement, remains of a significantly older site of the Middle Preceramic Period (8000-5000 BP) were discovered in 2005 and subsequently researched in an areal excavation of 400 m², which

Figure 4. Remains of a semi-subterranean dwelling (structure 11) with a burial (no. 50) placed in the abandoned hut (view: south; after: Reindel and Gorbahn 2016, fig. 9; Reindel and Gorbahn 2018, fig. 9).

we divided into two areas and excavated by following cultural layers. The distribution limits of the remains were detected in the north, east, and south of the excavation area. Towards the west, however, the superimposed remains of the walls of the Initial Period[2] were so dense that the preceramic remains below could not be excavated. The complete area of the preceramic site is estimated to be around 1200 m^2.

Various remains in the form of layers, pits, fireplaces, storage pits, *etc.* were documented during the excavations (Fig. 3).

This included the remains of 18 dwellings, which represented semi-subterranean, circular or oval huts with diameters of 2.5-3 m (see Fig 3. for locations and Fig. 4 for an example).

Additionally, 33 simple, primary inhumation burials containing 35 individuals, mainly in flexed positions, were discovered (see Fig. 4 for an example). About 2/3 of them had been buried in abandoned dwellings (see Fig. 3 for locations and Fig. 4 for an example), the rest in the open spaces between them. Numerous lithic, bone, basketry, wood, jewellery, and other artefacts were associated with the remains (Fig. 5).

---

2 The walls could not be removed according to Peruvian regulations of the preservation of archaeological monuments.

a
b
c
d
10 cm
e
i
l
f
m
g
n
j
k
h
10 cm
o
p
10 cm
q

Figure 5 (opposite page). Examples of artefacts of Pernil Alto: (a) mortar; (b) big ground stone; (c) very big handstone; (d) pestle; (e) projectile point; (f) cutting tool; (g) hammerstone; (h) notched piece; (i) spear thrower head; (j) braiding tool; (k) double-ended digging stick; (l) sea shell pendant; (m) discoidal sea shell beads; (n) oval sea shell beads; (o) textile remain; (p) mat remains; (q) possible net remain (after: Reindel and Gorbahn 2018, fig. 10 modified; see above).

Numerous botanical macroremains and faunal remains were recovered, since conservation conditions were ideal due to the extremely arid milieu. A total of 70 samples for radiocarbon analysis were obtained.

Following stratigraphic information, the ^{14}C-dates[3] were modelled in OxCal 4.2 and six phases could be distinguished. The artefacts were classified and then analysed by function, based on performed activities. The site was examined in spatial and functional terms in order to identify activity areas. The buried individuals were examined anthropologically with regards to age and sex.[4] In addition, measurements of strontium isotopes[5] were conducted. All botanical and faunal remains were analysed and species, weight, and plant or body parts were determined.[6]

The encompassing analytical approach for all these forms of analysis was based on a quantitative diachronic analysis that included all available information in a multi-proxy perspective. The core aim of the analysis was to quantify the available information and transfer it in quantified form to the phases as they were obtained from the stratigraphy and modelling of the ^{14}C data. Thus, the diachronic development of cultural components of Pernil Alto could be observed in a measurable and comparable form. An important aspect was the assumption that all cultural, natural, and archaeological/technical taphonomic processes affected the remains during all phases of the settlement in equal measure, so that the most meaningful results were not primarily due to the absolute numbers of components, but to the changing relations between them.

3 The radiocarbon measurements were conducted by laboratories in Heidelberg, Germany (Hd) and Mannheim, Germany (MAMS) by Bernd Kromer and his team. Some radiocarbon dates were given from this research group to a laboratory in Zürich, Switzerland (ETH), for control reasons. All datings are AMS-datings.

4 The recovered human remains were studied and determined by Elsa Tomasto Cagigao of the Pontificia Universidad Católica in Lima, Peru, and Lars Fehren-Schmitz, then of the Georg-August-Universität in Göttingen, Germany.

5 The analyses were conducted by Stefan Hölzl, Christian Dekant and Susanne Rummel, all then from the Bavarian State Collection of Paleontology and Geology, Munich, Germany.

6 The botanical remains were determined by Gabriela Bertone of the Museo Nacional de Historia Natural, Lima, Peru. The remains of the vertebrates were determined by Enrique Angulo and Carmen Rosa Cardoza of the Museo de Arqueología de San Marcos (Casona), Lima, Peru. The remains of the invertebrates were determined by Manuel Goritti Manchego.

Results

The remains dated to about 5800-5000 cal BP and could be divided into six consecutive chronological phases (0-5)[7]:

0: 5789-5291 cal BP
1: 5334-5266 cal BP
2: 5303-5150 cal BP
3: 5257-5064 cal BP
4: 5248-4985 cal BP
5: 5215-4819 cal BP

All remains were assignable to one of these six phases. Phase 0 was a particularly long phase that also differs culturally from the following phases. Phase 5 was poorly represented and all subsequent analysis steps ignore the remains of this phase, which probably represent a post-use period.

The dwellings served mainly as shelters for sleeping due to the associated internal contexts. The use of each dwelling by two or three people can be assumed. They did not exist simultaneously, but were erected successively around free places with abandoned dwellings serving as burial places. The dwellings were arranged around encircled areas. A larger central area was surrounded by six dwellings in the northeastern area of the site.[8] Three further smaller areas, consisting of four dwellings, were located in the north[9] and south.[10] The successive and arranged construction of the dwellings indicates a structured, planned settlement with a pattern of "circulating courtyards". Everyday activities took place outdoors in the areas surrounded by the dwellings.

The recovered botanical remains consisted of wild and cultivated plants of 11 species and 10 genera. Cultivated species were fully domesticated, so that domestication steps were not performed in Pernil Alto. The most important wild food plant was Prosopis (*Prosopis pallida*). Cultivated food plants included sweet potatoes (*Ipomoea batatas*), lima beans (*Phaseolus lunatus*), smaller proportions of edible canna (*Canna indica*), common bean (*Phaseolus vulgaris*), guava (*Psidium guajava*), jack-bean (*Canavalia sp.*), squash (*Cucurbita sp.*), and yam bean (*Pachyrrihzus sp.*). Another cultivated plant was the bottle gourd (*Lagenaria siceraria*), which was cultivated for industrial purposes as their dried fruits served as vessels.

Wild plants were collected in the riparian forest, while domesticated plants were probably cultivated on a river meander south of Pernil Alto. When directly compared, the weight of edible residues of wild plants makes up 34.49%, the weight of cultivated plants 65.51%. However, the proportions develop diachronically (see diagram in Fig. 6):

With 64.7%, wild plants represent the majority of plant residues in phase 0. Starting in phase 1, in comparison, the amount of cultivated plants reached 52% and increased to 74.5% in phase 4.

---

7 σ2-calibration.
8 See Fig. 3: formed by structures 7, 8, 9, 12, 13, and 16.
9 See Fig. 3: formed by structures 1, 2, 3, and 5; and by structures 4, 6, 10, and 11.
10 Less clear; see Fig. 3: formed maybe by structures 17, 18, and 19.

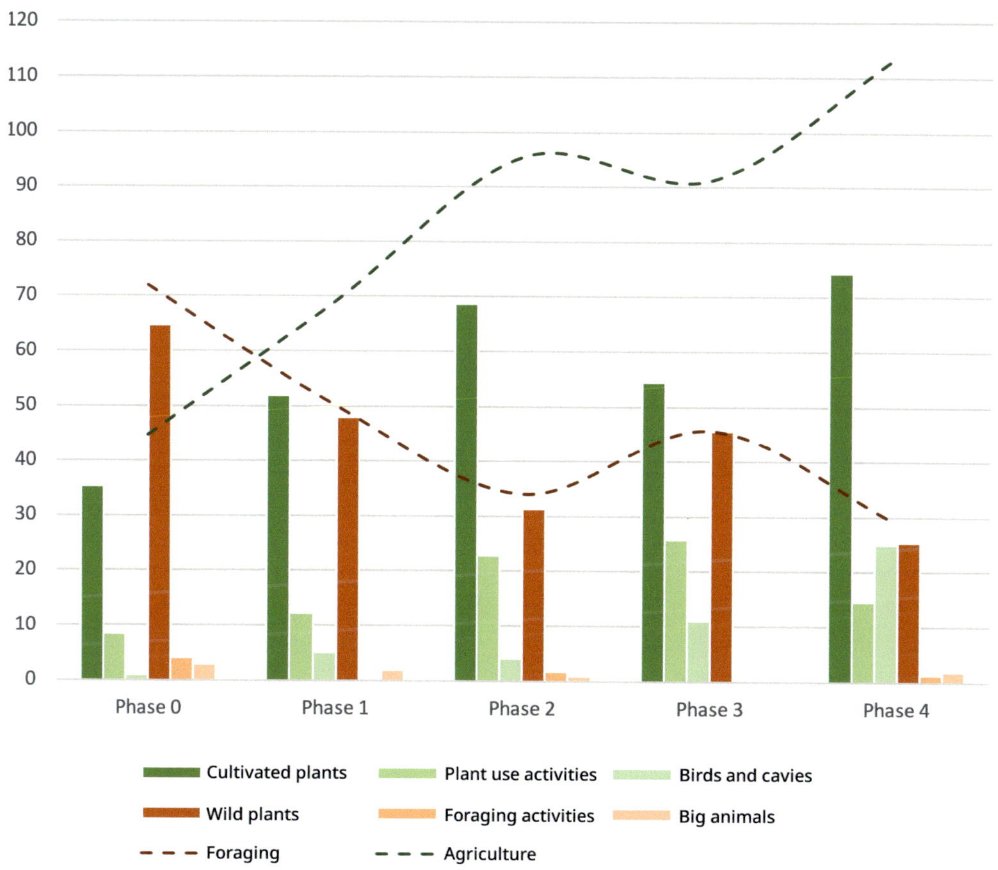

Figure 6. Diachronic development of the indicators of agriculture and foraging. The amounts for "cultivated plants", "plant use activities", "wild plants" are given in percentages. The amounts of "birds and cavies" and "big animals" are absolute numbers. The overall trendlines of "foraging" and "agriculture" indicate accumulated amounts (foraging = wild plants + foraging activities + big animals; agriculture = cultivated plants + plant use activities + birds and cavies) (diagram: H. Gorbahn and M. Reindel).

A similar development is identifiable in the faunal remains (see diagram in Fig. 6): Altogether, these are – in relation to places with clear evidence of hunting in the highlands (*e.g.* Aldenderfer 1998; Lavallée *et al.* 1985; Rick and Moore 1999) – poorly represented in Pernil Alto. Only the remains of 10 larger mammals (tarucas, guanacos, and other camelids) were detected. Besides these, the remains of 39 rodents and birds of different species were recovered. The larger animals can be considered as remains of hunted game. Their frequency decreases continuously from phase 0 onwards with only some occasional hunting activity in phase 4. Rodents and birds became increasingly more frequent. Most were found in the remains of phase 4. Hunting for larger animals – including guanacos, which descended from the highlands during the flowering period of the coastal fog oasis – can be assumed in the closer vicinity of Pernil Alto, but lost importance diachronically. The increasing amount of small game was probably connected to the increasing agricultural activity that attracted these animals, which were then "hunted" as an additional protein source or killed as pests on cultivated land. The remains of marine invertebrates are very sparse in Pernil Alto, except in processed jewellery. Mussels and sea fish were thus practically not consumed in Pernil Alto. However, there are some remains of freshwater shrimps originating directly from the Rio Grande.

The analysis of the artefact-expressed activities revealed that numerous activities were performed, which were combined into groups. This, in turn, enhanced the comprehensibility and comparability of the results.

The proportion of artefact-expressed activities related to foraging (projectile points, scrapers, spear thrower head, *etc.*; see Fig. 5b for examples) was low in relation to other activities on a whole, but also lost importance diachronically (see diagram in Fig. 6). In contrast, plant use-activities, expressed by specific artefacts (ground stones, mortars, handstones, pestles, digging sticks, *etc.*; see Fig. 5a and 5b for examples), increased continuously (see diagram in Fig. 6). Handcraft activities, evidenced by various artefacts (hammer stones, semi-products, cores, *etc.*), are relatively low in phase 0, but also increased continuously.

Raw materials were local and available within the vicinity of the site. Exotic materials were composed of sea shells and obsidian. The latter originates from the highlands and was only used in exceptional cases, with a continuously decreasing proportion. Sea shells were used for jewellery (mainly beads) and originated from the Pacific coast. Their amount increased diachronically.

The strontium signals measured in the human skeletal remains clearly indicate local signals, thus excluding longer stays in the highlands or on the coast.

The composition of the buried individuals probably corresponded to a living population. About 2/3 of them were young individuals (prenatal to infants 1); only 1/3 had become adult. There is a slight predominance of female individuals, but only seven could clearly be sex-determined. However, the burials are unequally distributed in the phases.

Based on local palaeoclimatic research (Eitel *et al.* 2005; Mächtle *et al.* 2010; Schittek *et al.* 2015), it seems clear that the mid-Holocene climate in the Rio Grande basin was distinctly more humid than today. The current precipitation in Palpa is about 5 mm/a (ONERN 1971), whereas in the mid-Holocene it has been estimated to have been more than 200 mm/a. This had an impact on the landscape surrounding Pernil Alto, providing the site with significantly more stream water, denser and more intensive riparian forests, and grasslands outside the river valleys (see Fig. 2 for a reconstruction of the landscape), which contrasts with today's extremely arid landscape.

Discussion

Following Bruce Smith (2001), subsistence economies of low-food-production and agriculture can be distinguished by the amount of produced food: Low-food-production systems are systems in which domesticated plants are cultivated, but whose main food source is foraging.[11] In contrast, cultivated plants constitute the major part of subsistence in agriculture. Deborah Pearsall (2003) has compared the information available from

11 Which includes, according to this definition, the use of the entire range of natural food resources like plant collecting, hunting, fishing, etc.

Southern Ecuador with that from the Central Andes to determine when agriculture first became the subsistence basis in the Central Andes. She included various aspects in a multi-proxy approach (Pearsall 2000; Pearsall 2009), contrasting more simple traditional approaches in which only the presence of domesticated plants was taken as an indicator of agriculture. Due to her results and data, it is likely that crop cultivation became the main subsistence strategy only from 4800 BP onwards (also cf. Zeidler 2008) and that it can only be from this point on that agriculture can be assumed. More recent research (Dillehay 2011) assumes that agriculture has existed since 7500 BP in the Nanchoc area in Northern Peru. However, concrete botanical macroremains are rather sparse (Rossen 1991; Rossen *et al.* 1996) and some interpretations are questionable from the authors' point of view (Piperno and Dillehay 2008). In the Nanchoc area, the dating of an irrigation channel from approximately 5600 BP (Dillehay *et al.* 2005; Dillehay *et al.* 2011) can be assumed to represent a more secure beginning of agriculture. However, the proportional relationship between plant cultivation and foraging is not clear. Furthermore, no village plans and settlements from this area and period are known.

If the definitions of Smith (2001) and the multi-proxy approach of Pearsall (2000; 2009) are transferred to the results of Pernil Alto described above (see Fig. 6), then the subsistence economy of Pernil Alto can be considered to have been a low-food-production system in phase 0. During this phase (ca. 5800-5300 cal BP), the focus of subsistence was wild plants, which accounted for 64.7% of the weight of plant residues, in contrast to 35.3% of cultivated plants. Hunting also had some importance. Moreover, logistical mobility seems to have been more pronounced, as obsidian was used in greater (albeit overall low) quantity in this phase compared to the following phases. In addition, foraging activities, as expressed by the artefacts, were still relatively frequent, while activities for plant use were already present, but not yet nearly as strong as in the following phases. Overall, a low-food-production subsistence with a focus on foraging and a still relatively strong logistic mobility seems to have been pursued in Pernil Alto during phase 0.

In contrast, the subsistence economy can be interpreted as agricultural in the following phases, starting at 5300 BP. From this time on, cultivated plants always account for more than 50% of the weight of the food plants. In phase 2, their amount even exceeds 2/3 and increases further with a slight backdrop in phase 3. Similarly, hunting for larger game decreases as reflected both in faunal remains and in artefact-expressed activities. In the latter, plant use activities increase and roughly correspond to the increase in the amounts of remains of cultivated plants. This proxy is thereby independent of that of the plant remains. The increase in small game can also be interpreted as an indication of agriculture now practiced as a subsistence basis: Rodents and birds were probably attracted by the larger and/or longer-used areas under cultivation and then killed by the inhabitants. The subsistence economy of Pernil Alto was therefore, from 5300 cal BP onwards, entirely agricultural, even if plant collecting still played a relevant role.

Pernil Alto's internal settlement pattern with circulating courtyards and the open spaces, probably used for communal/everyday activities, corresponds rather to that of a village and not to an agglomerated hamlet due to its structure and planning. The results of strontium analyses also show that the population was local and not mobile. In addition, the concentrated occurrence of archaeological evidence, verifying a permanent use of Pernil Alto in the form of the aforementioned village structure, agriculture by 5300 cal BP, the construction of graves and the particularly heavy artefacts (ground stones, mortars) as well as the local raw materials, clearly indicate that the population was sedentary. In addition, handcraft activities at the settlement increased and were not carried out externally (*e.g.* expeditions), which indicates a stronger presence at the settlement. The increase in jewellery made of marine materials also fits into the picture of this sedentism: With increasing sedentism, relations with the coast probably stabilised, which resulted in more intense exchange. Some sites, which are contemporaneous with Pernil Alto, such as Las Brujas (Vogt 2011; Vogt 2008; Vogt 2007) and Santa Ana (Engel 1981) (see Fig. 2), are known from the lower course of the Rio Grande. They are not yet fully researched, but provide indications of settlement activity during the Preceramic Period in these areas. Overall, Pernil Alto was a permanent and established agricultural village on the Andean foothills by 5300 cal BP.

This makes Pernil Alto the oldest hitherto known *agricultural* village of the Central Andes. The transition to agriculture that took place in Pernil Alto was obviously not triggered by changing environmental conditions. These were – in contrast to today – particularly favourable, whereas a significant improvement or deterioration of environmental conditions does not correlate chronologically with the changing mode of subsistence. It was rather an internal, socio-economic process that probably occurred, whose "trigger" – if any existed – could not be determined from the archaeological record of Pernil Alto. The abandonment of the settlement around 4900 cal BP was possibly due to a shifting riverbed, which often happens with the Peruvian coastal rivers under natural conditions. Already within the last phase – phase 5 – the archaeological remains are quite scarce and Pernil Alto probably only served as a burial place at this time.

Conclusion

Although Pernil Alto provides the oldest evidence of village agriculture in the Central Andes to date and this finding is important in itself, the findings furthermore represent a puzzle piece in the understanding of the multifaceted processes in which sedentism, agriculture, and ultimately the first complex societies based on it developed. Permanent villages on the Central Andean coast, such as La Paloma (Benfer 1990; Benfer 1999; Engel 1980; Quilter and Stocker 1983), Huaca Prieta (Bird and Hyslop 1985; Dillehay *et al.* 2012a; Dillehay *et al.* 2012b) or Chilca 1 (Engel 1988), already existed well before Pernil Alto. At these sites, however, rich marine resources were exploited, while plant cultivation was of minor importance. It is possible that older agriculture, from around 5600 BP, existed in Northern Peru in the Nanchoc area (Dillehay 2011), but no village structures have been found there yet. In addition, Pernil Alto was not a domestication place, since the cultivated food plant species already arrived in their fully domesticated form in Pernil Alto and originated botanically for the most part probably from Amazonia and/or Northern South America (see Piperno and Pearsall 1998). Research at Pernil Alto is, however, significant in that it has been proven that agricultural villages existed even before the emergence of complex societies on the Central Peruvian coast. There, at around 5000 cal BP, the established use of marine resources was combined with the – now demonstrably – already established agriculture into a marine-agricultural economy (Shady Solís 2006a; Shady Solís 2006b), in which cotton – for nets to increase the protein yield – and maize – to increase the carbohydrate production – were integrated. This "enhanced" double system then formed the economic basis for the first complex societies (see Reindel and Gorbahn 2016 for a more detailed description of the model), which left important archaeological remains in the form of early monumental structures and which were possibly already organised as proto-state societies (Shady Solís *et al.* 2000). They formed the cradle for the development of Central Andean civilisation. Pernil Alto represents a previous development that contributed to this development.

Overall, it can nevertheless be assumed that agricultural villages existed in other areas on the Andean foothills at least at the same time or even earlier than Pernil Alto. The results of research from the Nanchoc/Jequetepeque Valley (Dillehay 2011) provide strong evidence for very early developments of subsistence economy in these ecological zones. However, the foothills and western slope of the Andes have – despite admonishments by Peter Kaulicke since 1994 (Kaulicke 1994, 162) – still not been sufficiently researched. Future investigations on the Preceramic Period in this area could provide further important insights into the development of an agricultural economy in the Central Andes.

Acknowledgements

We would like to thank Artur Ribeiro and Eileen Küçükkaraca for the correction of the English. Still, all mistakes are our mistakes. We would like to thank Johny Isla and Judith Astahuamán for their collegial cooperation and support in Peru, Ingmar Unkel for helping in the production of the OxCal model, Bertil Mächtle for critically reviewing the landscape reconstruction, and the specialists Bernd Kromer, Elsa Tomasto Cagigao, Stefan Hölzl, Christian Dekant, Susanne Rummel, Gabriela Bertone, Enrique Angulo, Carmen Rosa Cardoza, and Manuel Goritti Manchego for their precise analyses, determinations, and fruitful discussions. Thank you very much!

References

Aldenderfer, M.S. 1998. *Montane Foragers: Asana and the south-central Andean archaic.* Iowa City: University of Iowa Press.

Benfer, R.A. 1990. The Preceramic Period Site of Paloma, Peru: Bioindications of Improving Adaption to Sedentism. *Latin American Antiquity* 1, 284-318.

Benfer, R.A. 1999. Proyecto de excavaciones en Paloma, Valle de Chilca, Perú, in: Kaulicke, P. (ed.), *El periodo arcaico en el Perú: Hacia una definición de los orígenes.* Boletín de Arqueología PUCP 3. Lima: PUCP, 213-237.

Benfer, R.A. 2008. Early Villages, in: Pearsall, D.M. (ed.), *Encyclopedia of archaeology.* Amsterdam: Elsevier, Academic Press, 368-380.

Bird, J.B. and Hyslop, J. 1985. *The preceramic excavations at the Huaca Prieta. Chicama Valley, Peru.* Anthropological papers of the American Museum of Natural History 62. New York: American Museum of Natural History.

Dillehay, T.D. 2011 (ed.), *From foraging to farming in the Andes: New Perspectives on Food Production and Social Organization.* Cambridge/New York: Cambridge University Press.

Dillehay, T.D., Bonavia, D., Goodbred, S., Pino, M., Vásquez, V.F., Tham, T.R. 2012a. A late Pleistocene human presence at Huaca Prieta, Peru, and early Pacific Coastal adaptions. *Quaternary Research* 77, 418-423.

Dillehay, T.D., Bonavia, D., Goodbred, S., Pino, M., Vásquez, V.F., Tham, T.R., Conklin, W., Splitstoser, J., Piperno, D.R., Iriarte, J., Grobman, A., Levi-Lazzaris. G., Moreira, D., Lopéz, M., Tung, T.A., Titelbaum, A., Verano, J.W., Adovasio, J.M., Scott Cummings, L., Bearéz, P., Dufour, E., Tombret, O., Ramirez, M., Beavins, R., DeSantis, L., Rey, I., Mink, P., Maggard, G.J., Franco, T. 2012b. Chronology, mound-building and environment at Huaca Prieta, coastal Peru, from 13700 to 4000 years ago. *Antiquity* 86, 48-70.

Dillehay, T.D., Eling, H.H., Rossen, J. 2005. Preceramic irrigation canals in the Peruvian Andes. *Proceedings of the National Academy of Sciences* 102, 17241-17244.

Dillehay, T.D., Maggard, G.J., Rossen, J., Stackelbeck, K.L. 2011. Technologies and Material Culture, in: Dillehay, T.D. (ed.*), From foraging to farming in the Andes. New Perspectives on Food Production and Social Organization*. Cambridge/New York: Cambridge University Press, 205-228.

Donnan, C.B. 1964. An Early House from Chilca, Peru. *American Antiquity* 30, 137-144.

Eitel, B., Hecht, S., Mächtle, B., Schukraft, G., Kadereit, A., Wagner, G.A., Kromer, B., Unkel, I., Reindel, M. 2005. Geoarchaeological evidence from desert loess in the Nazca-Palpa region, Southern Peru: Palaeoenvironmental changes and their impact on pre-Columbian cultures. *Archaeometry* 47, 137-158.

Engel, F.A. 1980. Paloma Village 613: A 6000 Year Old "Fog Oasis" Village in the Lower Central Andes of Peru, in: Engel, F.A. (ed.), *Prehistoric Andean ecology. Man, settlement and environment in the Andes*. Atlantic Highlands, N.J.: Humanities Press, 103-135.

Engel, F.A. 1980 (ed.), *Prehistoric Andean ecology. Man, settlement and environment in the Andes*. Atlantic Highlands, N.J.: Humanities Press.

Engel, F.A. 1981 (ed.*), Prehistoric Andean ecology. Man, settlement and environment in the Andes 2: The deep south*. Atlantic Highlands, N.J.: Humanities Press.

Engel, F.A. 1988. *Ecología prehistórica andina. El hombre, su establecimiento y el ambiente de los Andes, la vida en tierras áridas y semiáridas. Chilca, Pueblo 1. Implementos de hueso*. Lima: C.I.Z.A.

Fuchs, P.R. 2009. Del Arcaico Tardío al Formativo Temprano: las investigaciones en Sechín Bajo, valle de Casma, in: Kaulicke, P. and Onuki, Y. (eds.), *El Período Formativo: enfoques y evidencias recientes. Cincuenta años de la Misión Arqueológica Japonesa y su vigencia*. Boletín de Arqueología PUCP 13. Lima: PUCP, 55-86.

Gorbahn, H., 2013. The Middle Archaic site of Pernil Alto, Southern Peru: The beginnings of horticulture and sedentariness in Mid-Holocene conditions. *Diálogo Andino* 41, 61-82.

Haas, J. and Creamer, W. 2004. Cultural Transformations in the Central Andean Late Archaic, in: Silverman, H. (ed.), *Andean Archaeology*. Blackwell Studies in Global Archaeology 2. Malden, Mass.: Blackwell, 35-50.

Haas, J., Creamer, W., Ruiz, A. 2004. Power and Emergence of Complex Polities in the Peruvian Preceramic, in: Vaughn, K.J., Ogburn, D., Conlee, C.A. (eds.), *Foundations of power in the Prehispanic Andes* 14. Arlington, Va: American Anthropological Association, 37-52.

Harlan, J.R. 1971. Agricultural Origins: Centers and Noncenters. *Science* 174, 468-474.
Kaulicke, P. 1994. *Los orígenes de la civilización andina. Arqueología del Perú*. Historia general del Perú 1. Lima: Ed. Brasa.
Kaulicke, P. 1999 (ed.), *El periodo arcaico en el Perú: Hacia una definición de los origenes*. Boletín de Arqueología PUCP 3. Lima: PUCP.
Kaulicke, P. and Dillehay, T.D. 2006 (eds.), *Procesos y expresiones de poder, identidad y orden tempranos en Sudamérica*. Primera parte 10. Lima: Pontificia Univ. Católica del Perú.
Lavallée, D., Julien, M., Wheeler, J.C, Karlin, C. 1985. *Telarmachay: Chasseurs et Pasteurs Préhistoriques des Andes*. Editions Recherche sur les Civilisations, Synthèse 20. Paris: Inst. Français d'Etudes Andines.
Mächtle, B., Unkel, I., Eitel, B., Kromer, B., Schiegl, S. 2010. Molluscs as evidence for a late Pleistocene and early Holocene humid period in the southern coastal desert of Peru (14.5° S). *Quaternary Research* 73, 39-47.
Makowski, K. 2006. La arquitectura pública del Periodo Precerámico Tardío y el reto conceptual del urbanismo andino, in: Kaulicke, P. and Dillehay, T.D. (eds.), *Procesos y expresiones de poder, identidad y orden tempranos en Sudamérica*. Primera parte 10. Lima: Ponteficia Univ. Católica del Perú, 167-199.
ONERN. 1971. *Inventario, evaluación y uso racional de los recursos naturales de la costa. Cuenca del Río Grande (Nazca) I: Informe*. Lima: ONERN.
Pearsall, D.M. 2000[2] (ed.), *Paleoethnobotany: a handbook of procedures*. Walnut Creek: Left Coast Press.
Pearsall, D.M. 2003. Plant Food Resources of the Ecuadorian Formative: An Overview and Comparison to the Central Andes, in: Raymond, J.S. and Burger, R.L. (eds.), *Archaeology of formative Ecuador*. A symposium at Dumbarton Oaks, 7 and 8 October 1995. Washington, D.C.: Dumbarton Oaks Research Library and Collection, 213-257.
Pearsall, D.M. 2008 (ed.), *Encyclopedia of archaeology*. Amsterdam: Elsevier, Academic Press.
Pearsall, D.M. 2009. Investigating the Transition to Agriculture. *Current Anthropology* 50, 609-613.
Piperno, D.R. and Dillehay, T.D. 2008. Starch grains on human teeth reveal early broad crop diet in northern Peru. *Proceedings of the National Academy of Sciences* 105, 19622-19627.
Piperno, D.R. and Pearsall, D.M. 1998. *The origins of agriculture in the lowland neotropics*. San Diego, CA: Academic Press.
Plew, M.G. 1996 (ed.), *Prehistoric hunter-gatherer fishing strategies*. Boise, Idaho: Boise State University Dept. of Anthropology.
Quilter, J. and Stocker, J. 1983. Subsistence Economies and the Origins of Andean Complex Societies. *American Anthropologist* 85/3, 545-562.
Raymond, J.S. and Burger, R.L. 2003 (eds.), *Archaeology of formative Ecuador*. A symposium at Dumbarton Oaks, 7 and 8 October 1995. Washington, D.C.: Dumbarton Oaks Research Library and Collection.
Reindel, M. and Gorbahn, H. 2016. Arid Zones and the Rise of Complex Societies in South America, in: Reindel, M., Bartl, K., Lüth, F., Benecke, N. (eds.), *Palaeoenvironment and the development of early settlements*. Proceedings of the International Conferences: Palaeoenvironment and the Development of Early

Societies. Sanliurfa/Turkey, 5-7 October 2012: The Development of Early Settlement in Arid Regions. Aqaba/Jordan, 12-15 November 2013. Menschen – Kulturen – Traditionen Band 14. Rahden/Westf.: VML Verlag, 201-219.

Reindel, M. and Gorbahn, H., 2018.The rise of monumentality and complex societies in the Central Andes, Peru, in: Meller, H., Gronenborn, D., Risch, R. (eds.), Überschuss ohne Staat – politische Formen in der Vorgeschichte. 10. Mitteldeutscher Archäologentag vom 19. bis 21. Oktober 2017 in Halle (Saale) = *Surplus without the state – political forms in Prehistory.* 10th Archaeological Conference of Central Germany October 19-21, 2017 in Halle (Saale). Tagungen des Landesmuseums für Vorgeschichte Halle 18. Langenweißbach: Verlag Beier & Beran, 449-466.

Reindel, M. and Isla, J.A. 2006. Evidencias de culturas tempranas en los valles de Palpa, costa sur del Perú, in: Kaulicke, P. and Dillehay, T.D. (eds.), *Procesos y expresiones de poder, identidad y orden tempranos en Sudamérica. Primera Parte*. Boletín de Arqueología PUCP 10. Lima: PUCP, 237-283.

Rick, J.W. and Moore, K.M. 1999. El precerámico de la punas de Junín: El punto de vista desde Panaulauca, in: Kaulicke, P. (ed.), *El period arcaico en el Perú: Hacia una definición de los origenes*. Boletín de Arqueología PUCP 3. Lima: PUCP, 263-296.

Rossen, J. 1991. *Ecotones and Low-Risk Intensification: The Middle Preceramic Occupation of Nanchoc, Northern Peru*. Unpublished PhD thesis: University of Kentucky.

Rossen, J., Dillehay, T.D., Ugent, D. 1996. Ancient Cultigens or Modern Intrusions? Evaluating Plant Remains in an Andean Case Study. *Journal of Archaeological Science* 23/3, 391-407.

Sandweiss, D.H. 1996. The development of fishing specialization on the Central Andean Coast, in: Plew, M.G. (ed.), *Prehistoric hunter-gatherer fishing strategies*. Boise, Idaho: Boise State University Dept. of Anthropology, 41-63.

Schittek, K., Forbriger, M., Mächtle, B., Schäbitz, F., Wennrich, V., Reindel, M., Eitel, B. 2015. Holocene environmental changes in the highlands of the southern Peruvian Andes (14° S) and their impact on pre-Columbian cultures. *Climate of the Past* 11, 27-44.

Shady Solís, R. 1999. Los orígenes de la civilización y la formación del estado en el Perú. Las Evidencias Arqueológicas de Caral-Supe. Primera Parte. *Boletín del Museo de Arqueología y Antropología de la UNMSM* 2, 2-4.

Shady Solís, R. 2000. Los orígenes de la civilización y la formación del estado en el Perú. Las Evidencias Arqueológicas de Caral-Supe. Segunda Parte. *Boletín del Museo de Arqueología y Antropología de la UNMSM* 3, 2-7.

Shady Solís, R. 2006a. Caral-Supe and the North Central Area of Peru: The history of maize in the land where civilization came into being, in: Staller, J.E., Tykot, R.H., Benz, B.F. (eds.), *Histories of maize. Multidisciplinary approaches to the prehistory, linguistics, biogeography, domestication, and evolution of maize*. Walnut Creek: Routledge, 381-402.

Shady Solís, R. 2006b. La civilización Caral: Sistema social y manejo del territorio y sus recursos. Su trascendencia en el proceso cultural andino, in: Staller, J.E., Tykot, R.H., Benz, B.F. (eds.), *Histories of maize. Multidisciplinary approaches to the prehistory, linguistics, biogeography, domestication, and evolution of maize*. Walnut Creek: Routledge, 59-89.

Shady Solís, R. 2010. *Caral: La Primera Civilización de América/The First Civilisation in the Americas*. Chicago: University of Chicago Press.

Shady Solís, R. and Leyva, C. 2003 (eds.), *La cuidad sagrada de Caral-Supe. Los orígenes de la civilización andina y la formación del Estado prístino en el antiguo Perú*. Lima: Instituto Nacional de Cultura, Proyecto Especial Arqueólogico Caral-Supe.

Shady Solís, R., Dolorier, C., Montesinos, F., Casas, L. 2000. Los orígenes de la civilización en el Perú: El área norcentral y el valle de supe durante el arcaico tardío. *Arqueología y Sociedad* 13, 13-48.

Shady Solís, R., Machacuay Romero, M., Novoa Bellota, P., Quispe Loayza, E. 2014 (eds.), *Caral 20 años: recuperando la historia de la Civilización Caral para el Perú y el mundo, con responabilidad social*. Lima: Ministerio de Cultura, Zona Arqueológica Caral.

Silverman, H. 2004 (ed.), *Andean Archaeology*. Blackwell Studies in Global Archaeology 2. Malden, Mass: Blackwell.

Smith, B.D. 2001. Low-Level Food Production. *Journal of Archaeological Research* 9, 1-43.

Staller, J.E., Tykot, R.H., Benz, B.F. 2006 (eds.), *Histories of maize. Multidisciplinary approaches to the prehistory, linguistics, biogeography, domestication, and evolution of maize*. Walnut Creek: Routledge.

Stothert, K.E. 1985. The Preceramic Las Vegas Culture of Coastal Ecuador. *American Antiquity* 50, 613-637.

Vaughn, K.J., Ogburn, D., Conlee, C.A. 2004 (eds.), *Foundations of power in the Prehispanic Andes* 14. Arlington, Va: American Anthropological Association.

Vogt, B. 2007. Bajo Río Grande (Peru), in: Deutsches Archäologisches Institut (ed.), *Jahresbericht 2006 (2007)*, 207-208.

Vogt, B. 2008. Bajo Río Grande (Peru), in: Deutsches Archäologisches Institut (ed.), *Jahresbericht 2007 (2008)*, 295-297.

Vogt, B. 2011. Las Brujas, Bajo Río Grande (Peru), in: Deutsches Archäologisches Institut (ed.), *Jahresbericht 2010 (2011)*, 307-308.

Zeidler, J.A. 2008. The Ecuadorian Formative, in: Silverman, H. and Isbell, W.H. (eds.), *Handbook of South American Archaeology*. New York: Springer, 459-488.

Author addresses

Hermann Gorbahn
CRC 1266 "Scales of Transformation"
Kiel University
Leibnizstr. 3
24118 Kiel, Germany
hgorbahn@sfb1266.uni-kiel.de

Markus Reindel
Deutsches Archäologisches Institut/German Archaeological Institute (DAI)

Kommission für Archäologie Außereuropäischer Kulturen/
Commission for the Archaeology of Non-European Cultures (KAAK)
Dürenstr. 35-37
53173 Bonn, Germany
markus.reindel@dainst.de

About the authors

Hermann Gorbahn is currently a research coordinator of the CRC 1266 "Scales of Transformation" at Kiel University, Germany. He studied Prehistoric and Protohistoric Archaeology in Münster, Kiel, and Santiago de Chile and received his MA in 2008 and his PhD in 2016. He has worked in research projects of the Commission for the Archaeology of Non-European Cultures of the German Archaeological Institute in Peru and Brazil. From 2009-2012, he was a PhD student at the GS "Human Development in Landscapes" and from 2017-2019 he was a postdoctoral research fellow (both at Kiel University). In his PhD thesis, he investigated the site of Pernil Alto. One of his main research interests is the emergence of agriculture and the development of early complex societies in South America.

Markus Reindel is a senior researcher at the Americas division of the Commission for the Archaeology of Non-European Cultures (KAAK) of the German Archaeological Institute (DAI) and Honorary Professor at the Institute for American Anthropology of the University of Bonn, Germany. He studied American Anthropology, Ethnology, Geography and Spanish at the universities of Freiburg/i. Br., Madrid and Bonn, where he received his PhD in 1991. In the following years, he directed interdisciplinary research projects about settlement patterns and architecture in Ecuador (1992-1993), Mexico (1993-1997), Peru (1997-2015) and Honduras (2012-2019). Since 2006, he is the speaker of the Research Cluster I of the German Archaeological Institute (From Sedentariness to Complex Societies: Settlement, Economy, Ecology, Cult). Currently, he is engaged in archaeological projects on the north coast of Honduras and in landscape and settlement studies in Peru and Brazil.

Corded Ware and Bell Beaker between Rhine and Saale: Theories, Methods and Results

Ralph Großmann

Abstract

The Corded Ware and Bell Beaker phenomena were widespread appearances of the 3rd millennium BC, which were mostly spatially exclusive. However, in certain Central European regions both phenomena were located close by each other. These included the Upper/Middle Rhine region and the Thuringia region/Burgenland District. Based on an applied typo-chronology and chorology, these regions were analysed with the aim to reveal the dialectic and interrelation amongst these phenomena. Interrelations could be found, among other things, with respect to grave goods and ranges of sign systems to which the decoration motifs probably belonged. Shared elements occurred when spatial and temporal proximities of the phenomena were given. The sharing of material culture and symbols is interpreted as part of an exchange network between Corded Ware and Bell Beaker phenomena, which could be based on a gift giving character. Moreover, some burials overcame the Corded Ware and the Bell Beaker dichotomy and were regarded as hybrids.

Introduction

Within the 3rd millennium BC, the Corded Ware phenomenon and the Bell Beaker phenomenon dominated Europe's material culture. The distribution of the Corded Ware phenomenon that began around 2850 BC (Włodarczak 2009), ranged from the Middle Volga in the east to the Rhine in the west and over wide areas of Scandinavia. In the south, the phenomenon borders on the Alps and Carpathians. However, the Bell Beaker phenomenon spread from about 2700 BC from the Iberian Peninsula in the west to the Carpathian Basin and the Vistula River in the east and from Morocco in the south to Great Britain and southern Scandinavia in the north (Olalde *et al.* 2017; Heyd 2013; Lechterbeck *et al.* 2013).

in: Müller, J. and Ricci, A. 2020 (eds.), *Past Societies: Human Development in Landscapes*.
Sidestone Press: Leiden, 69-80.

The dissertation of the author pertaining to this topic included two work areas. First, the federal states of Hessen, Rhineland-Palatinate and northwestern Baden-Württemberg, which are summarised under the name Upper/Middle Rhine region, as well as the state of Thuringia and the Burgenland District. These areas were chosen due to extensive material bases that promised beneficial analytical studies. In addition, the selection of two work areas enabled a cross-spatial comparison and showed changes on the basis of different landscapes and cultural influences. Finally, two areas revealed evidence of possible diffusions of material cultures among regions.

The underlying thesis (Großmann 2016) addressed the question, whether relations between the Corded Ware phenomenon and the Bell Beaker phenomenon can be detected and, if so, in which manner these references have to be considered. Based on the axiom that spatial and temporal proximity indicate communication, further questions concerning chronology and distribution patterns were pursued. Moreover, questions about the cause of interrelations and about the meanings of decorative motifs were provided. In addition, theses about the transitions from the Late Neolithic to the End Neolithic and from the End Neolithic to the Early Bronze Age were postulated.

Material and Methods

The investigation was largely based on burial goods, which represent the most important source in the End Neolithic. Grave contexts were represented by single graves, sometimes covered by mounds (mostly in Corded Ware contexts). Often, burials were already partially or completely destroyed before they were documented and most burial mounds were preserved in forest areas (Messerschmidt and Ettel 2011, 19).

The corresponding sources for the Upper and Middle Rhine region were based on the catalogues of Gebers (1978) and Wiermann (2004); regarding Thuringia and the Burgenland District on catalogues by Löwe (1959), Feustel *et al.* (1966), Bach and Bach (1975), Matthias (1974; 1982; 1987), Bücke *et al.* (1989) and Hille (2012).

In addition to the material culture of the Corded Ware and Bell Beaker phenomena, the group of Giant Beakers was also part of the doctoral thesis, which had strong links to the Bell Beaker, Corded Ware and Single Grave cultures (see Wiermann 2004).

Chronologies for both phenomena and regions were created. Therefore, the studies by Gebers (1978; 1984) and Ullrich (2008) served as role models. Decoration motifs and beaker forms operated as bases for chronological analyses, which functioned as variables for correspondence analyses (Großmann 2016, 45-56). In contrast to Ullrich (2008) and Gebers (1978), no distinction was made in terms of decorating techniques, in order to underpin common motifs and not the techniques, which were applied.

The typologies of beakers and amphorae were chronologically proved by absolute data (^{14}C-data) and Bayesian ^{14}C models were added, which clarified and underpinned typochronologies. The results included phenomena of specific time periods for the respective work areas and justified assignments of the material cultures (beakers, amphorae) into the time periods (Großmann 2016, 59-116).

Furthermore, the dissertation contains distribution maps of material cultures in respective time periods, which also include kernel-density analyses made with Geographic Information System (GIS). Based on GIS, archaeological sites were also correlated with the predominant soil types and topographies. Moreover, distribution patterns of diverse typological vessel types were created, which were also presented in temporal depth (Großmann 2016, 119-176).

The references and interactions between the End Neolithic phenomena took centre stage in the thesis. Based on correspondence analytic studies of categories of grave goods, trans-phenomenon beaker forms and ornament motifs could be highlighted (Großmann 2016, 177-228).

Results

Regarding typo-chronologies, the following results were obtained: Both the Upper/Middle Rhine region as well as the Thuringia region and the Burgenland District provided an oldest, older, and middle Corded Ware phase. However, the oldest phase in the Thuringia region and the Burgenland District is very weakly pronounced. In addition, Thuringia and the Burgenland District demonstrated an additional younger phase (Fig. 1).

The oldest beakers (2800-2620 BC) were characterised by a bulbous s-profiled shape and short line-field ornamentations with final point decorations – beakers, which largely confirm the early onset of the so-called A-Horizon of the Corded Ware phenomenon (*e.g.* Ullrich 2008). Earliest amphorae included line bundle amphorae and amphorae carrying the Swiss Vinelzer motif. The early forms were mainly located in the Rhine-Main area with few further sites within the West Hesse Basin. Concerning Thuringia and the Burgenland District, a material continuity with and a temporal overlap to the Globular Amphora could be observed (Beran 1992; Müller

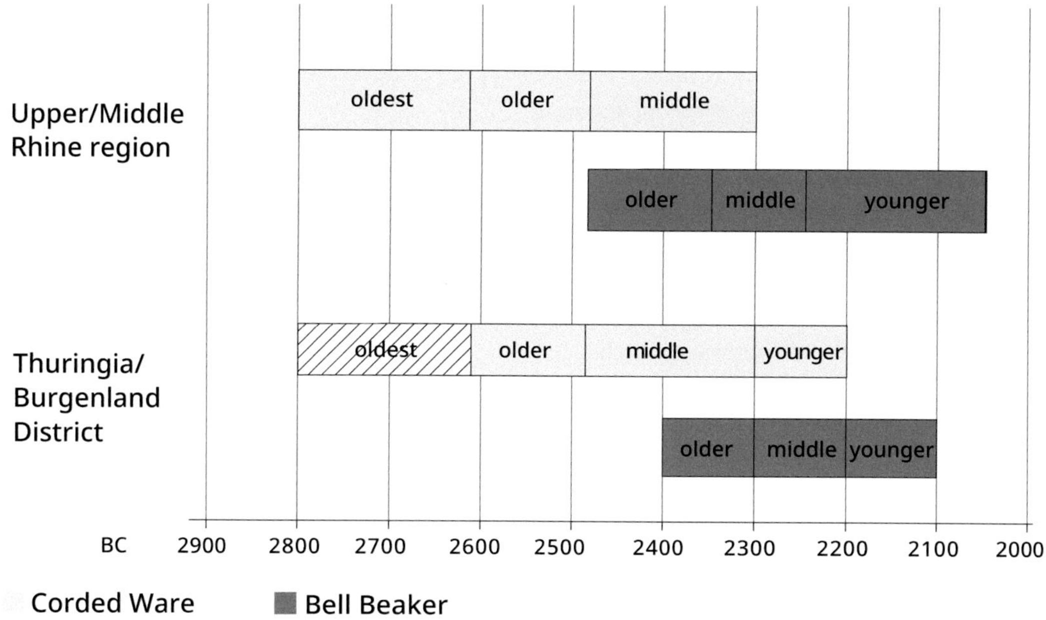

Figure 1. Chronological phases of Corded Ware and Bell Beaker in the work areas of the Upper/ Middle Rhine region and in the Thuringia region/Burgenland District, based on correspondence analyses and ^{14}C data (Großmann 2016, fig. 5.27, 112).

2001; Woidich 2014). No ^{14}C data from the oldest Corded Ware phase were provided and only a few beakers, which typologically correspond to the oldest phase, were located left of the Saale River and north of the Unstrut River (Großmann 2016, 129 fig. 6.7; 144 fig. 6.17).

In the Upper/Middle Rhine region, the older Corded Ware phase (2620-2480 BC) was represented, in particular, by the so-called herringbone ornamented beakers (*e.g.* Sangmeister 1951, 64). With the appearance of this type, the number of findings increased especially north of the Main. At this time, a wider range of style groups could be identified within Thuringia and the Burgenland District. The A-Horizon continued and further styles, such as the so-called Mansfeld style (mostly expressed by shaded triangles), herringbone, and fir branch ornamentations (Group II after Buchvaldek 1967), appeared. In addition, beaker forms were designed with a narrower and less s-shaped profile. The amphorae were still thickset and had high-seated handles and short necks. An enormous increase of sites was detectable and the phenomenon spread especially along the Saale River and the Weiße Elster River (Großmann 2016, 130 fig. 6.8; 145 fig. 6.18).

From 2480 BC, the Corded Ware vessels were characterised, in both regions, by complex ornaments (Mansfeld style, Groß-Gerau/Esch style; Köster 1966), which were combined with narrow vessel shapes (tulip beaker). In addition, long cylinder necks for beakers and amphorae had become predominant. At this time, amphorae were rather rhombic shaped, with handles placed on the middle of the vessels. In the Upper/Middle Rhine region, a significant southwest shift of the Corded Ware distribution to larger river estuary regions (Rhine-Lahn/Mosel, Rhine-Main and Rhine-Neckar) was documented. This spread was also accompanied by a preference for flatter areas. In the Thuringia/Burgenland District, the Corded Ware phenomenon had, when comparing it to the previous phase, a higher concentration within the Thuringia Basin at the upper reaches of the Saale and at the Pleise River (Großmann 2016, 131 fig. 6.9; 146 fig. 6.19).

From 2300 BC, Corded Ware findings could no longer be verified for the Upper/Middle Rhine region and less evidence was recorded north of the Unstrut River and west of the Gera River for Thuringia and the Burgenland District (Großmann 2016, 147 fig. 6.20). Vessel decorations were limited to spare horizontal line fields and zoned line decors. Cylinder neck vessels and beakers with handles continued to dominate the picture. *Ostharz* amphora belonged to the characteristic amphorae of this phase, which had only puncture and furrow engravings.

With respect to the Bell Beaker phenomenon, older, middle and younger phases were applied for the work areas, whereby the phenomenon started later and persisted a little bit shorter in Thuringia and in the Burgenland District than in the Upper/Middle Rhine region (Fig. 1).

In the Upper/Middle Rhine region, the first beakers (2480-2350 BC) included Maritime, CZM (Cord-Zoned-Maritime) and AOO (All-Over-Ornamented) vessels, which were especially recorded on the western side of the Rhine River within Rhine Hesse and the Anterior Palatinate region. The Bell Beaker phenomenon started in the Thuringia/Burgenland District around 2400 BC with few findings concentrated north and west of the Unstrut and Ilm rivers. In contrast to the Upper/Middle Rhine region, Maritime and CZM beakers were not recorded. Instead, Metope beakers, which display two broad ornamental zones, characterised the older phase (Großmann 2016, 135 fig. 6.10; 151 fig. 6.21).

From 2350 BC and 2300 BC, respectively, several regional Bell Beaker styles could be identified for both work areas, which were roughly represented by two styles: the Metope beakers and the Epi-Maritime beakers. In contrast to the previous phase, the Metope beakers were narrower. Instead of two, they had mainly three ornamental zones. Moreover, the variation of ornament motifs increased. Especially hourglass motifs characterised this middle phase. In the Upper/Middle Rhine region, the Bell Beaker phenomenon spread to the eastern side of the Rhine and occupied regions along the Main and Neckar. A strong increase of findings could also be recorded for the Neuwied Basin. In the Thuringia/Burgenland District, an enormous increase of findings and an expansion to the east toward the Weiße Elster River could be observed. Concentrations existed, in particular, at the Gera, Ilm, and Saale rivers. In both work areas, a process of suppression and replacement of the material culture of the Corded Ware phenomenon is recognisable (Großmann 2016, 136 fig. 6.11; 152 fig. 6.22).

From 2250/2200 BC, Bell Beakers had either complex decorations (Veluwe style) or were almost undecorated. The Neuwied Basin exhibited Giant Beakers and the material cultures of the Early Bronze Age groups (Adlerberg, Unitice) increasingly replaced the material culture of the End Neolithic groups – a development that is illustrated, in particular, by the increasing number of undecorated beakers and cups. Basically, this phase corresponds to a transitional horizon in which both the material culture of the Bell Beaker phenomenon and the material cultures of Early Bronze Age groups existed side by side (Großmann 2016, 136 fig. 6.12; 153 fig. 6.23).

With regard to the typological development, it should be emphasised that in both the Corded Ware and the Bell Beaker phenomena, forms of beakers and amphorae provide more indications regarding chronology than decorative motifs. Ornament motifs tend to cover a larger temporal corridor and reflect regional traditions (Fig. 2).

Corded Ware and Bell Beaker findings correlated across time and phenomena with fertile black soils and riverine meadowlands. In addition, sites of both phenomena were oriented on rivers, whereby Bell Beaker findings were more often oriented on larger ones. Overlapping zones could be identified, where people of both phenomena lived for about 200 years. This applied, in particular, to the large estuarine Rhine-Neckar and Unstrut-Saale regions. Thus, people of both phenomena had an interest in similar landscapes, which facilitated similar economic bases and convenient connections to communication networks (Großmann 2016, 142 fig. 6.16; 157 fig. 6.27).

In addition, there are indications of mutual contacts and possible interrelations between the two phenomena, which had already been described in other studies and have been interpreted as being opposite, dialectical, and sharing (Behrens 1969; Fischer 1976; Strahm 2002).

The submitted thesis concluded that some cultural elements of the Bell Beaker phenomenon, such as the north-south orientation of the burials, tanged arrowhead points, tulip-shaped beakers, and scratched line ornamentations, were adopted by the Corded Ware phenomenon. In addition, various decorative motifs entered the Corded Ware phenomenon (inside ornamentation, the zoning of the herringbone motif, standing line bundle motifs, cross motifs, and the zoning of the vessel surface with two-, three- or four-line bundles) (Großmann 2016, 177-228).

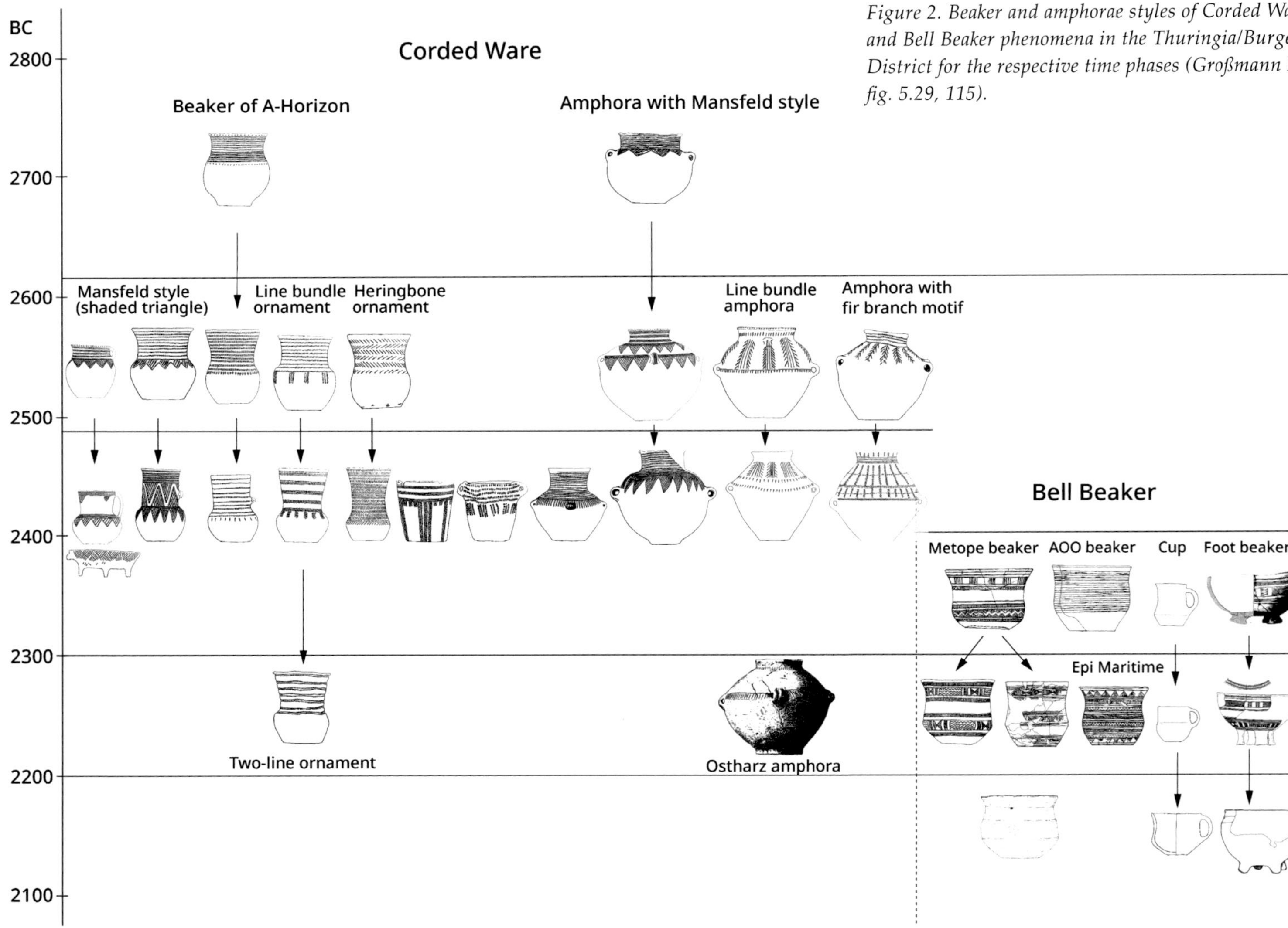

Figure 2. Beaker and amphorae styles of Corded Ware and Bell Beaker phenomena in the Thuringia/Burgenland District for the respective time phases (Großmann 2016, fig. 5.29, 115).

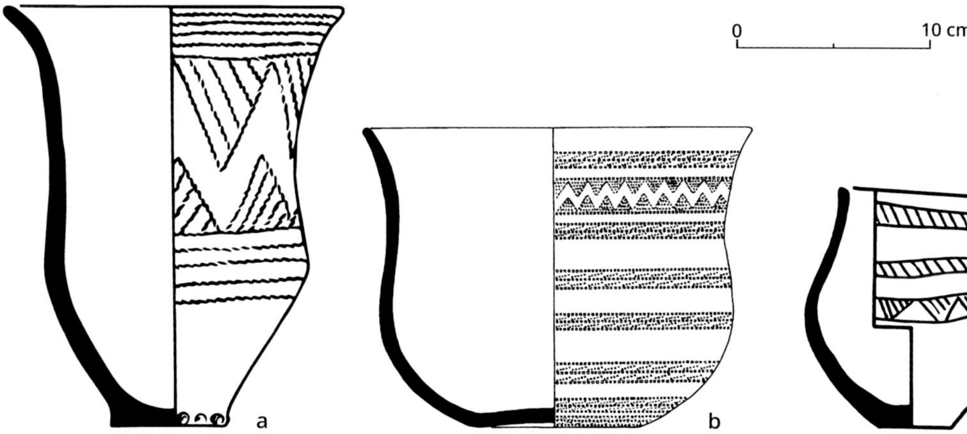

Figure 3. Motifs: Shaded triangle/spared angle band as examples for cross phenomena motifs: (a) Corded Ware: Mannheim-Seckenheim, Stadt-Mannheim (Gebers 1978, Taf. 3,3); (b) Bell Beaker: Mannheim, Stadt Mannheim (Wiermann 2004, Taf. 30,9); (c) Adlerberg Group (Early Bronze Age) Limburgerhof, Rhein-Pfalz-Kreis (Gebers 1978, 54,16).

Conversely, attributes were also adopted by the people of the Bell Beaker phenomenon from the Corded Ware phenomenon. This is shown by the east-west orientation of some burials and grave goods such as axes, arrowheads with concave bases, boar tusks, shell jewellery, bone antlers and *Komplementär-Keramik* = bowls, foot bowls, and cups (Strahm 2004). Various ornamentation techniques and motifs (cord and chisel stamp decorations, spared angle bands, shaded and interlocked triangular motifs) were also adopted by the Bell Beaker phenomenon. In addition, stone cist graves seem to be transmitted into the Bell Beaker phenomenon in connection with contacts to the Corded Ware phenomenon (Großmann 2016, 177-228).

Different elements, such as single graves, flat/stone cist graves, south-north orientations of the deceased, complementary ceramics (*Komplementär-Keramik*) and ornament motifs (shaded triangles, spared angle bands; Fig. 3), were also adopted by Early Bronze Age groupings (Unitice, Adlerberg).

Thus, there was a continuity, which also includes other regions such as the Lech Valley (cf. Knipper 2017; Schwarz 2015, 703). Another influence was recorded in the context of secondary burials of Bell Beakers in Corded Ware tombs, which were especially documented in the Thuringia/Burgenland District (Großmann 2016, 233-237 fig. 8.60).

Overall, there was not only a temporal proximity and overlap of both phenomena but distribution maps also showed a spatial proximity of common elements of the material culture that had been adopted by the respective phenomenon. This fact underpins the thesis that the occurrence of common elements was not a coincidental phenomenon, but the result of existing interrelations.

Discussion

Finally, it is questioned, which motives and backgrounds could be connected with these interrelations and why these references were expressed in an outward manner. Both phenomena preferred similar natural conditions and convenient locations. Thus, spatially-based references could hardly be avoided. Furthermore, the dimensions of burial grounds and settlements pointed to smaller communities (see Wattendorf-Motzenstein and Seregély 2008). Therefore, both Corded Ware and Bell Beaker groupings probably relied on common exchange networks. The resulting exchange character probably possessed an economic and a strategic background linked with exogamic practices (cf. Knipper 2017; Kristiansen *et al.* 2017) that did not put profit in the foreground, but rather produced connectedness and temporary alliances (Lévi-Strauss and Moldenhauer 1981; Mauss and Ritter 1990). Common elements of the material culture demonstrated that exchange networks had been established. In particular, symbols in the form of decoration motifs reflected this interaction. In some cases, this reference perhaps led to hybrid social identities, which were extracted both from the Corded Ware and Bell Beaker phenomena. Sometimes it is difficult to assign the material culture to people of the Corded Ware or the Bell Beaker phenomena; an indication that the polarisation and an allocation of material culture to one or another phenomenon frequently did not hardly correspond to reality (Großmann 2016, 233-251).

Conclusion

The Corded Ware and Bell Beaker phenomena were widespread appearances of the 3rd millennium BC, which were mostly spatially exclusive. However, in certain Central European regions – the Upper/Middle Rhine region and the Thuringia region/ Burgenland District – both phenomena were located nearby each other. Based on typo-chronologies and absolute data, phases could be disclosed and the spread of phenomena in the respective phases and work areas could be demonstrated. As a result, for both work areas a process of suppression and replacement of the material culture of the Corded Ware phenomenon is recognisable. However, references could also be detected, which had either a dialectic or a sharing character. These references could be found, among other things, with respect to grave goods and ranges of sign systems to which decoration motifs probably belonged. Shared elements occurred when spatial and temporal proximities of the phenomena were given. References in the material culture were interpreted as exchange activities, which probably included exogamic practices. Burials, which could not be assigned to one or the other phenomena, overcame the Corded Ware and Bell Beaker dichotomy and were regarded as hybrids.

Acknowledgements

The author is grateful to his supervisor, Prof. Dr. Johannes Müller, who offered valuable suggestions and advice and to the Graduate School "Human Development in Landscapes", which provided technical, skills-mediating and financial support. Moreover, the author would like to thank Prof. Dr. Martin Furholt and Prof. Dr. Antonia Davidovic-Walther for their supervision and Janine Cordts for support regarding publishing. The author would also like to thank the team from the "DB" for widening his horizon.

References

Bach, A. and Bach, H. 1975. Beiträge zur Kultur und Anthropologie der mitteldeutschen Schnurkeramiker II. *Alt-Thüringen*, 43-107.

Behrens, H. 1969. Westliche Einflüsse bzw. Einflüsse der Glockenbecherkultur bei den Becherkulturen der DDR, in: Behrens, H. and Schlette, F. (eds.), *Die neolithischen Becherkulturen im Gebiet der DDR und ihre europäischen Beziehungen*. Vorträge der Tagung 1967. Berlin: Deutscher Verlag der Wissenschaft, 143-154.

Beran, J. 1992. A-Horizont und Kugelamphorenkultur, in: Buchvaldek, M. and Chochol, J. (eds.), *Die Schnurkeramik in Böhmen*. Acta Universitatis Carolinae Philosophia et historica Monographia 19. Praha: Univ. Karlova, 35-41.

Feustel, R., Bach, H., Gall, W., Teichert, M. 1966. Beiträge zur Kultur und Anthropologie der mitteldeutschen Schnurkeramiker. *Alt-Thüringen*, 20-120.

Fischer, U. 1976. Die Dialektik der Becherkulturen. *Jahresschr. mitteldt. Vorgeschichte* 60, 235-245.

Gebers, W. 1978. *Das Endneolithikum und Frühbronzezeit im Mittelrheingebiet*. Bonn: Habelt.

Gebers, W. 1984. *Das Endneolithikum im Mittelrheingebiet*. Saarbrücker Beiträge zur Altertumskunde 27. Bonn: Habelt.

Großmann, R. 2016. *Das dialektische Verhältnis von Schnurkeramik und Glockenbecher zwischen Rhein und Saale*. Universitätsforschungen zur prähistorischen Archäologie 287. Human Development in Landscapes 8. Bonn: Habelt.

Heyd, V. 2013. Europe at the Dawn of the Bronze Age, in: Heyd, V., Kulcsár, G., Szeverényi, V. (eds.), *Transitions to the Bronze Age. Interregional interaction and socio-cultural change in the third millennium BC Carpathian basin and neighbouring regions*. Archaeolingua 30. Budapest: Archaeolingua Alapítvány, 9-66.

Hille, A. 2012. *Die Glockenbecherkultur in Mitteldeutschland*. Veröffentlichungen des Landesamtes für Archäologie 66. Halle (Saale): Landesamt für Denkmalpflege und Archäologie, Landesmuseum für Vorgeschichte.

Knipper, C., Mittnik, A., Massy, K. 2017. Female exogamy and gene pool diversification at the transition from the Final Neolithic to the Early Bronze Age in central Europe. *Proceedings of the National Academy of Sciences of the United States of America* 114/38, 10083-10088.

Köster, C. 1966. Beiträge zum Endneolithikum und zur Frühen Bronzezeit am nördlichen Oberrhein. *Prähistorische Zeitschrift* 43/44, 2-96.

Kristiansen, K., Allentoft, M.E., Frei, K.M. 2017. Re-theorising mobility and the formation of culture and language among the Corded Ware Culture in Europe. *Antiquity* 91/356, 334-347.

Lechterbeck, J., Kerig, T., Kleinmann, A. 2013. How was Bell Beaker economy related to Corded Ware and Early Bronze Age lifestyles? Archaeological, botanical and palynological evidence from the Hegau, Western Lake Constance region. *Journal of Environmental Archaeology* 19/2, 1-19.

Lévi-Strauss, C. and Moldenhauer, E. 1981[2]. *Die elementaren Strukturen der Verwandtschaft*. Suhrkamp Wissenschaft. Frankfurt am Main: Suhrkamp.

Loewe, G. 1959. *Thüringen. Kataloge zur mitteldeutschen Schnurkeramik*. Veröffentlichungen des Landesamtes für Denkmalpflege und Archäologie Sachsen-Anhalt – Landesmuseum für Vorgeschichte. Halle: Niemeyer.

Matthias, W. 1974 (ed.), *Kataloge zur mitteldeutschen Schnurkeramik. Teil 4: Südharz-Unstrut-Gebiet.* Berlin: Deutscher Verlag der Wissenschaft.

Matthias, W. 1982. *Kataloge zur mitteldeutschen Schnurkeramik. Teil 5: Mittleres Saalegebiet.* Berlin: Deutscher Verlag der Wissenschaft.

Matthias, W. 1987. *Kataloge zur mitteldeutschen Schnurkeramik. Teil 6: Restgebiete und Nachträge.* Berlin: Deutscher Verlag der Wissenschaft.

Mauss, M. and Ritter, H. 1990[1]. *Die Gabe. Form und Funktion des Austauschs in archaischen Gesellschaften.* Suhrkamp-Taschenbuch Wissenschaft 743. Frankfurt am Main: Suhrkamp.

Messerschmidt, K. and Ettel, P. 2011 (eds.), *Das schnurkeramische Gräberfeld und die eisenzeitlichen Siedlungsbefunde von Altenburg.* Jenaer Schriften zur Vor- und Frühgeschichte 4. Jena: Beier & Beran.

Müller, J. 2001. *Soziochronologische Studien zum Jung- und Spätneolithikum im Mittelelbe-Saale-Gebiet (4100-2700 v. Chr.): Eine sozialhistorische Interpretation prähistorischer Quellen.* Vorgeschichtliche Forschungen 21. Rahden/Westf.: Leidorf.

Olalde, I., Brace, S., Allentoft, M.E. 2017. The Beaker Phenomenon and the Genomic Transformation of Northwest Europe. *Nature* 555/7695, 190-196.

Sangmeister, E. 1951. *Die Jungsteinzeit im nordmainischen Hessen.* Schriften zur Urgeschichte. Melsungen: Heimatschollen-Verl.

Schwarz, R. 2015. Kultureller Bruch oder Kontinuität? – Mitteldeutschland im 23. Jh. v. Chr., in: Meller, H., Arz, H.W., Jung, R., Risch, R. (eds.), *2200 BC – ein Klimasturz als Ursache für den Zerfall der alten Welt?* 7. Mitteldeutscher Archäologentag vom 23.-26. Oktober 2014 in Halle (Saale). Tagungen des Landesmuseums für Vorgeschichte Halle 12/2. Halle (Saale): Landesamt f. Denkmalpflege u. Archäologie Sachsen-Anhalt, 671-713.

Seregély, T.F. 2008. *Studien zum dritten vorchristlichen Jahrtausend in Nordostbayern.* Universitätsforschungen zur prähistorischen Archäologie 154. Bonn: Habelt.

Strahm, C. 2002. Tradition und Wandel der sozialen Strukturen vom 3. zum 2. vorchristlichen Jahrtausend, in: Müller, J. (ed.), *Vom Endneolithikum zur Frühbronzezeit: Muster sozialen Wandels?* Tagung Bamberg 14.-16. Juni, 2001. Universitätsforschungen zur prähistorischen Archäologie 90. Bonn: Habelt, 175-194.

Strahm, C. 2004. Das Glockenbecher-Phänomen aus der Sicht der Komplementär-Keramik, in: Czebreszuk, J. (ed.), *Similar but different. Bell Beakers in Europe.* Poznań: Adam-Mickiewicz-University, 101-126.

Ullrich, M. 2008. *Endneolithische Siedlungskeramik aus Ergersheim, Mittelfranken. Untersuchungen zur Chronologie von Schnurkeramik- und Glockenbechern an Rhein, Main und Neckar.* Universitätsforschungen zur prähistorischen Archäologie 160. Bonn: Habelt.

Wiermann, R.R. 2004. *Die Becherkulturen in Hessen. Glockenbecher, Schnurkeramik, Riesenbecher.* Freiburger archäologische Studien 4. Rahden, Westf.: Leidorf.

Włodarczak, P. 2009. Radiocarbon and Dendrochronological Dates of the Corded Ware Culture. *Radiocarbon* 51, 737-749.

Woidich, M. 2014. *Die Westliche Kugelamphorenkultur. Untersuchungen zu ihrer raum-zeitlichen Differenzierung, kulturellen und anthropologischen Identität.* Topoi 24. Berlin: De Gruyter.

Author address

Ralph Großmann
Institute of Pre- and Protohistoric Archaeology/
Cluster of Excellence ROOTS
Kiel University
Leibnizstr. 3
24118 Kiel, Germany
rgrossmann@roots.uni-kiel.de

About the author

The author, born 1978 in Wertheim/Main, has been a member of the Graduate School "Human Development in Landscapes" since 2010. He published his PhD thesis *Das dialektische Verhältnis von Schnurkeramik und Glockenbecher zwischen Rhein und Saale* in 2016 as part of the series 'Human Development in Landscapes/ Universitätsforschungen zur prähistorischen Archäologie'. He wrote his Master's thesis at the University of Würzburg on social structures of the Early Bronze Age. Since 2017, the author has been dedicated to social inequalities in archaeological cultures.

Settlement History and Tell Formation Processes in the Birecik and Carchemish Sectors of the Euphrates River

Andrea Ricci

Abstract

This study investigates settlement trajectories in the Syro-Turkish region of the Middle Euphrates River Valley for the period between the 5th and the 3rd millennium BC. By applying a multi-scalar approach, which integrates published and original survey data with remote sensing analysis, this regional archaeological landscape study illustrates that longevity of settlement choices played a pivotal role in shaping the cultural landscape of the Birecik-Carchemish region. Both along the Euphrates and in the uplands, settlement continuity led to the formation of mounded sites as early as the 5th millennium BC.

Introduction

The application of a comprehensive idea of landscape implies documenting the overall archaeological landscape signature to reconstruct the on-site and off-site practices of past communities and individuals (Wilkinson 2003). As landscapes are the result of the interactions of environmental, social, economic and cultural factors through time, landscape archaeology must consider and integrate all of these components in order to reconstruct ancient landscape formation and transformation processes (*ibid.*). The present study attempts to find a balance between large-scale and micro-scale landscape analyses to address major archaeological issues concerning early social complexity in Northern Mesopotamia in the context of the Birecik and Carchemish sectors of the Euphrates River. This "medium-size" scale approach combines results from excavation and survey projects along the major river valley and the surrounding area and contextualizes them in a regional environmental framework of analysis defined by physi-

in: Müller, J. and Ricci, A. 2020 (eds.), *Past Societies: Human Development in Landscapes.* Sidestone Press: Leiden, 81-90.

cal-geographical boundaries. The result is a comprehensive regional reconstruction of the long-term settlement dynamics and landscape transformation processes for the 5th, 4th and 3rd millennia BCE in the Birecik and Carchemish sectors. The study shows how the longevity of settlement choices led to a nucleation on tell phenomena as early as the mid-Chalcolithic period.

The geographical setting

The region under study, also defined as the Birecik-Carchemish sector, is a sub-basin of the Middle Euphrates River Valley. It is located in Upper Mesopotamia between the southern piedmont of the Anti-Taurus range and the Syrian steppe. The modern Turkish town of Halfeti sets the northern limit of the research area, which extends south to an ideal line from Qara Qozaq/Qalat Nedjim Gorge over the Sajur-Euphrates junction and along the Sajur Valley for a total length of approximately 65 km (Fig. 1). Specifically, this research collates archaeological data from both Turkey and Syria in order to overcome the modern border, which has little, if any, physical geographical significance.

The current climatic conditions (*i.e.* the dry Late Holocene) were established between 4000 and 2000 years ago (Kuzucuoğlu 2007, 468). They are characterised by a hot dry season lasting from May through early October and a cooler winter period, which can start as early as late September and last until April. Nearly all precipitation

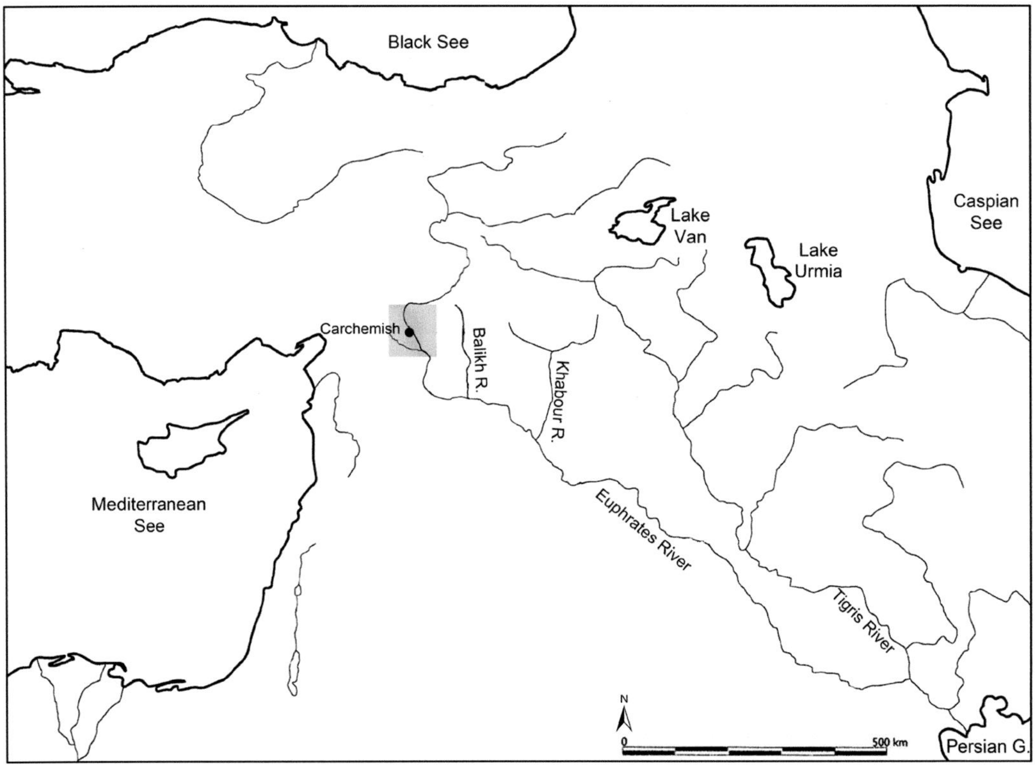

Figure 1. Map of Western Asia with an indication of the location of the Birecik-Carchemish region (map: A. Ricci).

occurs during the winter months. According to present conditions, the mean annual rainfall ranges between 480 and 330 mm, but inter-annual fluctuations can be as high as 50% or more (see Besançon and Sanlaville 1981, figs. 1-2; Wilkinson 2004, fig. 2.1). The precipitation is sufficient to support a dry-farming regime, however in drier years this is not successful and in the southern portion of the studied area cultivation and pasture are possible but risky (Wilkinson 2000, 3-6; see also Wilkinson *et al.* 2012, 147-148).

During the past four decades, the construction of a series of large dam projects for hydro-electrical and irrigation purposes has inundated large parts of this sinuous stretch of the Euphrates River Valley, north and south of the border between Turkey and Syria. These constructions provided the impetus for a number of rescue survey and excavation projects to document the endangered cultural heritage before it was forever lost under the water of the Euphrates. This concentration of archaeological investigations along the banks of the Euphrates has enriched the information on specific aspects of past occupation in the region (see Peltenburg 2007; del Olmo Lete and Montero Fenollós 1999), but has also left areas stretching east and west of the Euphrates Valley largely unexplored.

Methods of investigations

This study combines results of previous survey and excavation projects, original data from the Land of Carchemish Project (LCP), and analyses of historical and modern remote sensing datasets.

Published and unpublished results from five surveys conducted in the region over the past 35 years provide the primary data for this study (Fig. 2): the Algaze Survey (Algaze *et al.* 1994), the Özdoğan and Karul survey in Turkey (Özdoğan and Karul 2002), the Moore and Sanlaville-Copeland survey (Moore 1985), the McClellan and Porter survey (McClellan and Porter 1999), and the Land of Carchemish Project in Syria (LCP; Peltenburg *et al.* 2012; Wilkinson *et al.* 2016).

High-resolution satellite imagery includes historical images of the CORONAs project and contemporary images from GeoEye and Google Earth. The analyses of this imagery supported the identification of sites and off-site features for the field activities of the Land of Carchemish Project and in regions which had been previously investigated by other projects. SRTM data supported topographic analysis, whereas LANDSAT data were employed to generate large-scale maps, including soil or modern canopy coverage maps.

The collected data includes information on the location, topography, geomorphology, dimension, shape (*i.e.* flat scatter, flat settlement, cemetery, low mound, mound), and phase(s) of occupation of each site in order to make sites and site features statistically comparable. Great effort was devoted to provide fine chronological attributions of the occupations at each site within the frame of a comprehensive and coherent periodization scheme, and I conducted direct observations on artefacts when they were accessible. This enabled a fine chronological contextualization for the occupation of the 5th through the 3rd millennia BCE, supporting a detailed reconstruction of regional settlement dynamics.

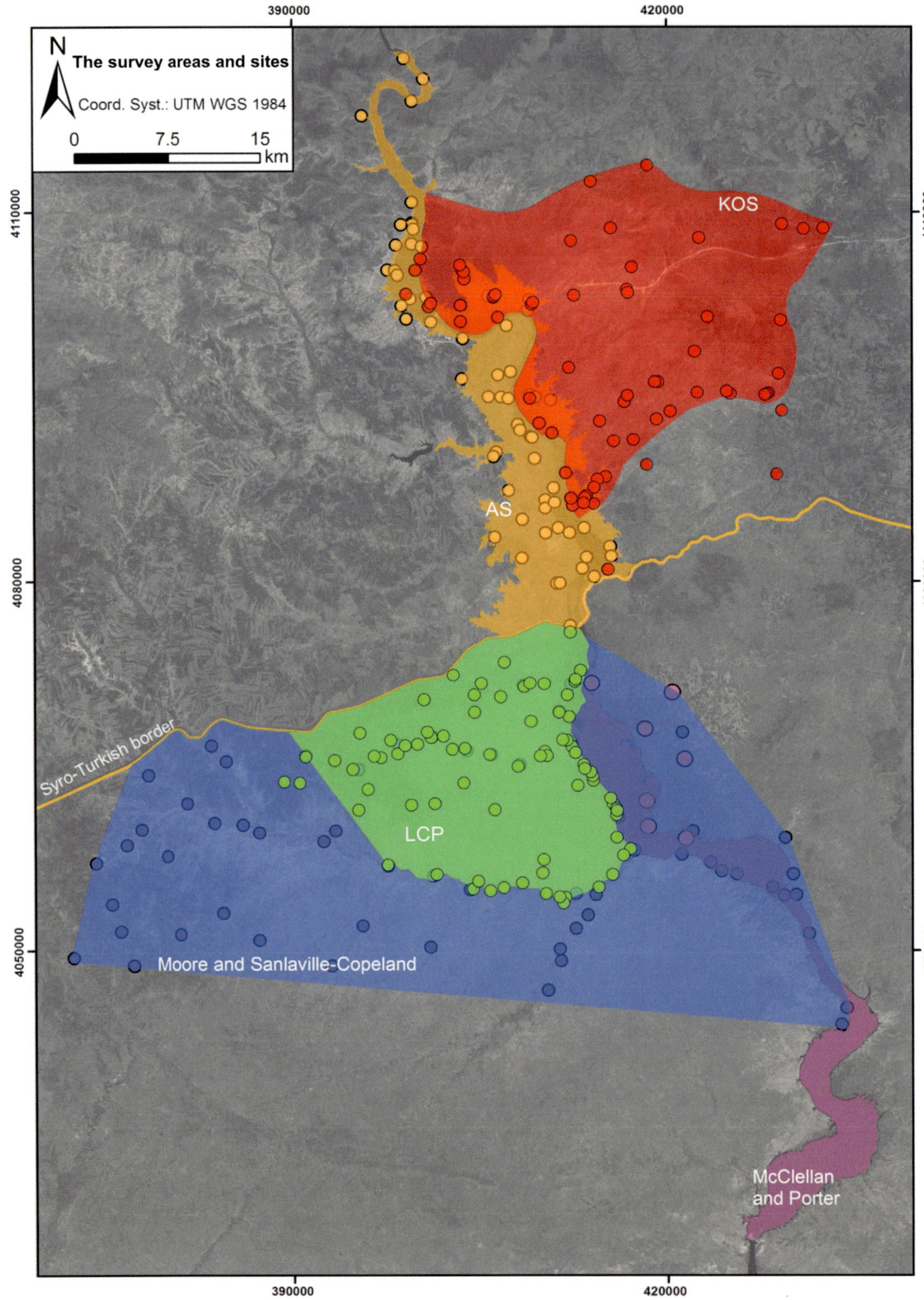

Figure 2. The five survey investigation areas and all surveyed sites considered in this study mapped over a Landsat 7 ETM+ image (band 1) (map: A. Ricci).

General regional settlement trends

There is a total of 21 recorded Ubaid occupations. It seems improbable that all of these sites were simultaneously and uninterruptedly occupied from 5200 to 4300 BC. Ubaid sites were generally small, the majority under 4 ha in size. Later, longer occupations resulted in significant stratigraphic sequences, which frequently hinder precise assessment of the extent of the Ubaid settlement. Therefore, the estimate of the total Ubaid occupied area – allegedly ca. 40 ha – remains uncertain. Several Ubaid settlements were established on previous Halaf locations. Both the Neolithic and Chalcolithic communities selected and continued to settle the same locations. This early phase of site foundation possibly led to a first stage of tell formation processes at several dispersed small settlements.

The overall regional population increased both in terms of the total settled area and the number of sites during the Local Late Chalcolithic (LLC) period (from approximately 4400-4350 BC until the first century of the 4th millennium BC). The fine dating of the LCP Chalcolithic sites, for which two sub-phases could be distinguished (*i.e.* LC 1-2 and LC 3), shows that a growth in the number of settlements occurred as early as the LC 1-2 phase without concurrent abandonment of any of the Ubaid occupations. However, human presence remained scarce, as the majority of LLC sites were small, extending less than 0.8 ha in size.

The Uruk period marked a major phase of site foundation and settlement expansion. The growth of the total settled area was robust (+33 ha), whereas the total number of occupations increased only slightly (+6). Settlement stability was high with occupation that continued at approximately half of the LLC sites. Specifically, in the area immediately north of Carchemish, several new large occupations appeared as early as the Middle Uruk period, *i.e.* around 3650 BCE. Further to the south, Uruk occupations continued to settle those locations that had already been selected during the previous period. The Uruk period marked a profound change in settlement organization. Administrative devices and so-called Uruk cones have been documented at Uruk settlements along the river (Algaze *et al.* 1994) and a three-tiered hierarchy emerged. However, the absence of beveled-rim bowls, an artefact linked to a centralized organization of labour, outside of the Euphrates River indicates the possibility that the Uruk system mainly orbited around the river valley itself. Outside of the valley, smaller communities seem to have lacked centralized administration.

In general terms, the Birecik-Carchemish region remained largely populated during the early phase of the Early Bronze Age period (EEBA) in the region, however divergent histories have been recorded. Settlement abandonment occurred in the Euphrates Valley, where the large Uruk sites were abandoned and a significant demographic decline occurred. By contrast, the number of sites increased in the lands to the northeast and the southwest of the valley. Certainly, in this phase regional settlement organization shifted from the centralized and highly hierarchical Uruk network of sites, with the largest centres along the Euphrates, to a much more ruralised landscape at the beginning of the Early Bronze Age with a high number of small dispersed sites and a lower degree or absence of hierarchical ties among settlements. The presence of cemeteries along the river valley also confirms a shift to a less structured organization within which high status charismatic men emerged among competing communities. The amount of metal objects in funerary contexts was probably not only a status indicator (Philip 2007), but also hints at the importance of the circulation and exchange of metal. The apparently ruralised and unstructured Birecik-Carchemish communities were, however, able

> *'to foster long-distance exchange and acquisitive social and political behaviours'* (Peltenburg 2007, 15; see also Cooper 2006, 278-279).

A dramatic increase in both the number of sites and total occupied area defines the peak in population by the middle of the 3rd millennium BC, when 30 new settlement foundations appeared along both the Euphrates and its tributaries. New sites have been recorded and, at the same time, the majority of sites (42, approx. 75%) continued to be inhabited. By ca. 2600 BC, small sites, extending less than 4 ha, dotted the Birecik-Carchemish landscape. Settlement also extended into areas apparently unfavourable for settlement, as in the southern portion of the region toward the Sajur River, where cultivation and pasture are possible but a risky undertaking (Wilkinson *et al.* 2012, 147-148). A more hierarchical structure emerged with the occupation of two larger sites (Tell Aarab Hassan and Tilardir Tepe) and the possible urban expansion of Carchemish. The regional settlement structure became more highly nucleated with possibly one central place, but also including a network of numerous small sites that maintained a degree of autonomy. However, the lack of precise information regarding the extent of Carchemish during the 3rd millennium BC hinders this discussion to some degree.

Towards the end of the 3rd millennium BC, both the number of sites and the estimated occupied area dropped. Carchemish remained inhabited and allegedly continued to be the principal regional centre, but significant depopulation occurred around the site. 40 sites were abandoned and the total number of occupied sites decreased by 50%, whilst the total settled area decreased by ca. 25%. Settlement stability was stronger along the river in the Birecik sector. Site abandonment is more evident to the west and east of the major river valley. Population decline specifically affected the small sites up to 2 ha in size, while settlement generally continued at the larger occupations. This trend might reflect a structural change at the village level rather than a total collapse of the settled area. It implies that at least parts of the population might have abandoned the smaller settlements and were concentrated at fewer sites, some of them large, by the end of the 3rd millennium BC.

Discussion

In the Birecik-Carchemish sector, longevity of settlement choice characterizes occupation both along the Euphrates Valley as well as in the lands stretching to the east and west of it. Of the sites dated to periods between the Ubaid and the LEBA, the majority (70) are multi-period settlements with at least two continuous phases of occupation, eight were uninterruptedly inhabited from the mid-Chalcolithic to the end of the Early Bronze Age, whereas only 27 were single phase occupations and six sites were resettled in two non-consecutive phases. When a location was selected for occupation, people frequently continued to settle the same place for millennia. This implies that the selected locations and their surroundings offered sufficiently stable conditions for settlement and successful primary economies. Settlement longevity seems weaker only

Figure 3. Site LCP 60, Tell Koundariyeh. A typical conical-shaped tell of the Birecik-Carchemish region (photo: A. Ricci).

in the southern portion of the study area, where environmental conditions may have influenced settlement choices. The Sajur Valley, lying below the 300 mm rainfall isohyet, experienced unstable cycles of occupation; after a limited LC 1-2 occupation, the valley remained largely unpopulated until the mid-3rd millennium BC when several settlements appeared. This growth did not last long as population almost completely deserted the Sajur corridor in the last centuries of the 3rd millennium BC (see Lawrence and Ricci 2016 for further discussion).

This longevity of settlement led to an early nucleation on tell phenomena at several locations. This process started as early as the mid-Chalcolithic period. Lower and higher tells formed the basic unit of settlement and remained the characterizing structural feature of the landscape of the region from the Ubaid through the LEBA periods. The shapes and dimensions of tells become more conspicuous around 2700-2600 BC. At this time, when regional population increased and interactions at the wider level among competing strong kingdoms (Mari, Ebla, Abarsal) intensified and might have episodically ended in conflicts, defensive structures were erected possibly to protect the population and the settlements (Liverani 2011, 172-175; Cooper 2006, 63-66). These constructions resulted in a change of the actual visual character of the mounds, which were constrained within clear borders and became prominently conical in shape (Fig. 3).

Conclusions

The tell, as a result of long, continued settlement of the same location, played a long-term role in shaping community dynamics of the Birecik-Carchemish sector from at least the Ubaid period onwards. It was not only the place where the population lived, economic activities were conducted, and defence was guaranteed, but it also represented a visual symbolic location.

Acknowledgements

My deep thanks go to the Graduate School "Human Development in Landscapes" at Kiel University for their support to conduct my doctoral research. My thanks also go to all members who created such a stimulating research environment. In particular, I would like to thank my supervisors, Johannes Müller and Rainer Duttmann, for their guidance and fruitful discussions, which luckily are still continuing today. Special thanks go to Dan Lawrence and Marcella Frangipane for the constant opportunity for discussion.

My sincere gratitude goes to Tony J. Wilkinson and Eddie Peltenburg, not only for entrusting me with the study of the Ubaid, Late Chalcolithic and Early Bronze Age materials of the Land of Carchemish Project, but also for their constant support as I worked through my PhD dissertation and beyond. They will be always a great source of inspiration.

References

Algaze, G., Breuninger, R., Knudstad, J. 1994. The Tigris-Euphrates Archaeological Reconnaissance Project: Final Report of the Birecik and Carchemish Dam Survey Area. *Anatolica* 20, 1-96.

Besançon, J. and Sanlaville, P. 1981. Aperçu géomorphologique sur la vallée de l'Euphrate syrien. *Paleorient* 7/2, 5-18.

Cooper, L. 2006. *Early Urbanism on the Syrian Euphrates*. Oxon: Routledge.

Kuzucuoğlu, C. 2007. Climatic and environmental trends during the third millennium BC in Upper Mesopotamia, in: Kuzucuoğlu, C. and Marro, C. (eds.), *Sociétés humaines et changement climatique à la fin du trosième millénaire: une crise a-t-elle eu lieu en haute Mésopotamie?* Actes du Colloque de Lyon, 5-8 décembre 2005. Paris: De Boccard, 459-480.

Lawrence, D. and Ricci, A. 2016. Long Term Settlement Trends in the Birecik-Carchemish Sector, in: Wilkinson, T.J., Peltenburg, E., Wilkinson, E. (eds.), *Carchemish in Context*. BANEA Monograph Series. Oxford: Oxbow, 38-67.

Liverani, M. 2011 (first edition 1988). *Antico Oriente. Storia società economia*. Roma-Bari: Laterza.

McClellan, T.L. and Porter, A. 1999. Survey of Excavations at Tell Banat, in: del Olmo Lete, G. and Montero Fenollós, J.L. (eds.), *Archaeology of the Upper Syrian Euphrates. The Tishrin Dam Area*. Aula Orientalis Supplement 15. Barcelona: Editorial Ausa, 107-116.

Moore, A.M.T. 1985. The archaeological survey of 1977, in: Sanlaville, P. (ed.), *Holocene settlement in north Syria: résultats de deux prospections archéologiques effectuées dans la région du nahr Sajour et sur le haut Euphrate syrien*. Oxford: BAR International Series 238, 45-66.

Özdoğan, M. and Karul, N., 2002, Şanlıurfa, Birecik-Suruç Arkeolojik Envanter Raporu, in: Başgelen, N. (ed.), *Birecik-Suruç Türkiye Kültür Envanteri Pilot Bölge Çalışmaları*, Tüba Tüksek yay. No. 1/1. Istanbul: Arkeoloji ve Sanat Yay, 1-101.

Peltenburg, E. 2007. New perspectives on the Carchemish sector of the Middle Euphrates River Valley in the 3rd Millennium BC, in: Peltenburg, E. (ed.), *Euphrates River Valley Settlement. The Carchemish Sector in the Third Millennium BC*. Levant Supplementary Series 5. Oxford: Oxbow Books, 3-24.

Peltenburg, E., Wilkinson, T.J., Ricci, A., Lawrence, D., McCarthy, A., Wilkinson, E.B., Newson, P., Perini, S. 2012. The Land of Carchemish (Syria) Project: The Sajur Triangle, in: Curtis, J., Fletcher, A., Glatz, C., Matthews, R., Seymour, M., Simpson, J., Taylor, H. (eds.), *Proceedings of the 7th ICAANE Conference held in London in 2010.* Wiesbaden: Harrassowitz, 191-204.

Philip, G., 2007. The metalwork of the Carchemish region and the development of grave repertories during the third millennium BC, in: Peltenburg, E. (ed.), *Euphrates River Valley Settlement – The Carchemish Sector in the Third Millennium BC.* Levant Supplementary Series 5. Oxford: Oxbow Books, 187-197.

Wilkinson, T.J. 2000. Settlement and land use in the zone of uncertainty in upper Mesopotamia, in: Jas, R. (ed.), *Rainfall and Agriculture in Northern Mesopotamia.* Leiden: Nederlands Historisch-Archaeologisch Instituut te Istanbul, 3-35.

Wilkinson, T.J. 2003. *Archaeological Landscapes of the Near East.* Tuscon, Ariz.: The University of Arizona Press.

Wilkinson, T.J. 2004. *Excavations at Tell Es-Sweyhat, Syria 1: On the Margin of the Euphrates: Settlement and Land Use at Tell Es-Sweyhat and in the Upper Lake Assad Area, Syria.* Oriental Institute Publications 124. Chicago, Ill.: Oriental Institute of the University of Chicago.

Wilkinson, T.J., Galiatsatos, N., Lawrence, D., Ricci, A., Dunford, R., Philip, G. 2012. Late Chalcolithic and Early Bronze Age Landscapes of Settlement and Mobility in the Middle Euphrates: A Reassessment. *Levant* 44/2, 139-185.

Wilkinson, T.J., Peltenburg, E., Wilkinson, E. 2016 (eds.), *Carchemish in Context.* BANEA Monograph Series. Oxford: Oxbow.

Author address

Dr. Andrea Ricci
Graduate School Human Development in Landscapes
Kiel University
Leibnizstr. 3
24118 Kiel, Germany
aricci@roots.uni-kiel.de

About the author

Andrea Ricci is an archaeologist specialised in the study of the prehistory of Southwestern Asia. He completed his first MA studies at La Sapienza University in Rome (Italy) and then he received a second MA degree at Durham University (UK). After completing his PhD in the framework of the Graduate School "Human Development in Landscapes" at Kiel University, he held a post-doctoral position at the Eurasia Department of the German Archaeological Institute. He is currently one of two scientific coordinators of the Cluster of Excellence ROOTS at Kiel University. He has been conducting research in southwest Asia, including Azerbaijan, Georgia, Iran, and Syria, over the last ten years.

His main research topics include the investigation of Holocene human-environmental dynamics, the process of neolithisation, and the emergence of the first forms of social and economic complexity.

Writing the History of 'Peoples without History': The Case of the Zagros in the First Millennium BCE

Silvia Balatti

Abstract
The purpose of this paper is to shortly present the results of my PhD thesis entitled *Mountain Peoples in the Ancient Near East: The Case of the Zagros in the First Millennium BCE*, which was written in the framework of the Graduate School "Human Development in Landscapes" and recently published in the series *Classica et Orientalia* of the Harrassowitz Publishing House. In this contribution, special attention is paid to methodological and theoretical issues rather than to content matters. The book on the ancient peoples of the Zagros Mountains provides a significant example of how to write a political, socio-economic and cultural history of 'silent' peoples using a wide range of sources and data available for the study of the past. This interdisciplinary approach broadens the horizons of the historical discipline, which usually still concentrates on societies and social groups who produced a large number of written records.

Introduction
The Zagros Mountains are a thousand five hundred-kilometre-long mountain range, which separates the modern countries of Iraq and Iran. Starting from Southeastern Anatolia, it extends southeastwards to the Straits of Hormuz. From an ecological perspective, the Zagros Mountains constitute, together with the Taurus Mountains of Eastern Anatolia, a vast highland ecoregion which supports open forests of deciduous oaks, almonds and pistachios, interspersed by a diverse steppe flora (Zohary 1973, 87, 169, 181, 198). This ecoregion, which Zohary characterises as Kurdo-Zagrosian steppe-forest, is particularly important for biodiversity since it is characterised by high rates of endemism and many plant and animal species were first domesticated there,

in: Müller, J. and Ricci, A. 2020 (eds.), *Past Societies: Human Development in Landscapes*.
Sidestone Press: Leiden, 91-98.

thus enormously contributing to the development of early agriculture in the neighbouring Mesopotamian lowlands (Riehl *et al.* 2013; Zeder and Hesse 2000).

Steadily inhabited by village communities since ca. 8500-7500 BCE, the Zagros Mountain region early experienced the development of different forms of mobile pastoralism (Abdi 2003), which has continued to be practiced together with small-scale agriculture, horticulture, hunting and gathering for millennia. Although being situated near the Mesopotamian plains and acting as a place of cultural and economic connectivity between the lowlands to the west and the highlands to the east, the Zagros Mountains have always been environmentally, economically and socio-culturally different but complementary to Mesopotamia. With the only partial exception of the mountain areas of Khuzestān and Fārs in the Southern Zagros – which were always strongly connected with the lowlands of Khuzestān and its socio-cultural dynamics and economy (Potts 2015) – the Northern and Central Zagros did not experience processes of urbanism and urbanisation, productivity, social stratification and division of labour comparable to those which took place in other areas of the Ancient Near East. It follows that the majority of the peoples of the Zagros probably did not use any writing system which, as we know, was initially created in Lower Mesopotamia to respond to the administrative requirements of complex societies (Nissen *et al.* 1993). Only very few and short written records – whose majority is ascribable to contacts with the lowlands – have been discovered in Iran for the pre-Achaemenid period (before 550 BCE). Even in the Achaemenid and later periods, when writing was used by the authorities basically only for administration, political propaganda and religious matters, orality likely remained the dominant form of communication and transmission of knowledge in ancient Western Iran (Madreiter 2018).

Beyond the royal court, the local population and in particular the small communities of the Zagros Mountains probably did not need to extensively use writing in their everyday life. Their lack of writing is, however, a great obstacle for historians who investigate ancient societies primarily using documentary sources. Thus, it is no surprise that the history of the peoples of the Zagros, such as that of many other 'silent' peoples, has been neglected by historians in favour of well-documented regions, groups and time periods. The result of this tendency is that peoples living at the 'margins' of 'core regions' of the ancient world, who often inhabited remote, sparsely populated and environmentally challenging territories, such as steppes, mountains and deserts, have received very little attention in historical research at least until the 1970s. Even when these peoples started to enter historical discourse as the consequence of the spread of anthropological methods in historical studies, they were mainly investigated in relation to state institutions and analysed using core-periphery models characterised by patterns of dominant cores and subordinate peripheries (Briant 1976; 1982). In the last decades, especially new archaeological and ethnographic research in the liminal areas of the ancient world – I think, for example, of Central Asia – have shown the inconsistency of the core-periphery models as they were previously conceived, and demonstrated the key role of 'marginal' peoples in political, cultural, social and economic transformations involving the centre, thus opening new directions of research (Frachetti 2009; Paul 2013).

The role that these peoples played in transformations of societies is also detectable several times in the history of the Near East. With regard to our study area, the

Zagros, the mountain dwellers were not infrequently involved in processes of social and cultural changes. In the mid-1st millennium BCE, for example, the inhabitants of 'peripheral' Fārs, a mountain region of the Zagros characterised by a strong and long-lasting connectivity to the lowlands, created the new political entity known as the Achaemenid Empire, which became the largest empire in the history of the Ancient Near East until then (Wiesehöfer 1998). This shows that a historical study on the ancient peoples of the Zagros Mountains is a very useful supplement – not only for the study of 'peripheral' areas of the ancient world and their dynamics but also for an investigation of the processes that triggered the creation and maintenance of the Achaemenid Empire.

Sources and Methods

As befits a historical work, this study started with the analysis of the available documentary sources. This statement seems to contradict what was stated in the previous section – namely that the peoples of the Zagros did not produce written documents. However, this is only an apparent contradiction. In fact, there is a relatively large number of sources produced by foreign state institutions that refer to the Zagros Mountains and their inhabitants in different contexts and for different purposes. References to the mountain dwellers of the Zagros can be found in Mesopotamian documentary sources since the 3rd millennium BCE (Balatti 2017, 5-9 with references). However, they became particularly numerous from the early 1st millennium BCE onwards, when the Assyrians started their imperial expansion into the mountainous territories to the north and to the east of Upper Mesopotamia.

The texts which mention the peoples of the Zagros in the 1st millennium BCE were produced by the main authorities on the political chessboard of the Near East at that time and include Assyrian royal letters and official inscriptions, Urartian royal inscriptions, Elamite administrative and political texts, Babylonian administrative and 'historical' documents, Achaemenid inscriptions and administrative tablets and Greco-Roman 'historical' records (Balatti 2017, 11-22 with references). Although very different in scope and in nature, all these documentary sources provide us with an external and often biased view of the peoples of the Zagros, which perfectly fit in a dichotomous model of core and periphery with an advanced and dominant centre in the lowlands and a barren and barbarous periphery in the mountains. In absence of local documents, which can question this model, research methodology becomes extremely important to investigate the 'realities' of the peoples of the mountains and to understand their contribution to the history of the Ancient Near East.

First of all, it was necessary to analyse the texts and investigate the scope and nature of every textual typology in order to identify ideological representations and stereotyping. This textual analysis alone just allows the formulation of hypotheses on the socio-political organisation, lifestyle, costumes and beliefs of 'silent' peoples. Evidence on the reliability or unreliability of the textual information can be, however, obtained juxtaposing them with data coming from other disciplines. These data must be accurately collected, selected and interpreted according to the specific research methods and theoretical frameworks of each discipline. In doing this, one should also be aware of the current debate within each discipline; debates that have sometimes led to important methodological and theoretical rethinking, as demonstrated, for example, by new important studies on the archeology of pastoral nomadism (Honeychurch and Makarewicz 2016; Arbukle and Hammer 2018). In the case of the mountain peoples of the Zagros, I considered the use of socio-anthropological theories on pastoral societies, ethnographic observations, archaeological and archaeozoological records, and palaeobotanical studies particularly relevant for interpretations and synthesis with data provided by documentary sources.

Results and Discussion

As mentioned in the introduction, pastoralism has been the primary mode of subsistence in the Zagros Mountains over many millennia and pastoral groups continue to perform their seasonal movements between valleys and high pastures until the present (Potts 2014; Tapper and Thompson 2002). Thus, a theoretical framework based on anthropological and sociological theories on pastoral societies and historical and ethnographic case studies turned out to be a very important tool to interpret the evidence available for ancient societies. Socio-anthropological theories and ethnographic observations, in particular, show the complexity of the relations which involve the members of pastoral societies and their continuous oscillations between more nomadic or more sedentary lifestyles (Salzman 2004; Leder and Streck 2005). This put into question many of the categories that we commonly use to interpret reality and urges a more reasoned and flexible use of them. In doing so, I could better comprehend some of the characteristics of the societies described in the documentary sources such as the importance of social solidarity among the societal members, the lack of institutions (and writing), their way of fighting as a 'society in arms' and fluid subsistence strategies (Balatti 2017, 343-352).

Many hypotheses on social and economic phenomena that emerged from the textual analysis can be proven thanks to an interdisciplinary synthesis. Archaeological data demonstrate, for example, the presence of fortresses in the Zagros in the first half of the 1st millennium BCE and show clear changes in settlement pattern in the following periods, thus corroborating and adding information to the textual analysis (Balatti 2017, 260-264). The discovery of several metal objects in sites and especially in tombs in the Central Zagros Mountains as well as the excavation of mine sites on the neighbouring Western Iranian Plateau reveal that metallurgy was one of the primary handicraft activities of the peoples of the Zagros (Balatti 2017, 290-296). Zooarchaeological material confirms that especially sheep, goats, horses and cattle were bred in the region (Balatti 2017, 273-286) and shows that hunting was part of the local subsistence economy (Stronach and Roaf 1978, 24-28; Mashkour and Mohaseb Karimlu 2011). As the archaeological and iconographic evidence suggests, the latter was also performed by the local élites, probably as a display of force and power, thus adding information on socio-cultural values and indigenous conceptions of authority (Balatti 2017, 286-287). Palaeobotanical data confirm that conifer timber was one of the main natural resources exploited in the Zagros Mountains in antiquity, both by foreign imperial officials and by the locals (Balatti 2017, 318-320). Moreover, pollen analysis, especially when combined with geoarchaeological surveys and soil sediment analyses, clearly demonstrates the implementation of agriculture and arboriculture in the intermontane plains of the Southern Zagros in the Achaemenid periods (Djamali *et al.* 2016).

An interdisciplinary synthesis is also useful to uncover literary *topoi* and biased views of the peoples of the Zagros in the documentary sources. The infertility and poverty of the Zagros region, which is often related to barbarous life-ways and banditry in the Greek and Latin sources, is refuted by the ecological and palaeoecological evidence. Several edible plants grow even spontaneously in the Zagros, species-rich grasslands are abundant and water is moderately available, today as well as in antiquity (Balatti 2017, 303-318). Moreover, ethnographic observations of pastoral groups in the mountains of the Middle East show that the group members often rely on different subsistence strategies, including animal husbandry and farming, but also hunting, gathering and robbery – a practice that the political authorities always consider a despicable act, worthy only of contempt, but that is generally the reaction to an aggressive exploitation policy by the states or to phases of acute economic crisis (Salzman 2004, 9-10). The pursuit of multiple subsistence strategies is often a specific choice rather than a real need in the context of the pastoral societies and must not necessarily be linked to famine, poverty or lack of civilisation (Balatti 2017, 328-338).

Biased details recorded in the texts can also be uncovered juxtaposing the data at our disposal. The archaeological evidence and local iconographic material prove, for example, that the peoples of the Zagros did not commonly wear fur and animal skins, as the Assyrian sources suggest, but proper clothes made of wool, fur and leather (Balatti 2017, 297-298). Palaeobotanical data demonstrate that, in contrast to what is recorded by the Roman author Curtius Rufus in his work on Alexander the Great (Curt. 5.4.4-6), thick and inaccessible forests never covered the Southern Zagros Mountains in ancient times and, consequently, that Alexander's march towards the heartland of the Persian Empire was not so perilous as generally assumed (Balatti 2017, 325-326). These examples show how the documentary (and iconographic) sources – especially if they are elaborated in the context of the official propaganda or for literary purposes – can be biased and conceal fictional information in every little detail. This phenomenon clearly depends on the intent of the communicators, which in the case of official propagandistic texts was, generally speaking, to praise the deeds of the state authorities and their loyal subjects, the majority of which permanently lived in cities and villages, and in the case of the literary texts was to arouse emotions and sensations rather than to describe the historical reality.

Conclusions

The research project on the ancient peoples of the Zagros Mountains shows that an interdisciplinary approach in historical studies can successfully: 1) enrich the theoretical framework, 2) demonstrate hypotheses and add information to the mere textual analysis, and 3) uncover misunderstandings and biased views provided by the written sources, thus significantly helping historians to reflect on the reasons behind imprecise or fictional representations of particular events or phenomena. Although interdisciplinarity is a useful and effective tool in every historical work, it is absolutely necessary for the study of 'silent' peoples and their societies, whose investigation is irremediably compromised by a lack of documents. As the case of the peoples of the Zagros in antiquity demonstrates, the synthesis of the available data on society, economy and environment provides a plausible, though highly fragmentary picture of ancient peoples' life-ways and enables the detection of changes in a diachronic perspective. I could write about their mode of subsistence, socio-political structures, military organisation, settlement patterns and local exploitation of natural resources and even make assumptions on their languages, values, patterns of attire and religious beliefs. Moreover, comparing the results of the interdisciplinary synthesis with the representations of the described peoples in official texts, I could gain information on the relationship between the mountain groups of the Zagros and the foreign political authorities, who ruled over the mountainous territories or came in contact with the peoples inhabiting the region.

As this study shows, historians who work interdisciplinarily must not necessarily limit their research interest to neighbouring disciplines – a practice that has become customary since the break with traditional historiography operated by the *Annales*-school, which strongly fostered the use of social scientific methods by historians – but can also broaden their perspective to even include the natural sciences. However, since the methodical modes to think and the problems that must be faced when interpreting the data are undeniably different in the human and natural sciences, I am convinced that a constant dialogue among experts should be maintained in order to correctly run data analyses and produce coherent and integrated research work.

Acknowledgements

My PhD work would not have been possible without the guidance and support of my first supervisor, Prof. Josef Wiesehöfer, to whom I am extremely grateful. I would also like to offer my special thanks to my second supervisor, Dr. Oliver Nelle, and to Dr. Morteza Djamali, Dr. Marjan Mashkour and Prof. Daniel Potts. Their advice has been a great help for my interdisciplinary work. I am also grateful to all the members of the Graduate School "Human Development in Landscapes", with whom I have had the pleasure to work with during the last years. At the GS, I encountered an excellent working environment, inspiring scientific exchange and very nice colleagues.

References

Abdi, K. 2003. The Early Development of Pastoralism in the Central Zagros Mountains. *Journal of World Prehistory* 17/4, 395-448.

Arbukle, B.S. and Hammer, E.L. 2018. The Rise of Pastoralism in the Ancient Near East. *Journal of Archaeological Research* 27/3, 1-59.

Balatti, S. 2017. *Mountain Peoples in the Ancient Near East: The Case of the Zagros in the First Millennium BCE.* Wiesbaden: Harrassowitz Verlag.

Briant, P. 1976. "Brigandage", dissidence et conquête en Asie Achéménide et Hellénistique. *Dialogues d'histoire ancienne* 2/2, 163-258.

Briant, P. 1982. État et pasteurs au Moyen-Orient ancien. Paris: Éditions de la Maison des sciences de l'homme.

Djamali, M., Jones, M.D., Migliore, J., Balatti, S., Fader, M., Contreras, D., Gondet, S., Hosseni, Z., Lahijani, H., Naderi, A., Shumilovskikh, L.S., Tengberg, M., Weeks, L. 2016. Olive cultivation in the heart of the Persian Achaemenid Empire:

new insights into agricultural practices and environmental changes reflected in a Late Holocene pollen record from Lake Parishan, SW Iran. *Vegetation History and Archaeobotany* 25/3, 255-269.

Frachetti, M.D. 2008. *Pastoralist Landscapes and Social Interaction in Bronze Age Eurasia.* Berkeley/Los Angeles: University of California Press.

Honeychurch, W. and Makarewicz, C.A. 2016. The Archaeology of Pastoral Nomadism. *Annual Review of Anthropology* 45, 341-359.

Leder, S. and Streck, B. 2005. *Shifts and Drifts in Nomad-Sedentary Relations.* Wiesbaden: Reichert.

Madreiter, I. 2018. Der Raum alltäglicher weiblicher Literalität im Achaimeniden-Reich, in: Kolb, A. (ed.), *Literacy in Ancient Everyday Life.* Proceedings of a conference in Zurich, 2016. Berlin/Boston: De Gruyter, 113-142.

Mashkour, M. and Mohaseb Karimlu, A.F. 2011. Hunting and Husbandry in the Ozbaki Archaeological Zone (Savojbolagh Plain) from the 6th Millennium until the Iron Age: Archaeozoological Study of Jeiran Tepe, Maral Tepe, Doshan Tepe and Tepe Ozbaki, in: Majidzadeh, Y. (ed.), *Kavoshhaye Mohavateyeh bastani Ozbaki.* Jeld 1. Honar va Me'mari. Tehrān: Iranian Cultural Heritage Organisation and Tourism, 273-302.

Nissen, H.J., Damerow, P., Englund, R. K. 1993. *Archaic Bookkeeping: Early Writing and Techniques of Economic Administration in the Ancient Near East.* Chicago: University of Chicago Press.

Paul, J. 2013. *Nomad Aristocrats in a World of Empires.* Wiesbaden: Reichert.

Potts, D.T. 2014. *Nomadism in Iran: From Antiquity to the Modern Era.* Oxford/New York: Oxford University Press.

Potts, D.T. 2016[2]. *The Archaeology of Elam.* New York: Cambridge University Press.

Riehl, S., Zeidi, M., Conard, N.J. 2013. Emergence of Agriculture in the Foothills of the Zagros Mountains of Iran. *Science* 341/6141, 65.

Salzman, P.C. 2004. *Pastoralists: Equality, Hierarchy, and the State.* Boulder/Oxford: Westview Press.

Stronach, D. and Roaf, M. 1978. Excavations at Tepe Nush-i Jan. *Iran* 16, 1-28.

Tapper, R. and Thompson, J. 2002. *The Nomadic Peoples of Iran.* London: Azimuth Ed.

Wiesehöfer, J. 1998. *Das antike Persien. Von 550 v. Chr. bis 650 n. Chr.* Düsseldorf/Zürich: Artemis & Winkler.

Zeder, M.A. and Hesse, B. 2000. The Initial Domestication of Goats (*Capra hircus*) in the Zagros Mountains 10,000 Years Ago. *Science* 287/5461, 2254-2257.

Zohary, M. 1973. *Geobotanical Foundations of the Middle East.* Stuttgart: Fischer.

Author address

Silvia Balatti
Institute of Classics
Kiel University
Leibnizstraße 8
24118 Kiel, Germany
balatti@email.uni-kiel.de.

About the author

Silvia Balatti is currently an Assistant Professor at the Institute of Classics of Kiel University. After studying Ancient History and Ancient Near Eastern Studies at the University of Pavia, she moved to Kiel, where she attended the Graduate School "Human Development in Landscapes" and earned her PhD in 2014. Her PhD thesis was honoured with the Johanna Mestorf Award in 2015 and with the World Award for the Book of the Year of the Islamic Republic of Iran in 2018.

Iron Age Landscapes of Power in the Middle Rhine-Moselle Region

Manuel Fernández-Götz

Abstract

The completed PhD project addressed the transformation of Iron Age and early Roman societies in Northeastern Gaul, with a particular focus on the Middle Rhine-Moselle region. From a theoretical and methodological perspective, the work adopted a holistic approach that combined different sources in order to analyse issues of identity and power relations among the communities of the study area. Among the main topics explored are the multidimensional levels of socio-political organisation, the role of cemeteries as places of memory and performance, the cycles of centralisation and decentralisation, the emergence of the *oppida*, and the role of sanctuaries in the construction of collective identities.

Introduction

The aim of my PhD was to analyse the transformation of Iron Age and early Roman communities in Northeast Gaul (ca. 600 BC-AD 70), particularly in the Middle Rhine-Moselle region, with special attention paid to questions of social identity. The project was carried out as a binational PhD (*cotutelle*) between Kiel University in Germany and the Complutense University of Madrid in Spain and titled *Identidad y Poder: la Galia Nororiental de la Primera Edad del Hierro a la Romanización* (*Identität und Macht: Nordostgallien von der frühen Eisenzeit bis zur Romanisierung*). This work has been published as a monograph in Spanish by the Royal Academy of History (Fernández-Götz 2014a), and a revised and reduced version was also published in English by Amsterdam University Press (Fernández-Götz 2014b). In addition, several articles and book chapters address and expand on some of the topics studied within the PhD (*e.g.* Fernández-Götz 2014c, 2014d, 2016a, 2016b).

in: Müller, J. and Ricci, A. 2020 (eds.), *Past Societies: Human Development in Landscapes*.
Sidestone Press: Leiden, 99-108.

Sources and Methods

In what follows, I will present, from a narrative perspective, some of the main approaches and results developed in the thesis. Further references can be found in the above-mentioned publications but, as a kind of summary, I would like to highlight here some of the main sources of inspiration and documentation: for social identities and the notion of power the works by A. Hernando (2002) and M. Foucault (1980); for the different socio-political levels of Late Iron Age Gaul the monographs by N. Roymans (1990) and S. Fichtl (2012); and for the archaeological record of the study area the volumes by A. Haffner (1976), J. Metzler (1995), N. Roymans (2004), R. Gleser (2005), D. Krausse (2006) and S. Hornung (2008).

The two key concepts around which the work was structured are identity and power, *i.e.* the power relationships that existed between the various identity-based categories. Methodologically, a holistic and multidimensional approach was adopted, combining archaeological information (burials, settlements, environmental data) with anthropological and historical references (Fig. 1).

The concept of power was heavily influenced by the thinking of M. Foucault. According to this perspective, power is omnipresent, pervading the entire social body. This means that identities cannot be studied without also analysing the complex power networks within and between them. In the Iron Age, power was expressed through the

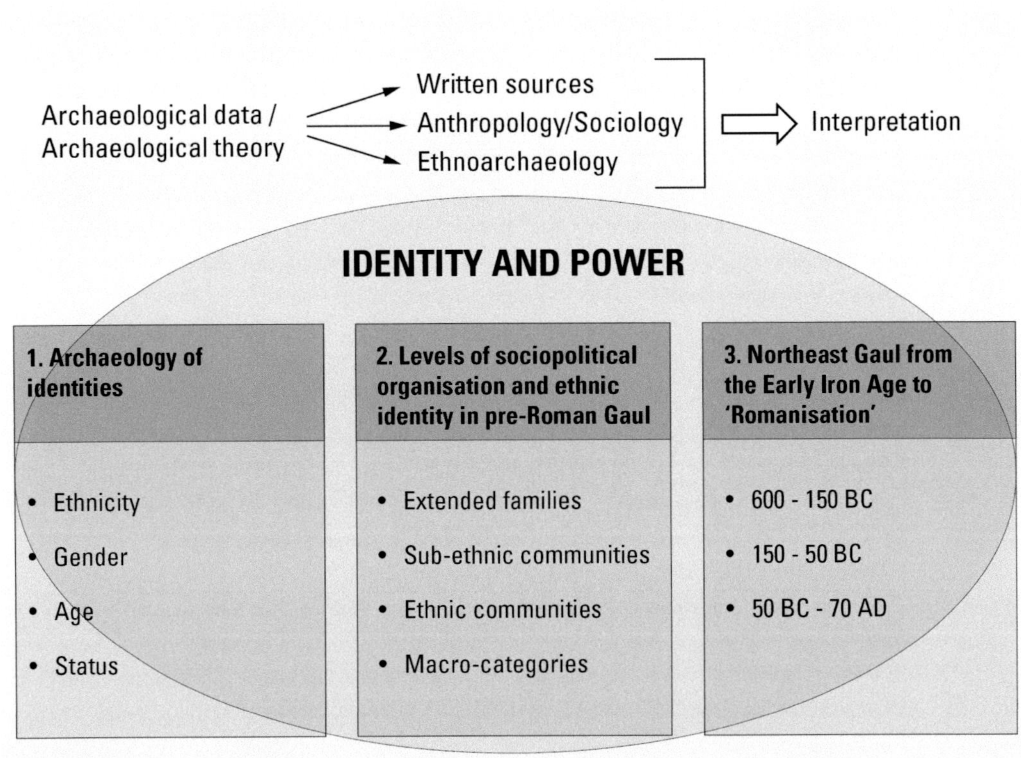

Figure 1. Research strategy used in the PhD and three major blocks of analysis (diagram: M. Fernández-Götz).

ties of clientage that existed between persons and communities, but also through the architecture and internal organisation of the settlements, the increasing standardisation observed in material culture and the erection of monumental *tumuli*, to name just some of the examples explored in the work.

The thesis was organised into three main parts, starting from the more general and moving on to the specific, with a particular emphasis on the last:

1) The first part presented a theoretical and methodological review of the different types of social identity – such as ethnicity, gender, age and class – as well as the central concept of 'power'. Together with an explanation of definitions and key concepts, each section also included a series of historical and anthropological examples, as well as a discussion about the limitations and possibilities of an archaeological exploration of major identity categories. Moreover, a central point was the distinction between different degrees of relational and individualised identities.

2) The second block offered a detailed study of the different superimposed and integrated levels of socio-political organisation and ethnic identity in non-Mediterranean Gaul at the end of the Iron Age. According to written and archaeological sources, the three main socio-political levels that can be distinguished are, in ascending order: extended family groups comprising several households, sub-ethnic communities (*pagi*) and ethnic communities (*civitates*). The complex relationships between the different groupings, the features of real and fictive kinship ties, the dual nature of pre-Roman *pagi* and *civitates* as both political and ethnic entities, the evolution of political institutions, such as public assemblies and aristocratic senates, the all-embracing character of clientship networks and the changing border dynamics were some of the topics discussed (Fig. 2). Furthermore, a critical reappraisal of macro-ethnic categories, like Gauls, Belgae, Celts and Germans, was made, following a distinction drawn between ethnic categories, ethnic networks and ethnic communities.

3) Finally, the third and longest part of the work comprised the diachronic analysis of the cultural changes experienced by the societies of Northeastern Gaul from approximately 600 BC until AD 70, *i.e.* from the beginning of demographic growth in the Early Iron Age to the consequences of the Batavian revolt. Although the Middle Rhine-Moselle region was the principal area of study, neighbouring regions were also considered, *e.g.*, the Champagne, the Belgian Ardennes and the Lower Rhine regions. Some of the main issues addressed through specific case-studies were the cycles of centralisation and decentralisation, the origins of the La Tène culture, the emergence of the *oppida* and the distinction between different types of social landscapes within the study area.

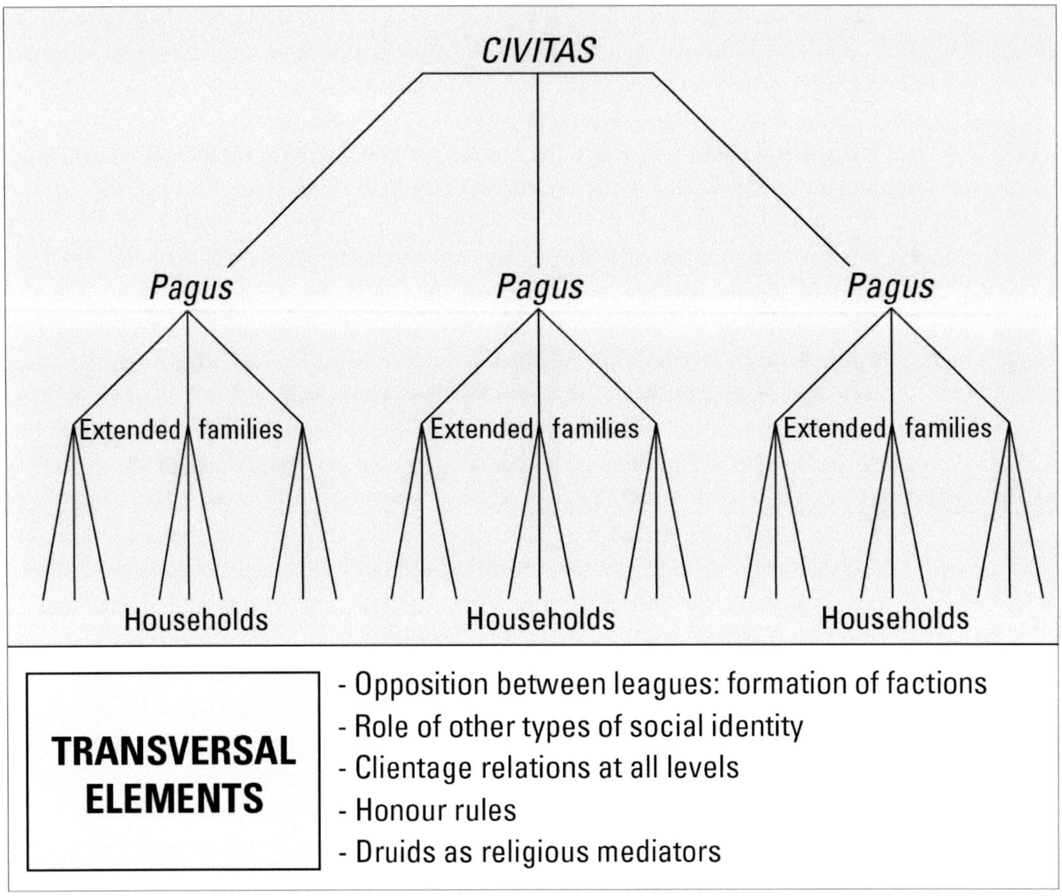

Figure 2. Top: simplified schema depicting the socio-political structure of Late Iron Age Gaul. Bottom: transversal elements fundamental for an understanding of Gallic societies (diagram: M. Fernández-Götz, based on Roymans 1990 and Verger 2009).

Results

The developed narrative starts around the end of the 7th century BC, when a process of demographic growth began in the landscapes of the Middle Rhine-Moselle, as indicated both by archaeological data and pollen analysis. Approximately a century later, the first fortified centres – small hillforts known as *Burgen* with an area of just a few hectares – as well as the first elite burials appeared. Both elements testify to a process of increasing social hierarchisation, which must have gone hand in hand with demographic growth. The elite burials became even more sumptuous in the decades that followed with the erection of some of the most prominent tombs of the Early La Tène period in the region, containing elements such as chariots, weapons, Mediterranean imports and gold artefacts. More or less in parallel, the second half of the 5th and first half of the 4th centuries BC saw the appearance or consolidation of a network of large hilltop centres on the same sites that would be occupied by the Treveran *oppida* of the Late La Tène period several centuries later. These sites of supra-local importance would have served as central places for different entities, whose relations with each other could be described as peer polity interaction. All these developments reflect a process of increasing 'social density', *i.e.*, a growth in the frequency of communications and interactions between individual persons and groups. This would have led to increasing pressure on resources, the establishment of growing inequalities both between and within groups, and the integration of persons and communities into wider socio-organisational networks.

This multidimensional transformation of Iron Age societies in the study area towards greater hierarchisation and centralisation came to an end in the course of the 4th century BC. The stage of centralisation was followed by a phase of decentralisation and a decrease in vertical social differentiation in what constitutes a specific case-study of the non-linear nature of history. Population decline is attested both by the archaeological record and pollen data, and can be interpreted, at least in part, as the result of the emigration of part of the population in the course of the so-called 'Celtic migrations' of the 4th to 3rd centuries BC, as also occurred in the neighbouring Champagne and in the Belgian Ardennes regions. Although the specific causes of these migrations are still poorly understood, all the evidence points to a combination of factors. The consequences of the worsening climate linked to a reduction in solar activity could clearly have played a part, but factors of socio-ideological nature can also be put forward: in particular, the possible role of population movements as mechanisms that regulated power relations in the sense that they would contribute to lowering levels of social inequality. In fact, throughout history numerous societies have developed strategies aimed at counteracting the excessive intensification of coercive powers, the fission of part of the group being a frequently used solution. Be that as it may, the lands of the Middle Rhine-Moselle never became completely uninhabited, as the continuity observed in some cemeteries of the Hunsrück and the emergence of a second generation of small hillforts testify.

A new trend towards centralisation began in the 2nd century BC, which led to the development of the Treveran *oppida* of the Late La Tène period. Spaces for religious practices and assemblies have been documented in six of these seven sites, which, together with their almost regular distribution across the territory and the evidence of coin production found there, underlines their role as centres of the various *pagi* that comprised the Treveran *civitas* (Fig. 3).

These places, which had already been frequented and in some cases even fortified in the Early La Tène period, would have been true places of memory (*lieux de mémoire*) in which practices were pursued that were fundamental to groups' social cohesion, for example, voting on political matters or ceremonial performances. Taking a wider view, it can be seen that the prime mover for the development of many of the *oppida* of temperate Europe was a politico-religious component, since several cases have been found in which the presence of cult and/or assembly places pre-dates the concentration of a stable population on the sites. In a context of improving climate, demographic growth, increased production and the flourishing of contacts with the Mediterranean world, religion must have been the principal cohesive force through which the integration of communities into broader socio-political groupings was structured.

Both the increasing standardisation observed in the production of objects and the progressive division of the landscape demonstrate the advance of individualising trends during this period. Given the fractal relationship that exists between persons and culture, the construction of enclosures would express, in spatial terms, the progressive

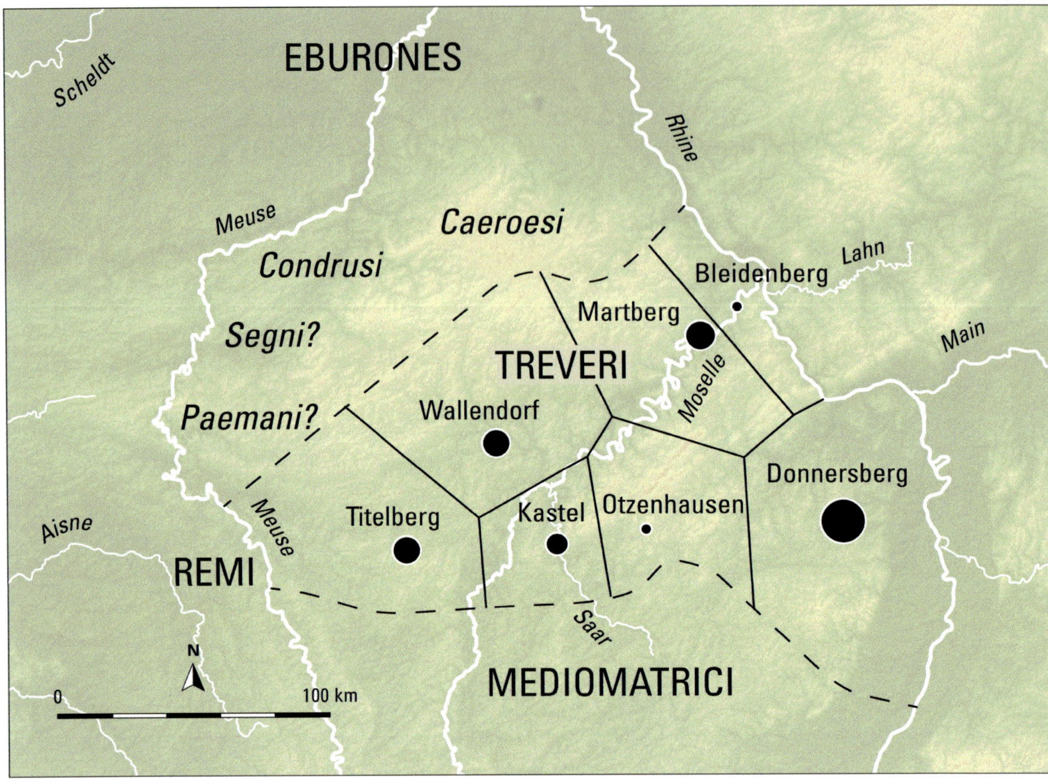

Figure 3. Organisation of the Treveran territory in the 1st century BC based on the application of the Thiessen polygons method (distribution map: M. Fernández-Götz).

establishment of limits and distinctions within and between communities. What is more, from the identitary perspective proposed here, the *oppida* can also be seen as a new technology of power, their emergence being a means of strengthening social cohesion and political control. In a good proportion of the Gallic polities, power was concentrated in the hands of aristocratic oligarchies that were at the head of a social organisation underpinned by clientship. Members of the elite included both men and women, who can be seen, for example, in the sumptuous burials of the Treveran territory. These elite burials are sometimes found within larger cemeteries belonging to local communities, but on other occasions they were built in isolated places, demonstrating a separation that was both spatial and social. Interestingly, the distribution pattern of elite graves indicates that in many cases aristocrats did not live in fortified hilltop settlements permanently, but rather in their rural domains.

Over and above the apparent homogeneity suggested by concepts such as 'civilisation of the *oppida*', the socio-political landscape of Late La Tène Gaul displays considerable heterogeneity with groups that came to form early states and others that continued to maintain more decentralised and less hierarchised structures. Thus, a supra-regional comparison reveals various convergences and divergences between the communities of the Middle Rhine-Moselle region and the societies situated immediately to the south and to the north. Broadly speaking, two major types of 'economies

Treveri	Mediomatrici	Eburones
Territory strongly structured around the *oppida*	Territory strongly structured around the *oppida*	Absence of *oppida* (although presence of supralocal sanctuaries)
Presence of Mediterranean imports	Presence of Mediterranean imports	Absence of Mediterranean imports
Abundance of tombs, marked social differences	Scarcity of graves	Scarcity of graves
Diversified minting of coins from early dates	Diversified minting of coins from early dates	Very late minting of coins, absence of fiduciary coinage
Early state	Early state?	Complex chiefdom

Table 1. Comparative table summarising some of the principal characteristics of the Treveri, Mediomatrici and Eburones in the Late La Tène period (table: M. Fernández-Götz).

of power' can be defined: on the one hand, societies with territories that were tightly structured around the *oppida*, accompanied by the presence of Mediterranean products and the minting of coins from an early date (*e.g.* Treveri or Mediomatrici) and, on the other hand, more decentralised communities that were more resistant to external influences (including the Eburones and Nervii) (Tab. 1).

However, it has to be remembered that there were many internal variations within each of these two macro-zones, for example, between the western and eastern Treveran areas. Similarly, new research shows that Eburonean communities can no longer be characterised as passive and egalitarian.

The PhD project ended with a brief look at 'Romanisation', revealing not only the transformations experienced by the Middle Rhine-Moselle populations after their forced incorporation into the Roman Empire, but also the continuities. Perhaps the most important feature is the variation in rhythms and stages within this process that were the result of geographical differences, the distinction between city and countryside, and between elites and peasants. Moreover, the study of relatively novel research fields, such as culinary traditions or customs of dress, helps to provide a more complete picture that investigates people's daily lives beyond the official narratives.

Conclusion

By way of a final evaluation, from the point of view of the history of culture, the ten main contributions made by the work included:

1) recognising the otherness of the past based on the lessons provided by the concept of materiality and the distinctions between more relational and individualised identities;
2) providing an up-to-date compendium of the different types of social identity and their potential for archaeological exploration;
3) presenting a practical example of the multidimensional and situational nature of identity ascriptions through an analysis of the various socio-political and identitary levels of Late Iron Age Gaul;
4) synthesising the debate concerning migrations in the past as recognised by archaeology, discussing the modalities they take and the mechanisms involved;

5) offering a new look at the origin of urbanisation processes in temperate Europe and the cycles of centralisation and decentralisation;
6) evaluating the key role of sanctuaries in the construction of collective identities;
7) developing a model of 'bottom up' ethnogenesis processes, based on the integration of households and extended families into broader networks;
8) applying the concepts of 'economies of power' and 'ethnic markers' in order to reveal the diversity of synchronous social formations;
9) rethinking macro-categories such as Celts and Germans;
10) contributing to the current debate on 'Romanisation' from the perspective of identities.

The result is a revised view of Iron Age societies in temperate Europe and, at a more general level, a step forward in the complicated but fascinating task of constructing an archaeology of identities.

Acknowledgements

I would like to thank my PhD supervisors, Prof. Dirk Krausse and Prof. Gonzalo Ruiz Zapatero, for their continuous encouragement and help during my studies. Special thanks also go to Prof. Johannes Müller, the Kiel Graduate School "Human Development in Landscapes" and Joanna Zygo for their support.

References

Fernández-Götz, M. 2014a. *De la familia a la etnia: Protohistoria de la Galia Oriental.* Bibliotheca Archaeologica Hispana 41. Madrid: Real Academia de la Historia.

Fernández-Götz, M. 2014b. *Identity and Power: The Transformation of Iron Age Societies in Northeast Gaul.* Amsterdam Archaeological Studies 21. Amsterdam: Amsterdam University Press.

Fernández-Götz, M. 2014c. Reassessing the Oppida: The Role of Power and Religion. *Oxford Journal of Archaeology* 33/4, 379-394.

Fernández-Götz, M. 2014d. Central places and the construction of collective identities in the Middle Rhine-Moselle region, in: Popa, C. and Stoddart, S. (eds.), *Fingerprinting the Iron Age. Approaches to Identity in the European Iron Age.* Oxford: Oxbow Books, 175-186.

Fernández-Götz, M. 2016a. Revisiting migrations in Archaeology: The Aisne-Marne and the Hunsrück-Eifel Cultures, in: Erskine, G., Jacobsson, P., Miller, P., Stetkiewicz, S. (eds.), *Proceedings of the 17th Iron Age Research Student Symposium* (IARSS). Oxford: Archaeopress Publishing, 1-11.

Fernández-Götz, M. 2016b. The power of the past: Ancestral cult and collective memory in the Central European Iron Age, in: Sîrbu, V., Jevtić, M., Dmitrović, K., Ljuština, M. (eds.), *Funerary Practices during the Bronze and the Iron Ages in Central and Southeast Europe.* Belgrade/Čačak: University of Belgrade National Musem, 165-178.

Fichtl, S. 2012. *Les peuples gaulois. IIIe-Ier siècle av. J.-C.* Paris: Editions Errance.

Foucault, M. 1980. *Power/Knowledge: Selected Interviews and Other Writings.* New York: Vintage Books.

Gleser, R. 2005. *Studien zu sozialen Strukturen der historischen Kelten in Mitteleuropa aufgrund der Gräberanalyse.* Bonn: Habelt.

Haffner, A. 1976. *Die westliche Hunsrück-Eifel-Kultur.* Römisch-Germanische Forschungen 36. Berlin: De Gruyter.

Hernando, A. 2002. *Arqueología de la Identidad.* Madrid: Akal.

Hornung, S. 2008. *Die südöstliche Hunsrück-Eifel-Kultur: Studien zu Späthallstatt- und Frühlatènezeit in der deutschen Mittelgebirgsregion.* Universitätsforschungen zur prähistorischen Archäologie 153. Bonn: Habelt.

Krausse, D. 2006. *Eisenzeitlicher Kulturwandel und Romanisierung im Mosel-Eifel-Raum.* Mainz: von Zabern.

Metzler, J. 1995. *Das treverische Oppidum auf dem Titelberg (G.-H. Luxemburg). Zur Kontinuität zwischen der spätkeltischen und der frührömischen Zeit in Nord-Gallien.* Dossiers d'Archéologie du Musée National d'Histoire et d'Art 3. Luxembourg: Musée National d'Histoire et d'Art.

Roymans, N. 1990. *Tribal Societies in Northern Gaul. An Anthropological Perspective.* Cingula 12. Amsterdam: Universteit van Amsterdam.

Roymans, N. 2004. *Ethnic Identity and Imperial Power: The Batavians in the early Roman Empire.* Amsterdam: Amsterdam University Press.

Verger, S. 2009. Société, politique et religion en Gaule avant la Conquête. Éléments pour une étude anthropologique. *Pallas* 80, 61-82.

Author address

Manuel Fernández-Götz
School of History, Classics and Archaeology
University of Edinburgh
William Robertson Wing
Old Medical School, Teviot Place
Edinburgh EH8 9AG, United Kingdom
M.Fernandez-Gotz@ed.ac.uk

About the author

Dr. Manuel Fernández-Götz is Head of Archaeology at the University of Edinburgh. After completing his PhD, he worked as coordinator of the Heuneburg project at the State Office for Cultural Heritage Baden-Württemberg. He joined the University of Edinburgh in September 2013, being appointed as Chancellor's Fellow in Archaeology. In 2016, he was awarded the prestigious Philip Leverhulme Prize, and in 2017 promoted to Reader. He has authored ca. 200 publications and held visiting scholar positions at the universities of Oxford, Cambridge and Brown, among others. Recent fieldwork projects include the sites of Monte Bernorio, Huerta Varona, Sasamon and Puig Ciutat in Spain, Ardoch in Scotland and Arras in England. Since 2018, he co-directs research at the Early Iron Age site of Kaptol and its surroundings (Croatia).

Meteorological Medicine in the Hippocratic Corpus

Anne Liewert

Abstract

This research project focused on one of the oldest and most famous writings of the Hippocratic corpus, which includes a discourse on the influence of the environment on human health, the physical form, human character and culture. This complex medical theory, which finds confirmation in many other works of the collection, is closely related to the theory of the humors, which had a deep impact on western medicine and social theory and stands for one of the earliest examples in European thinking for "Human Development in Landscapes".

Material and methods

The Hippocratic Corpus contains more than 60 books on several medical disciplines, which were published under the name of Hippocrates of Kos, the so-called father of medicine, from the 5th to the 1st century BC. Hippocratic medicine is widely famous for its ground-breaking humoral pathology, which implies that human health is determined by the harmony and balance of a certain number of humors inside the human body. But an important issue, which has hardly been researched (see, *e.g.*, the leading study of Schöner 1964), is the cause for the respective humor ratios and the influence of environmental factors. This was one major aim of the research project presented here (Liewert 2015), since the well-known humoral pathology can just be fully understood within this context.

When studying the ancient concept of environmental factors and their impact on a person's condition, research used to focus on the short treatise *On Airs, Waters and Places,* which contains the first extensive disquisition on medical climatology and ethnography in the European history of science. This text shows how one can predict in which manner the health or a present illness of a person will develop, only by regarding his/her environment. This environment is distinguished by physical, political and cul-

in: Müller, J. and Ricci, A. 2020 (eds.), *Past Societies: Human Development in Landscapes.*
Sidestone Press: Leiden, 109-114.

tural factors. The concept also includes long-term effects on people according to their general constitutions and, of course, short-term effects such as diseases.

In spite of this interesting content, the treatise had merely been analysed regarding its authorship, unity and dating, but not regarding the complexity of the comprehensively developed environmental typology (see, *e.g.*, Edelstein 1931; Diller 1934; Jouanna 1996). Furthermore, confining research to just one text of the large corpus has been, of course, very short-sighted.

After taking stance on the mentioned philological problems concerning this treatise, it was therefore necessary to compile a few hundred related passages within the Hippocratic Corpus and to collate the contents. The analysis showed that *On Airs, Waters and Places* is just one (even though the most extensive) instance for the environmental concept. Several other texts, such as *On Regimen*, *On the Humors* and *Aphorisms,* endorse this milieu theory by providing more information, partly compliant with the first treatise, partly additional.

On this basis, it was possible to reconstruct the whole Hippocratic tenet, consisting of four main environmental factors, which influence the humor ratio and thus a person's health, but also his/her physical form, character and culture: The first factor is the wind, mostly linked with the cardinal points north, south, east and west (for the wind see, *e.g.*, *On Airs, Waters and Places,* 3-6; *On Regimen,* 2, 37f.; *On the Sacred Disease,* 10, 13). The texts pay the most attention to the north and the south wind, which reveals a hidden dualism. These winds, originally cold and wet, change their qualities by blowing over huge land masses. In Greece, the north wind is usually perceived as cold and dry, whereas the south wind is said to be warm and humid. Phlegm is connected with the south wind, which loosens up the human body; the north wind activates the bile and dries out the body. People with a high proportion of bile have dry, warm and firm bodies, and healthy heads, but problems with their digestion. They are constantly hungry, thirsty, brave, obstinate and wild and tend to have inner heat, which causes inflammations. People with a lot of phlegm have humid, cold and slack bodies. They are rather weak and less fertile, sometimes even corpulent and have a gentle character. Regarding the winds, humidity therefore forms the major connection between this environmental factor and the medical consequences – and we will later see that humidity plays a major role in the whole reconstructed theory. The other two winds are less important, although dawn always has a positive connotation and the sunset a negative one.

The second environmental factor is highly interrelated to the winds: the seasons (for the seasons see, *e.g.*, *On Airs, Waters and Places*, 10f.; *Aphorisms*, 3,1-23; *On the Nature of Man* 7f.; *On Regimen*, 1,32; 3,68 and *On Hebdomads*, 4; 18-22). Springtime is portrayed as the ideal climate when temperatures and humidity are moderate. People living under such climatic conditions are supposed to be very healthy and balanced in every way. The other seasons are pathogenic because of their extreme characteristics. Like the winds, the seasons are regarded mainly referring to the greatest contrast between them, which can be found between summer and winter, since the summer is much too hot and too dry and the winter too cold and too wet. Again, we see a basic dualistic structure and the use of the elemental qualities for a precise description. The main humors, phlegm and bile, are assigned to these two seasons according to – again – their moisture content: Phlegm occurs mostly in humid winters and bile in dry summers. To emphasise the specific climate of each season, the Hippocratic authors use the above-mentioned winds. Therefore, not every year has the same course, but is influenced and characterised by the winds and their qualities. In addition, astronomical phenomena form important moments during the year because of the climate's changes.

The third environmental factor, water, is set out in the treatise *On Airs, Waters and Places*, in particular (see chapter 7-9 and additionally in *On the Nature of the Child*, 24-26). The subject of this treatise involves three types of water, which are used as drinking water and therefore have an impact on a person's health: The best water is light, fine, fresh and clear. It has a pleasant smell, a moderate temperature and is very digestible. You find this good water in rivers, especially those with its source towards the east, and in boiled rainwater. Persons with a high proportion of bile are recommended to drink this best type of water. The second type is murky water, which has a higher weight because of its solid particles and an unfavourable temperature. In some instances, it even has a bad smell and dark colour. This type occurs in standing and in defrost waters and is generally not recommended for use as it causes several diseases. This murky water activates bile in summer and phlegm in winter, which has a negative effect on human health, since the specified humors are overproduced in these seasons anyway. Hard water is the third type, which comes from mineral rich springs or rocks. It is hard to digest and rather salty and is therefore recommended for persons with a high proportion of phlegm. The basis of this water theory is the famous principle '*contraria contrariis*', according to which you need to consume substances opposite to your physical constitution.

The soil is the fourth environmental factor, which stands for the landscape that surrounds a person (for the soil see, *e.g.*, *On Airs, Waters and Places*, 12-24, especially the last chapter; *On Regimen*, 2,37; *On the Nature of the Child*, 24-26). The ancient texts connect three different theories regarding this topic to explain how our physical forms and our characters are influenced by the landscape. First, two different types of soil are distinguished, which are determined by their water content and climate: Type 1 is thick, soft and rich in water, and the climate is balanced. People who live there have a lot of phlegm in their bodies. As a contrast, type 2 is bare, dry and rough, and the weather is very changeable. This countryside favours the production of bile. As a second theory concerning the soil, this research project could identify the analogy of macrocosm and microcosm: Accordingly, people correspond to their surrounding landscape with regard to their physical form, for example, tall people can be found in mountainous regions and small people in low-lying areas. The third aspect that the authors include pertains to changes of the climate. On the one hand, big changes cause the production of bile and form the tough type of people. On the other hand, they effect diversity within the population of one region. Accordingly, a balanced climate may provoke the forming of the soft type of people and similarity within a population.

In short, the above summarised analysis showed that there is a close connection between the different environmental factors in the Hippocratic theory of meteorological medicine. In particular, the winds and the seasons form an influential constellation, which we refer to today as 'climate', and they define the conditions of the air that humans breathe. Therein, the seasons are strongly dependent on the winds in that the occurrence of a particular type of wind brings a major change in the original qualities of a season. In contrast, the analysis detected hardly any dependence, but rather that just the character of each wind varies a little from season to season, as its temperature and humidity are determined by the radiation of the sun and the (linked) ground heat. In this way, the north wind is, for example, less cold in summer than in winter, when it even causes snowfall and frost. But the climate also has effects on the soil, as seen in humidity levels, the vegetation, and on the water, as is explained in *On Airs, Waters and Places* using the example of four model cities (chapter 3-6). Beyond that, the two named factors are characterised by their own independent nature: River water, for example, is always presented with a positive and sump water with negative attributes, since their main characteristics are assigned to a good respectively bad water type. Moreover, the altitude of one place is not directly dependent on the climate.

While analysing all these different factors and their connections, it was very important to keep in mind that the whole theory was written by and for physicians. This also explains the two major aims of the concept: First of all, physicians were supposed to be able to understand that different patients have a tendency to react to medication and treatments in different ways as they have different constitutions. Secondly, by observing the natural environment of their patients, doctors should be enabled to diagnose illnesses and also predict which illnesses may occur under the respective local circumstances. Therefore, they would have the opportunity to institute preventive measures and diets.

The medical background explains why all the mentioned factors have an impact on people and why the reference point on the part of a human person is always his/her health and, additionally, also the individual physical form and the inner being. In this context, the physiological basis of every nosological etiology is – as already mentioned at the beginning – humoral pathology. The concentration on two main humors, instead of four, indicates the very early date of origin of meteorological medicine, which already evolved in the 5th *c.* BC. Accordingly, the factors wind, seasons and soil also each show two main manifestations, which correspond to the two humors – bile and phlegm. Only water does not follow this dualistic schematism, but nevertheless has a close connection to the humors. The two main characteristics of each factor form extremes, which deviate from the ideal. The ideal is presented as a golden mean, where every aspect is balanced and people are completely healthy. According to the Hippocratic concept, these ideal circumstances can be found during springtime, towards dawn, in digestible water or in moderate conditions of the soil. These explanations of ideal climate conditions and the indication of a specific region led, interestingly, to discussions about the Hippocratic world view and the question where exactly to locate the centre of the world (see, *e.g.*, Schubert 2000, 212-216). We can be quite sure about the assumption of three main regions: one very cold in the north, one moderate in the middle (where southern Europe and Asia Minor are located) and one very hot in the south. But the centre of the world, according to the Hippocratic concept, cannot be located for sure.

One major result of the analysis of the very complex theory is the conclusion that the main connection between the environment and the humor ratio is formed by humidity. Earlier, some researchers looked for a link according to temperature, but wondered why, for example, the warm south wind and the hot summer do not activate the same humor (see, *e.g.*, Diller 1934, 26 and Joly 1966, 187). We found the answer in the different levels of humidity, whereby temperature plays a subordinate role. This result proves that the natural environment is one of the main basic elements at the beginning of a cause-and-effect chain, which in the end sets a person's medical condition, when one of the humors has an increased level for a longer period of time.

Another achievement of this research project is the evidence of the analogy of macrocosm and microcosm in the context of meteorological medicine. Previously, this had been regarded just roughly or in a very general way (see, *e.g.*, Grensemann 1979, 436 and Le Blay 2005, 253). The current analysis proved that the entire human being consists of diverse components, such as the surrounding environment, and can be described by the exact same qualities. Both the constitution of humans and the environmental conditions are very individual and also changeable in a dynamic way.

Linked with the analogy is the therapeutic principle '*contraria contrariis*', which was already mentioned above for the example of the factor 'water'. Since people are a product of their environment, this circumstance can be the best remedy for their illnesses: By consuming substances opposite to their constitutions and diseases with regard to specific qualities and efficacies, they will receive relief.

Finally, there is one fifth factor – in addition to the environmental ones – that also has an impact on humans: everyone's lifestyle regarding the customs of a specific community. After the natural environment sets the foundation of human constitution and character, there is still a possibility to change this determination. There are several examples of tribes in the Hippocratic Corpus, especially in the treatise *On Airs, Waters and Places* (chapter 12-24), to clarify this principle. This completes the complex theory and again points to the individuality of everyone's determination.

This combination of ancient milieu theory and humoral pathology, which was reconstructed in this research project, had a deep impact on western medicine (*e.g.* Galen and Avicenna) and social theory alike (*e.g.* Herodotus and Montesquieu), and stands for one of the earliest examples in European thinking for "Human Development in Landscapes".

References

Diller, H. 1934. Wanderarzt und Aitiologe, Studien zur hippokratischen Schrift περὶ ἀέρων, ὑδάτων, τόπων. *Philologus Suppl.* 26/3, 1-120.

Edelstein, L. 1931. Περὶ ἀέρων *und die Sammlung der hippokratischen Schriften.* Problemata 4. Berlin: Weidmann.

Grensemann, H. 1979. Das 24. Kapitel von De aeribus, aquis, locis und die Einheit der Schrift. *Hermes* 107, 423-441.

Joly, R. 1966. *Le niveau de la science hippocratique, Contribution à la psychologie de l'histoire des sciences.* Paris: Soc.d'éd. 'Les belles lettres'.

Jouanna, J. 1996 (ed.), *Hippocrate, Tome II, 2e partie, Airs, Eaux, Lieux.* Paris: Les Belles Lettres.

Le Blay, F. 2005. Microcosm and Macrocosm, The Dual Direction of Analogy in Hippocratic Thought and the Meteorological Tradition, in: van der Eijk, P. (ed.), *Hippocrates in Context, Papers Read at the XIth International Hippocrates Colloquium.* University of Newcastle upon Tyne, 27-31 August 2002. Leiden/Boston: Brill, 251-269.

Liewert, A. 2015. *Die meteorologische Medizin des Corpus Hippocraticum.* Berlin/ München: De Gruyter.

Schöner, E. 1964. *Das Viererschema in der antiken Humoralpathologie.* Wiesbaden: Steiner.

Schubert, C. 2000. Konstruktionsprinzipien des Weltbildes, Die Hippokratische Schrift De aeribus und die Suche nach der Mitte der Welt. *Medizinhistorisches Journal* 35, 201-218.

Author address

Anne Liewert
Universitäts- und Landesbibliothek Düsseldorf
Geb. 24.41
Universitätsstraße 1
40225 Düsseldorf, Germany
Anne.Liewert@ulb.hhu.de.

About the author

After completing her studies in Classics and Theology, Anne Liewert earned her doctorate in Greek Philology at Kiel University in 2013. Afterwards, she completed a library traineeship at the Herzog August Bibliothek at Wolfenbüttel. Since 2015, she is the head of the Special Collections at the University and State Library of Düsseldorf.

Do as the Romans do? Human-Environmental Interactions in Ancient Southern Latium

Michael Teichmann and Hans-Rudolf Bork

Abstract

In the framework of this contribution, the relationship of humans to their surrounding landscape in southern Latium (Central Italy) during Roman antiquity is discussed. Results on geoarchaeological issues, on forms of land use in antiquity and on settlement-related processes, which could be obtained using a broad basis of different sources, are presented. They enable a better understanding of interaction and adaptation processes in the surroundings of Rome, a core area of the Roman Empire.

Introduction

Within the scope of the dissertation titled *Mensch und Landschaft im südwestlichen Latium in der römischen Antike* (*Humans and Landscape in Southern Latium in Roman Antiquity*) – following the main theme of the Graduate School "Human Development in Landscapes" – the complex human-environment-relationship in ancient Central Italy was investigated (Teichmann 2017; Teichmann and Bork 2012) within an interdisciplinary approach at the interface of archaeological research and other scientific disciplines. The study concentrated on a time span from the 4th/3rd century BC to the 3rd/4th century AD, and thus on a timeframe from the mid-republican period to the Late Roman imperial period.

The core area of investigation ranges from the Tiber Valley in the north to the westward-facing slopes of the Alban Hills, the Lepini and the Ausoni Mountains and to Terracina in the southeast (Fig. 1).

In the west, the Tyrrhenian Sea formed the natural border. In the investigated region, areas with various natural characteristics are found close together: the mostly sandy and partly rocky coast, the Tiber Valley consisting of alluvial soil, the hilly Campagna Romana just to the south of Rome, the Pontine Plain, which was partly

in: Müller, J. and Ricci, A. 2020 (eds.), *Past Societies: Human Development in Landscapes*. Sidestone Press: Leiden, 115-128.

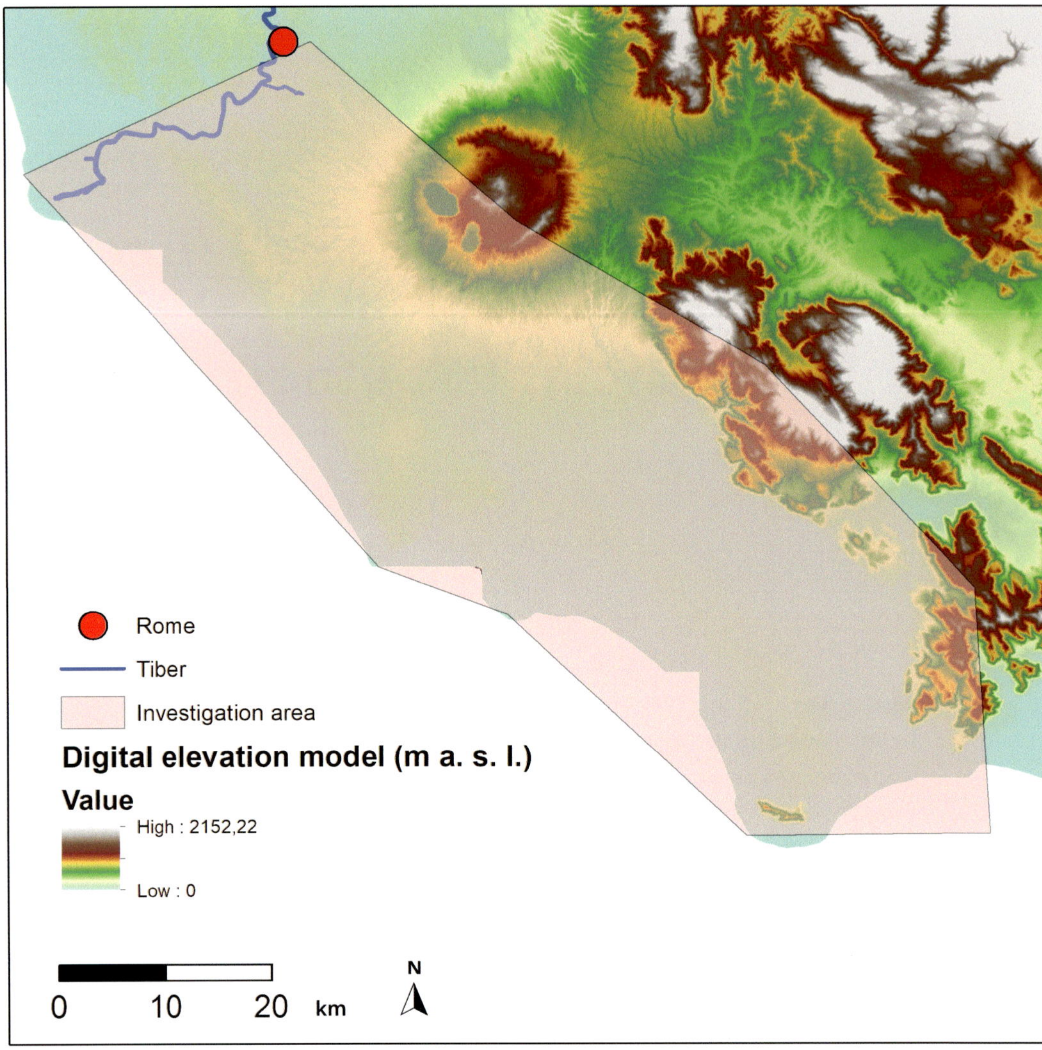

Figure 1. Overview map of the investigation area (map: M. Teichmann).

marshy in ancient times, the volcanic Alban Mountains as well as the Ausoni and Lepini Mountains and the Monte Circeo as limestone massifs.

From a historical point of view, the study area was very important in view of its strong connections to Rome as the capital and centre of the Roman Empire. A part of the investigated area belonged to the direct hinterland of the ancient metropolis with which it interacted economically, socially and demographically.

From a variety of questions, some of the central issues are exemplarily chosen and presented here (Teichmann 2017, 13).

1) Geoarchaeological issues: How did human action affect landscape alteration processes? Was human use of the landscape sustainable or were strong erosion processes triggered by excessive use? To what extent are anthropogenic causes and to what extent are climatic causes formative for today's landscape?

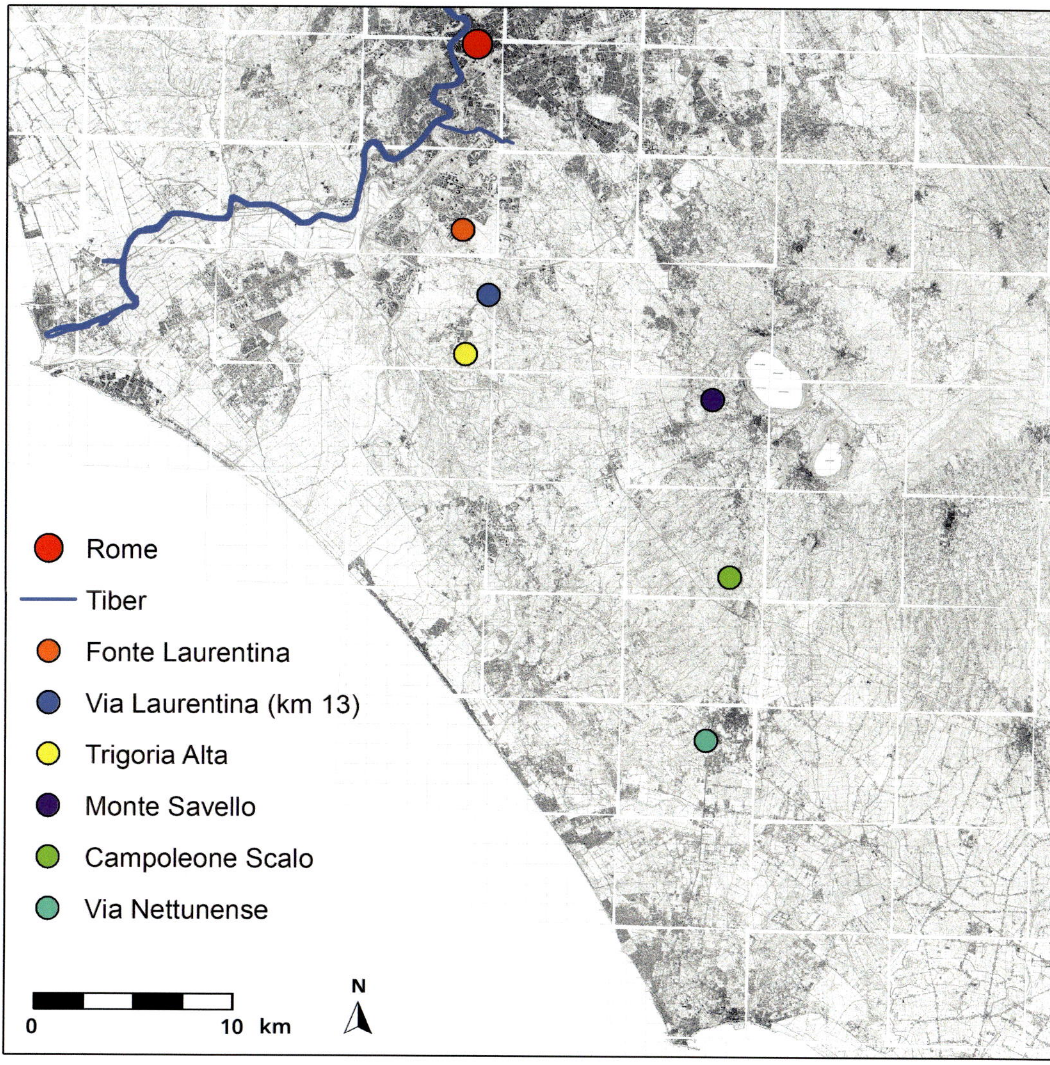

Figure 2. Geoarchaeological sites (map: M. Teichmann).

2) Questions on landscape use: What evidence do we have about forms of land use in the investigated area during Roman times? What characterises the plant spectra? What role did animal husbandry play?
3) Questions on settlement archaeology: Which cultural and natural spatial factors were decisive for the human choice of sites of use? How were cultural and ecological factors weighed against each other in the choice of locations?

Material and Methods

In order to answer the posed scientific questions, a variety of methods were implemented: In 2009, a geoarchaeological overview survey was conducted to reconstruct (post-) depositional processes from documented soil profiles in the field (Teichmann and Bork

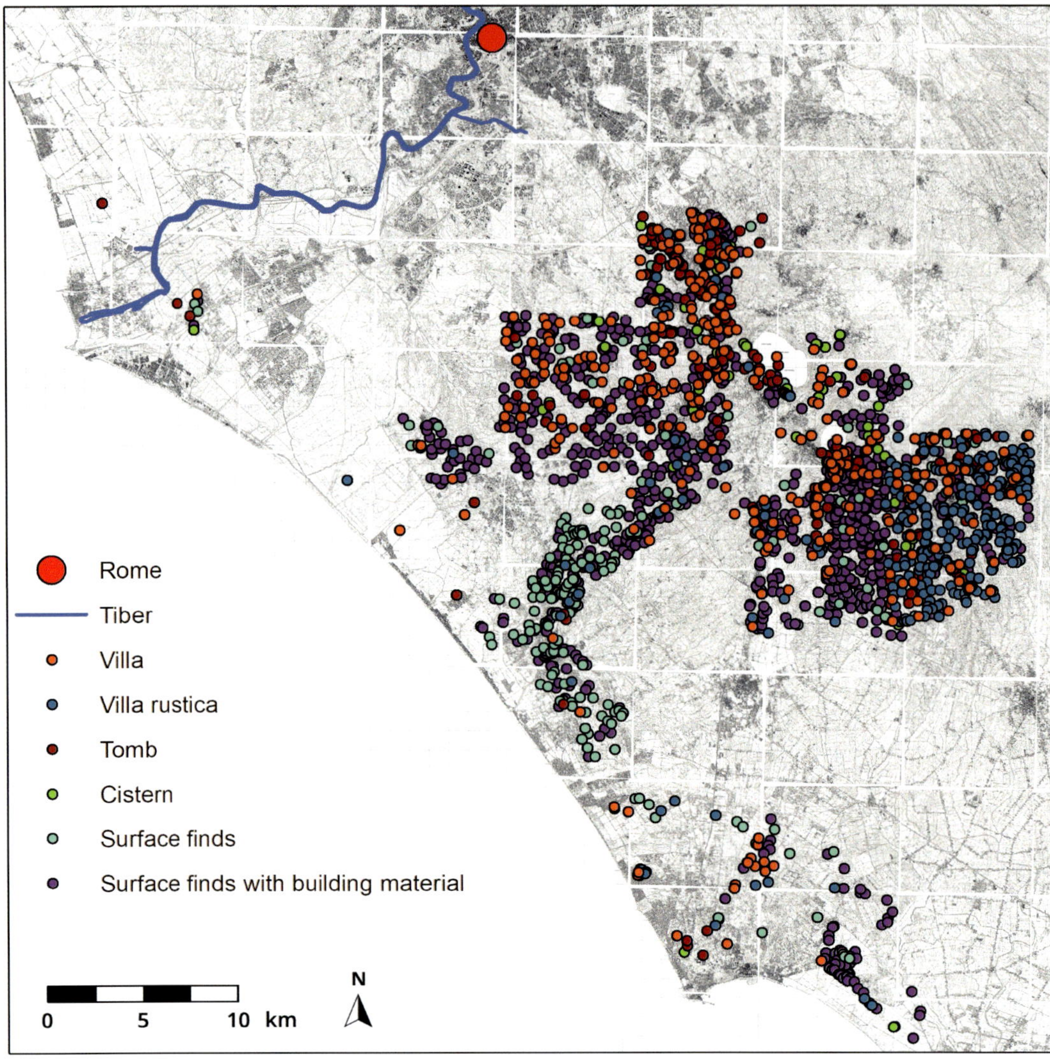

Figure 3. All sites used for the quantitative site location analysis (map: M. Teichmann).

2012). Bork's (2006) four-dimensional, ecosystem analysis approach, which considers all temporal and spatial factors that lead to sediment deposition, was implemented. Geoarchaeological sites on the Via Laurentina, at Fonte Laurentina, on the Via Nettunense, at Trigoria Alta and at Monte Savello were investigated in detail (Fig. 2).

For questions of land use, ancient text sources were compared with published finds and features from the study area. Source categories, such as pollen analyses, macro remains, cultivation traces, and archaeological finds related to agriculture and archaeozoological findings, were included.

For archaeological questions concerning settlement, published site data for the southern Province of Rome was geo-referenced and compiled in a GIS. The data include 991 sites with architectural fragments, 332 sites with scattered finds, 307 villas (205 of these with earliest age determinations in republican times, 62 in imperial times), 273 *villae rusticae*, 261 graves and 104 cisterns (Fig. 3).

The data quantity is statistically significant for all the investigated site categories. Quantitative investigations included descriptive site location analyses, viewshed analyses and density cluster analyses.

Results

Geoarchaeological questions

The geoarchaeological findings differ significantly from one another at the individual investigation sites: early findings, particularly with regard to salt extraction around Portus, are of interest, where a freshwater environment became a brackish water environment around 600 BC – possibly caused by human action (Giraudi *et al.* 2007). The scientific sources confirm the historical view of the early onset of salt production (Bellotti *et al.* 2011, 1114-1115). The geoarchaeological findings are also significant in order to provide an explanation for the absence of findings and finds of a very early settlement – mentioned by Livy (1,33,9) for the year 640 BC and, according to legend, founded by Ancus Marcius – in the area of Ostia of republican and imperial times. Due to a shift of the mouth of the river, a location approximately in the area of the later Portus – hidden today under massive sediments – may be assumed (Giraudi *et al.* 2009). In addition, there is an indication from palynology that the environmental conditions were too instable for a larger settlement in the 7th *c.* BC (Bellotti *et al.* 2011, 1114). Around 450 BC, human influence became increasingly perceptible: Crop plants of this period included *Olia* (olea), *Vitis* (grapevine), *Cannabis* (cannabis), Cereals, *Mercurialis* (mercuries), *Juglans* (walnut) *Castanea* (chestnut) as well as *Pinus pinaster/ pinea* (stone pine) (Di Rita *et al.* 2010; Bellotti *et al.* 2011). The tree population near the coasts was dominated from 600 BC-600 AD by evergreen oaks. Inland, a mixed forest existed. Zones of anthropogenic induced macchia and isolated mixed forest were established on the coast. Over time, macchia decreased. *Chenopodium* (goosefoots) grow well in a salty environment and clearly spread out from the 1st *c.* AD, which is associated with intensified salt production in the area of Ostia (Di Rita *et al.* 2010; Bellotti *et al.* 2011, 1112). Evidence of massive erosion processes can be encountered at numerous sites indicating a variety of heavy rainfall events: For the Torre-Spaccata area, the original interpretation of Gioia *et al.* (2010) with regard to volcanic activities with lahar eruptions around the 4th *c.* BC can be disputed due to the state of research on Lake Albano (D'Ambrosio *et al.* 2010). Instead, the findings suggest a secondary deposition of the lahar material, which is only conceivable in the context of huge erosion processes, especially since the authors assume a single deposition process. The shifting processes were possibly caused by the meltwaters of the extreme winter of 400 BC, which is mentioned in ancient written sources (Liv. 5,2,7; Dion. Hal. Ant. 12,8,1-3). The findings could fit into this chronological framework, although neither archaeological nor geoarchaeological methods enable corresponding precise dating.

In the Marcandreola area, massive erosion led to the abandonment of a road in the 3rd *c.* BC (Betori and Fischietti 2010, 233). In the Torre-Spaccata area, only little fine-grained sediments were deposited from the 3rd/2nd *c.* BC to the 4th *c.* AD, indicat-

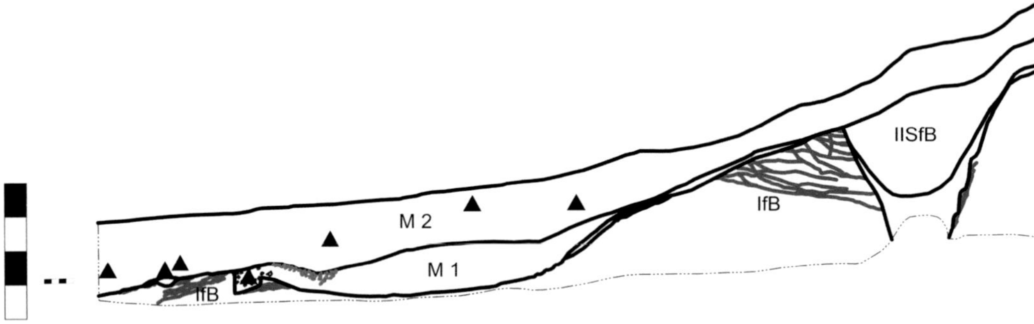

Figure 4. Soil profile along the Via Laurentina near the km 13 point. Length of scale bars: 2m (horizontal scale 1:100, vertical scale 1:20). M2: Homogeneous colluvium with ceramic fragments. M1: Stratified colluvial layer. The stratification is the result of depositional events as a consequence of numerous heavy rainfall events. IISfB: Gully system in which reddish-brown loamy soil developed during a warm period in the Middle or Late Pleistocene. IfB: Reddish-brown residue of a loamy soil, which developed during a warm period in the middle Pleistocene (profile: M. Teichmann and H.-R. Bork 2012, 215).

ing largely consistent conditions with soil-protecting vegetation (Gioia *et al.* 2010). A similar sediment pattern is observed in the Tiber Valley around the Ponte Galeria (Arnoldus-Huyzendveld and Pellegrino 2000, 223) and also on the Pontine Plain near the Tratturo Caniò sanctuary (Cassieri *et al.* 2013, 397), where soil formation started in republican times. Soil formation processes, which are not exactly dated, but perhaps fall into a similar timeframe, were recorded in our own geoarchaeological work at the geoarchaeological profile close by the Via Nettunense (Teichmann and Bork 2012).

The excavations on a dam in the Magliana area exhibit traces of two floods from the early 1st *c.* AD, after which the dam was built, and sediments for which no exact dating is mentioned (Arnoldus-Huyzendveld and Pellegrino 2000, 221). In front of the dam, material was deposited until the 4th *c.* AD. The dam was overrun by massive erosion in post-ancient times.

The increase in overflow levels in Terracina and Ostia in the 1st *c.* AD due to an increased groundwater table testifies more humid conditions (Cassieri and Innico 2009, 380; Pellegrino 2000, 15). A shift in the course of the Tiber at the end of the 1st *c.* AD is an indication for another flood event during this period (Arnoldus-Huyzendveld and Pellegrino 2000, 222). On the Amaseno River, there was a strong flood in the 1st or 2nd *c.* AD (Feiken 2014, 217).

In the peri-urban *suburbium* near the Via Asinaria, strong erosion processes can be observed around the middle of the 3rd and the early 4th *c.* AD (Rea 2014, 16). The surface erosion processes at the sites of Fonte Laurentina and Via Laurentina (Fig. 4) probably also indicate the imperial period, but exact chronological limitation is difficult.

Comparing the observed geoarchaeological evidence with the climatic indicators from the villa of Faragola in Apulia, an apparent discrepancy between the findings is evident (Caracuta 2011, 275). One could assume that the floods primarily occurred in the particularly humid climatic phases. However, extreme heavy precipitation in the entire Mediterranean region is the result of specific weather conditions lasting for a few hours to a few days, independent of longer-range weather conditions. Heavy precipitation occurs predominantly in the fall and spring months and occasionally also in winter. Thus, numerous floods, which are well-documented in written sources, occurred in Rome during a phase of reduced wetness at the end of republican times in the late 1st *c.* BC (Camuffo 1990). During the dry-phase from the 2nd half of the 4th *c.* and the beginning of the 5th *c.* AD, strong erosion processes occurred on the Via Asinaria.

In contrast, there is no available evidence in the study area of increased erosion processes for the phase of increasing humidity at the end of the 2nd and the beginning of the 3rd *c.* BC. These findings suggest that individual events played a more prominent role than general climate trends.

Furthermore, when observing the geoarchaeological findings, it is striking that these hint at very different erosion events, which had very lasting effects on a local scale and led, in some cases, to the abandonment of former land use. Indications of relatively stable conditions and low sedimentation rates from about the 2nd *c.* BC are merely found as a common element in a number of findings in Rome's surroundings in the Torre-Spaccata area, in the Tiber Valley and on the Pontine Plain.

Sedimentation rates from Rome's surroundings, the Tiber Delta (Bellotti *et al.* 1989) and on the coast near the Vicus Augustanus (Hansom 1998; Rendell *et al.* 2007) verify a marked increase in the sedimentation of material since Roman times. When comparing ancient Roman landscape changes with processes of landscape changes in post-antiquity, the verifiable younger processes moulded and reshaped the landscape far more strongly at numerous locations than erosion processes in antiquity. As anthropogenic factors, the abandonment of artificial drainage systems and deforestation played a role in this, although extreme weather events combined with intensive land use until recent times are most strongly responsible for landscape alteration processes.

Land use issues

Since erosion processes are closely connected to the forms of land use and given that it makes a huge difference, if water falls on sheltered wooded or cleared and used land, considerations about ancient land use are a thematically related field: Archaeological sources indicating land use are found in the form of agricultural terraces, cisterns used for the irrigation of fields, centuriation and traces of cultivation. Indirect evidence is provided by millstones as well as oil and wine presses.

Republican agricultural terraces in the mountainous areas of Terracina, Cori and Segni verify early efforts to protect the soil from erosion. Viticulture is well-documented by republican cultivation traces in the surroundings of Rome (Santangeli Valenzani and Volpe 2012, 62-64; Di Blasi *et al.* 1999, 111; Aglietti 2007; Aglietti and Cuccurullo 2014, 136; Arena and Ebanista 2013, 16-20). This was carried out with the use of intercropping. Grain cultivation and the production of olive oil are evidenced by mills and presses, but also by pollen profiles and by macro remains like legumes and fruits.

Most traces of cultivation from the surroundings of Rome date to republican times. Direct in the *suburbium*, at the Via Asinaria, winegrowing of the imperial era was replaced by horticulture, which promised higher returns and, due to the perishability of the products, had to be produced in the immediate vicinity of the city.

Figure 5. Fish breeding enclosure at the Villa La Banca north of Torre Astura (photo: M. Teichmann).

Wood as a natural resource played a prominent role in ancient times both as a building material and as a source of fuel. Charcoal findings from Valmontone demonstrate the selective choice of wood for the production of charcoal in republican times (Bellini 2008, 1619).

The pollen profiles from the Alban Hills verify an increase in crop plants, such as chestnut, olive, walnut, cereals and cannabis, in Roman times (Bonatti 1963; Alessio *et al.* 1986; Magri and Celant 2009). The cultivation of cannabis in the Alban Hills, probably for the production of ropes or textiles, was a special feature of the 1st and 2nd *c.* AD, which is only documented in such pronounced form here in Central Italy (Marzano 2013, 29-30).

In the Roman diet, pork was very popular. Cattle were especially used as draft animals in the middle republican period and were not allowed to be slaughtered for consumption (Varro rust. 2,5,4; Mazzorin and Minniti 2010, 55). Sheep and goats appear often in findings, but mostly in smaller quantities. They were held as suppliers of wool and milk rather than as meat suppliers. With an increasing production of pork for an urban market, the form of pig husbandry changed from extensive wood pasture to intensive fattening (Meyer *et al.* 2004). This was accompanied by a change from the high-legged to the compact pig (Meyer *et al.* 2004). Plinius (epistle 2,17,3) confirms the practise of inverse transhumance in the early imperial period for the area of his villa on the coast of the Vicus Augustanus.

Poultry and game belonged, as well as hazel dormice for which there is archaeological evidence of breeding around Rome, to those foods that were reserved for wealthy classes (Colonnelli *et al.* 2000, 321).

Fish farming as a delicatessen for the urban elite played an important role in the late republican and the early imperial period (Fig. 5).

Saltwater fish was clearly preferred to freshwater fish (Plaut. Truculentus 1,1,35; Varro 3,17,2; Marzano 2013, 210-211). Villas on the coast sometimes had impressive fish farms that are archaeologically documented. Fish farming was a pastime for the elite as well as a profitable source of income.

Isotope analyses show that the population of the port city of Portus tended to consume more maritime proteins than the population further inland, although there is an overlap in the consumption behaviour of both groups (Prowse *et al.* 2004). The inhabitants of Portus also primarily consumed terrestrial proteins. Adults had better diets in comparison to children, and men consumed more protein-rich foods than women (Prowse *et al.* 2004).

Issues of settlement archaeology

Quantitative analyses on preference factors, spatial distribution and visual relations show the role of different natural and cultural preference factors, which were decisive for the development of a specific settlement pattern:

Numerous ancient sites are found at higher elevations (Fig. 6), on more inclined slopes and with an orientation to the east, sometimes also to the south.

These locational attributes were meant to guarantee good air circulation and to help to avoid particularly damp locations. An analysis of the curvature values verifies this finding. Southern slope locations used the sunshine particularly well. Eastern slopes were relevant in view of prevailing winds. Sites were often located at low cost-distance to the nearest river from which utility water could be taken. They were rarely located on alluvial soil and were often found on sandstone with marl that was mixed with loamy marl. This finding could partly be due to the fact that sites under alluvial soil are more difficult to locate. However, this likely reflects an ancient preference for less flood-prone and mosquito-infested sites on locations with more solid ground. Among the cultural factors, low cost-distance to the next road, to the next sanctuary and cult place can be observed for numerous sites of various types. An individual study with regard to cities and sanctuaries shows that many sites were located at a low cost-distance to Velitrae, Aricia and to a lesser extent also to Lanuvium, whereas good accessibility to the smaller towns of Ardea and Antium on the coast were of less relevance for the investigated sites.

Density analyses show the spatial structure of settlement patterns, whereby both chronological and typological-functional differences in land use strategies were observed.

The field of view analysis shows close visual relations between villas of similar size (in the same category) and (larger) luxury villas – the latter belonging to a higher order in settlement hierarchy. It is obvious that landscape perceptions and the concept "to see and be seen" played a decisive role.

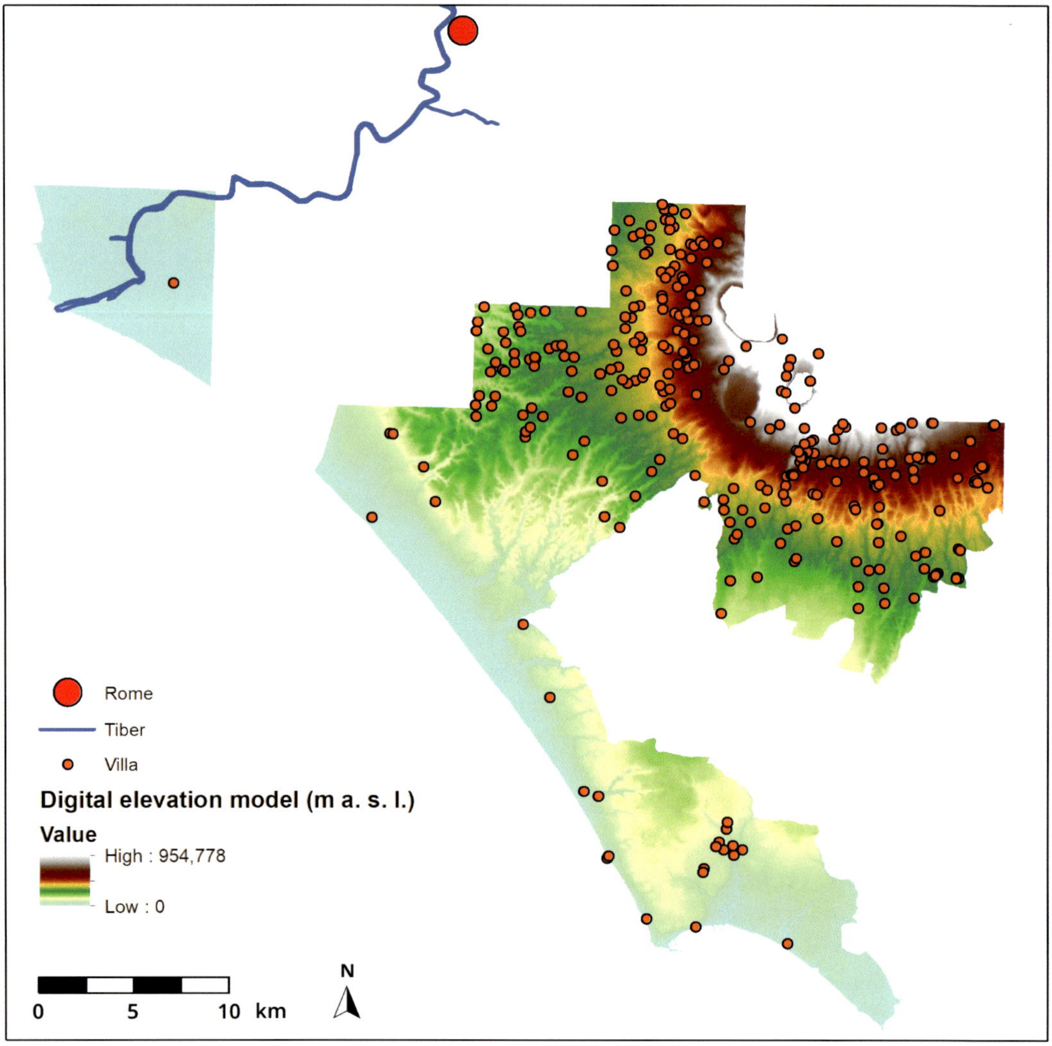

Figure 6. Villas in relation to the variable "altitude above sea level" (map: M. Teichmann).

Conclusion

The interaction of humans with their surrounding landscape in ancient times has been investigated in this study in various ways. Thus, a coherent picture of human life in the ecosystem could be presented.

As always in an investigation of past times, the available source material is fragmentary and the informative power is temporally and spatially limited. Moreover, every scientific discipline has its limits with regard to temporal and spatial resolution. The combination of results from different scientific disciplines is a necessary prerequisite for the solution of innovative questions concerning the relationship of humans to the surrounding environment.

Acknowledgements

The study described above was financially supported by a grant from the Graduate School "Human Development in Landscapes" (GSHDL) of Kiel University, by a short-term grant from the German Academic Exchange Service (DAAD), by a Visiting Fellowship granted by the Digital Institute for Archaeology at the University of Arkansas and by an Ernst-Mach-Fellowship from the Austrian Exchange Service (OeAD) for a research visit at the University of Vienna. The German Archaeological Institute (DAI) supported the study from 2012-2015, when M. Teichmann was employed as a scientific research assistant at the Rome Department. All of these institutions, their staffs and numerous further colleagues are warmly thanked for their support.

References

Aglietti, S. 2007. Rinvenimenti archeologici e numismatici dagli scavi della Tangenziale ai Castelli Romani ad Albano Laziale, in: Ghini, G. (ed.), *Lazio e Sabina 4.* Atti del Convegno: Quarto Incontro di studi sul Lazio e la Sabina. Rome: De Luca, 181-186.

Aglietti, S. and Cuccurullo, E. 2014. La villa Romana "ai Cavallacci" ad Albano Laziale (RM): strutture dell'impianto e nuove acquisizioni dall'area. *Amoenitas* 3, 123-139.

Alessio, M., Allegri, L., Bella, F., Calderoni, G., Cortesi, C., Dai Pra, G., De Rita, D., Esu, D., Follieri, M., Improta, S., Magri, D., Narcisi, B., Petrone, V., Sodori, L. 1986. 14C dating, geochemical features, faunistic and pollen analyses of the uppermost 10 m core from Valle di Castiglione. Rome, Italy. *Geologica romana* 25, 287-308.

Arena, A.P. and Ebanista, L. 2013. Via della Cogna, Località Campo di Carne: rinvenimento di un impianto rustic, in: Panella, S. (ed.), *Scavi ad Aprilia.* Viterbo: BetaGamma Ed., 13-42.

Arnoldus-Huyzendveld, A. and Pellegrino, A. 2000. Traces of historical landscapes preserved in the coastal area of Rome. Tracce di paesaggi storici conservati nell'area costiera di Roma, in: Gisotti, G. and Zarlenga, F. (eds.), *Memorie descrittive della Carta Geologica d'Italia 54.* Rome: Istituto Poligrafico e Zecca dello Stato, 219-226.

Bellini 2008: I siti archeologici, in: Piccininno, M. (ed.*), Il Museo di Valmontone e il Palazzo Doria Pamphilj.* Pescara: Carsa, 16-43.

Bellotti, P., Calderoni, G., Di Rita, F., D'Orefice, M., D'Amico, C., Esu, D., Magri, D., Preite Martinez, M., Tortora, P., Valeri, P. 2011. The Tiber river delta plain (central Italy): Coastal evolution and implications for the ancient Ostia Roman settlement. *The Holocene* 21/7, 1105-1116.

Bellotti, P., Carboni, M.G., Milli, S., Tortora, P., Valeri, P. 1989. La piana deltizia del Tevere: analisi di facies ed ipotesi evolutiva dall'ultimo low stand glaciale all'attuale. *Giornale di Geologia* 51/1, 71-91.

Betori, A. and Fischietti, A.L. 2010. Rinvenimenti archeologici in loc. Marcandreola a Ciampino (Roma), in: Ghini, G. (ed.), *Lazio e Sabina 6.* Atti del Convegno: Sesto Incontro di Studi sul Lazio e la Sabina, Roma, 4-6 marzo 2009. Rome: Edizioni Quasar, 229-236.

Bonatti, E. 1963. Stratigrafia pollinica dei sedimenti postglaciali di Baccano, lago craterico del Lazio. *Atti della Società Toscana di Scienze Naturali*, Ser. A 70, 40-48.

Bork, H.-R. 2006. *Landschaften der Erde unter dem Einfluss des Menschen.* Darmstadt: Wissenschaftliche Buchgesellschaft.

Camuffo, D. 1990. Clima e uomo. Milan: Garzanati.

Caracuta, V. 2011. Ambiente naturale e strategie agroalimentari in Puglia settentrionale tra tardo antico e alto medioevo: l'esempio di Faragola (FG). *PCA* 1, 275-295.

Cassieri, N. and Innico, P.C. 2009. Terracina. La città bassa. Elementi di topografia urbana, in: Ghini, G. (ed.), *Lazio e Sabina 5.* Atti del Convegno Quinto Incontro di Studi sul Lazio e la Sabina, Roma, 3-5 dicembre 2007. Rome: L'Erma di Bretschneider 2009, 369-381.

Cassieri, N., van Leusen, M., Feiken, H., Anastasia, C., Tol, G. 2013. Ricerche geoarcheologiche nell'area di Tratturo Caniò (Sezze, Latina), in: Ghini, G. and Mari, Z. (eds.*), Lazio e Sabina 9.* Atti del Convegno Nono Incontro di Studi sul Lazio e la Sabina, Roma, 27-29 marzo 2012. Rome: Quasar, 393-398.

Colonnelli, G., Carpaneto, G.M., Cristaldi, M. 2000. Uso alimentare e allevamento del ghiro (myoxus glis) presso gli antichi Romani. Materiale e documenti, in: Associazione Italiana di Archeozoologia (ed.), *Atti del 2. Convegno nazionale di archeozoologia,* Asti, 14-16 novembre 1997. Forlì: Abaco, 315-325.

D'Ambrosio, E., Giaccio, B., Lombardi, L., Marra, F., Rolfo, M. F., Sposato, A. 2010. L'attività recente del centro eruttivo di Albano tra scienza e mito: un'analisi critica del rapporto tra il vulcano e la storia dell'area albana, in: Ghini, G. (ed.), *Lazio e Sabina 6.* Atti del Convegno: Sesto Incontro di Studi sul Lazio e la Sabina, Roma, 4-6 marzo 2009. Rome: Edizioni Quasar, 211-222.

Di Blasi, L., De Marco, L., Fellak, M., Foddai, E. 1999. *Elementi e linee ricostruttive di un paesaggio agrario del suburbio di Roma.* Atlante Tematico di Topografia Antica 8. Rome: L'Erma di Bretschneider, 95-114.

Di Rita, F., Celant, A., Magri, D. 2010. Holocene environmental instability in the wetland north of the Tiber delta (Rome, Italy): Sea-lakeman interactions. *Journal of Paleolimnology* 44, 51-67.

Feiken, H. 2014. *Dealing with biases. Three geo-archaeological approaches to hidden landscapes of Italy.* Groningen: Barkhuis Groningen University Library.

Gioia, P., Arnoldus-Huyzendveld, A., Celant, A., Rosa, C., Volpe, R. 2010. Archaeological investigations in the Torre Spaccata valley (Rome): human interaction with the recent activity of the Albano Maar, in: Funicello, R. and Giordano, G. (eds.), *The Colli Albani Volcano.* London: Geological Society, 355-382.

Giraudi, C., Tata, C., Paroli, L. 2007. *Carotaggi e studi geologici a Portus: il delta del Tevere dai tempi di Ostia Tiberina alla costruzione dei porti di Claudio e Traiano.* www.fastionline.org/docs/FOLDER-it-2007-80.pdf.

Giraudi, C., Tata, C., Paroli, L. 2009. Late Holocene Evolution of the Tiber River Delta and Geoarchaeology of Claudius and Trajan Harbor, Rome. *Geoarchaeology* 24/3, 371-382.

Hansom, J. 1998. Insediamenti costieri di età romana ed evoluzione della linea di costa a Castelporziano. Rapporto preliminare, in: Lauro, M.G. (ed.), *Castelporziano III, Campagne di scavo e restauro 1987-1991.* Rome: Viella, 157-160.

Magri, D. and Celant, A. 2009. Paesaggi vegetali dei Colli Albani dalla Preistoria al Medioevo, in: Drago Troccoli, L. (ed.), *Il Lazio dai Colli Albani ai Monti Lepini tra preistoria ed età moderna.* Rome: Ed. Quasar, 29-37.

Marzano, A. 2013. *Harvesting the sea: the exploitation of marine resources in the Roman Mediterranean.* Oxford: Oxford University Press.

Mazzorin, J. De Grossi and Minniti, C. 2010. L'utilizzazione degli animali nella documentazione archeozoologica a Roma e nel Lazio dalla Preistoria recente all'età Classica, in: Drago Troccoli, L. (ed.), *Il Lazio dai Colli Albani ai Monti Lepini tra preistoria ed età moderna.* Rome: Ed. Quasar, 39-64.

Meyer, H., Franke, P.R., Schäffer, J. 2004. *Hausschweine in der griechisch-römischen Antike. Eine morphologische und kulturhistorische Studie.* Oldenburg: Isensee.

Pellegrino, A. 2000. Ostia antica. Führer zu den Ausgrabungen. Rome: Abete.

Prowse, T., Schwarcz, H.P., Saunders, S., Macchiarelli, R., Bondioli, L. 2004. Isotopic paleodiet studies of skeletons from the Imperial Roman-age cemetery of Isola Sacra, Rome, Italy. *Journal of Archaeological Science* 31/3, 259-272.

Rendell, H.M., Claridge, A.J., Clarke, M.L. 2007. Late Holocene Mediterranean coastal change along the Tiber delta and Roman occupation of the Laurentine shore, central Italy. *Quaternary Geochronology* 2, 83-88.

Santangeli Valenzani, R. and Volpe, R. 2012. Paesaggi agrari della viticoltura a Roma e nel suburbia, in: Ciacci, A., Rendini, R., Zifferero, A. (eds.), *Archeologia della vite e del vino in Toscana e nel Lazio. Dalle tecniche dell'indagine archeologica alle prospettive della biologia molecolare.* Florence: All'Insegna del Giglio, 61-69.

Teichmann, M. and Bork, H.-R. 2012. Geo- and Landscape archaeological investigations in south-western Lazio (Italy): An approach for the identification of man-made landscape transformation processes in the hinterland of Rome, in: Kluiving, S. and Guttmann-Bond, E. (eds.), *Landscape Archaeology between Art and Science. From a Multi- to an Interdisciplinary Approach.* Amsterdam: Amsterdam University Press, 211-222.

Teichmann, M. 2017. *Mensch und Landschaft im südwestlichen Latium in der römischen Antike.* Vienna: Phoibos-Verlag.

Author addresses

Michael Teichmann
Kirchbachstraße 35
65191 Wiesbaden, Germany
mbwteichi@web.de

Hans-Rudolf Bork
Institute for Ecosystem Research
Kiel University
Olshausenstraße 75
24118 Kiel, Germany
hrbork@ecology.uni-kiel.de

About the authors

Michael Teichmann studied Classical Archaeology in Vienna and Rome as well as "Landscape Archaeology" at the University of Birmingham. During his PhD studies at Kiel University, he completed longer research stays at the German Archaeological Institute in Rome. He was a Visiting Fellow at the University of Arkansas (Fayetteville) and an Ernst-Mach fellowship holder at the University of Vienna. Further on, he was employed as a researcher at the German Archaeological Institute in Berlin. He is currently conducting research at the LBI ArchPro in Vienna as a DAAD postdoctoral fellow.

Hans-Rudolf Bork studied Geography, Soil Science, Geology and Rural Water Management in Gießen and Braunschweig. After his doctorate and habilitation at the TU in Braunschweig, he was appointed as Professor of Regional Soil Science at the TU Berlin in 1989. From 1992 to 1999, Hans-Rudolf Bork headed the Leibniz Centre for Agricultural Landscape Research in Müncheberg. Since 2000, he has been Professor of Ecosystem Research at Kiel University. Bork researches the dynamics of human-environment relations since the Neolithic with a focus on pedological and geoarchaeological methods. Regionally, he focuses on Central, Southern and Eastern Europe, East Africa, China, the Chilean Atacama, Easter Island, Robinson Crusoe Island and Palau in Micronesia. He has written 15 scientific books and more than 200 articles in peer-reviewed scientific journals.

Palynological Investigations on the Deposits of a Well Shaft from the Roman Iron Age with Special Reference to Non-Pollen Palynomorphs

Magdalena Wieckowska-Lüth and Dieter Bischop

Abstract

This study presents the results of palynological analyses of the backfill layers of a well from the Roman Iron Age at Bremen-Kirchhuchting. It reveals that the deposits do not only include pollen grains but also a great number of diverse non-pollen polymorphs (NPPs). While the pollen signal therein primarily mirrors the local surroundings, the NPP evidence represents the depositional environment of the immediate site. This illustrates the high significance of NPPs in the reconstruction of site relations and additionally underlines the large potential of the combination of pollen and NPP data in conjunction with archaeological contexts.

Introduction

In connection with archaeological research, pollen analysis represents a completely independent method and provides the opportunity to observe and interpret single features from a different perspective. The investigation of the pollen found in archaeological features can, for example, lead to knowledge about the use of the immediate settlement area, the local site conditions as well as the spatial and economic organisation of a settlement. In addition to "classical pollen analysis", the application of additional, more precise indicators on a small scale can be very helpful in order to more accurately reconstruct the type of anthropogenic use at a particular site. With the establishment of the analysis of non-pollen palynomorphs (NPPs: for example, fungal remains, eggs of parasites, remains of algae, shells of amoebae,

in: Müller, J. and Ricci, A. 2020 (eds.), *Past Societies: Human Development in Landscapes*.
Sidestone Press: Leiden, 129-140.

remains of invertebrates, *etc.*), new possibilities for detailed site characterisation in connection with archaeological contexts arose (*e.g.* Bosi *et al.* 2011; Brinkkemper and van Haaster 2012; Chichinadze and Kvavadze 2013; Kvavadze and Kakhiani 2010; Revelles *et al.* 2016; Święta-Musznicka *et al.* 2013; van Geel *et al.* 1983; 2003). Many of these micro remains are characterised by the fact that they only occur under specific conditions, for example, with the presence of plant material, wood or manure or together with parasitic infestation, after fire and erosion events, under dryness or waterlogging conditions, and along with increased nutrient input or water pollution. Therefore, the identification of these indicators that are more precise on a micro level in excavation features are useful in order to grasp how they were used. Against this background, the aim of the present palynological study was to provide new insights for a more detailed site reconstruction. For this purpose, pollen and NPP analyses were conducted on archaeological deposits of a well filling at the site of Bremen-Kirchhuchting from the Roman Iron Age.

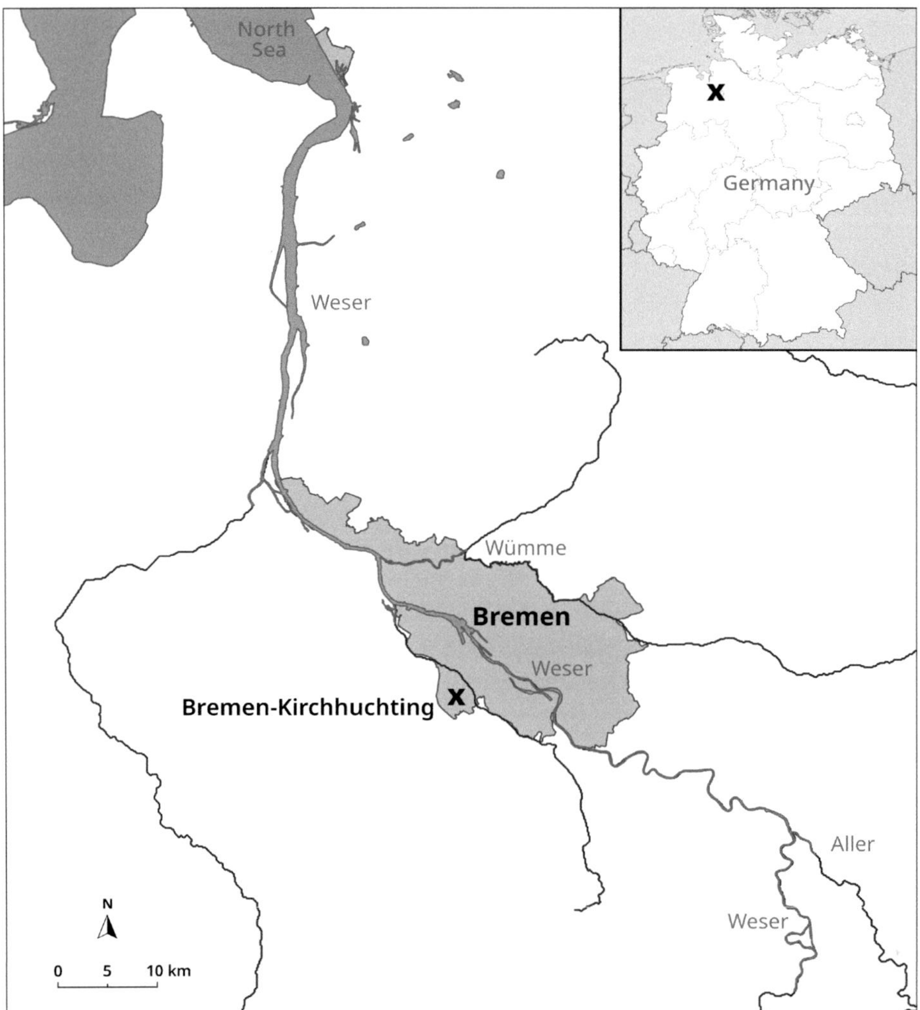

Figure 1. Location of the investigation area in Bremen-Kirchhuchting, Northwest Germany (map: P. Lüth, Archäologie und Beratung).

Figure 2. The wooden box well (finding no. 189) buried in the in-situ dune sand at the excavation site Bremen-Kirchhuchting (photo: J. Geidner, Landesarchäologie Bremen).

Archaeological site

Archaeological monitoring during the construction of a refugee transitional home in Bremen-Kirchhuchting (Fig. 1) provided – in addition to a few Late Bronze Age/Early Iron Age settlement traces – above all evidence of multi-aisled post structures and pits of the Roman Iron Age and the early Migration Period (Bischop 2017).

One of the five wooden wells of this settlement was identified as a box well. Into its corner posts, crosspieces were mortised, on which flat oak planks were mounted like a picket fence (Fig. 2). As an extension of the well shaft, a hollow oak log was buried at the bottom of the well (Fig. 3).

A piece of wood from the well box was dendrochronologically dated by the DAI Berlin to 249 AD as the year that the used tree was felled. From the filling of the well, a ring-shaped weaving weight made of clay, a glass bead and sherds of Saxon bosses pottery, *i.a.*, were recovered. They indicate a longer phase of utilisation of the Late Roman Iron Age well, possibly back to the abandonment of the settlement in the early Migration Period.

Material and methods

For palynological analyses, five samples (1, 20, 34, 50 and 66 cm) (Fig. 3) were taken from humous backfill layers of the well (finding no. 189) into which sandy layers were continuously interposed. In the range at a depth of 34 cm, the humous deposits also contained remnants of wood. All samples were prepared according to the standard techniques outlined by Moore *et al.* (1991). Tablets containing a known number of

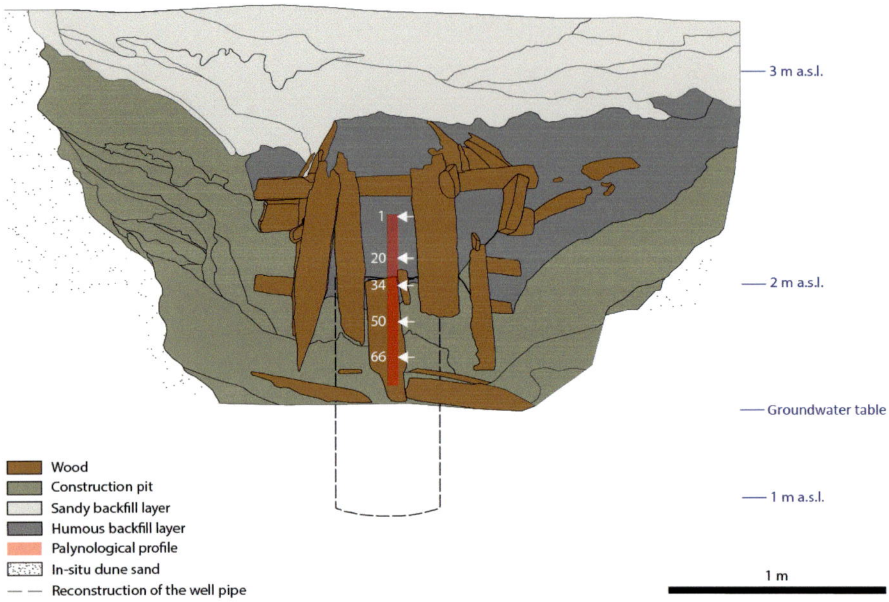

Figure 3. Position of the palynological profile in the well findings (finding no. 189) of Bremen-Kirchhuchting (profile: after J. Geidner, Landesarchäologie Bremen, modified by the authors).

Lycopodium spores were added to enable calculation of concentrations. The samples were characterised by relatively high pollen and NPP concentrations, whereas the preservation was moderate to good. The calculation of pollen percentages is based on the total terrestrial pollen sum (trees, shrubs and dwarf-shrubs + pollen of herbaceous terrestrial plants), with an average value of 500. Data from microscopic charcoal analysis are expressed as concentration per cubic centimetre of sediment. The pollen and NPP diagrams were produced with the help of the program CountPol (Feeser unpublished) (Fig. 4).

Nomenclature of pollen types follows Beug (2004) and that of spores follows Moore *et al.* (1991). NPPs were identified using a reference catalogue at Kiel University and available literature (Andreev *et al.* 2014; Booth *et al.* 2010; Cugny *et al.* 2010; Dietre *et al.* 2012; Égüez *et al.* under review; Florenzano *et al.* 2012; Gelorini *et al.* 2011; Guarro *et al.* 2012; Jones *et al.* 2016; Le Bailly *et al.* 2007; Miola *et al.* 2006; van Geel and Aptroot 2006; van Geel *et al.* 1983; 2003; Vánky 2013; Wieckowska-Lüth and Heske 2019). Nomenclature of NPP-types follows the HdV-no. system (Miola 2012). During the microfossil analysis, some unknown NPPs were recorded. These types were termed using the code "KIU-xxx" (KIU = Kiel University, Germany; -xxx = sequential number). Selected NPP finds are illustrated in figure 5.

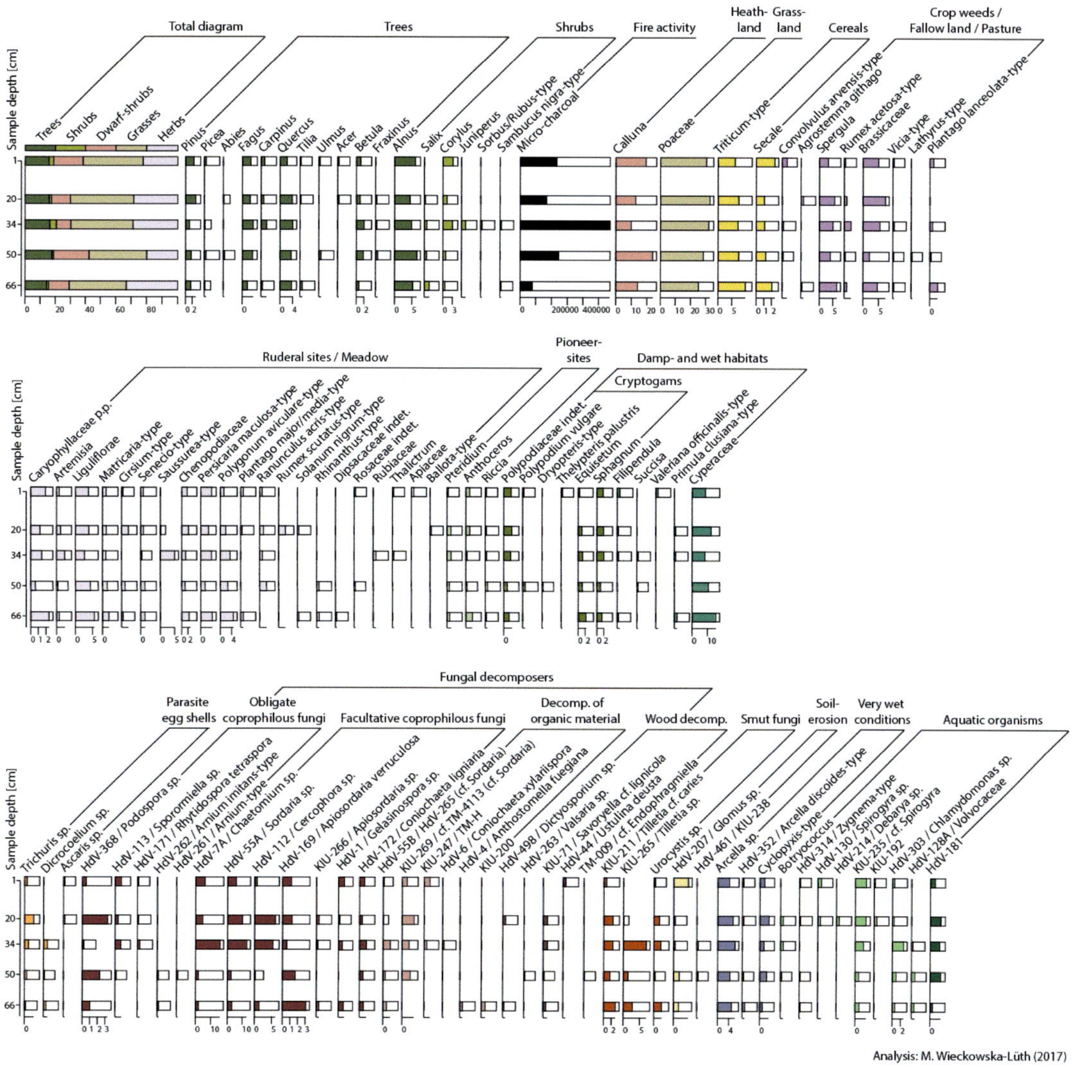

Figure 4. Pollen, spores and NPP diagram (in %) for the profile from the well finding of Bremen-Kirchhuchting. The results of the micro-charcoal analysis are presented in the upper section of the diagram (in particle/cm³) (diagram: M. Wieckowska-Lüth).

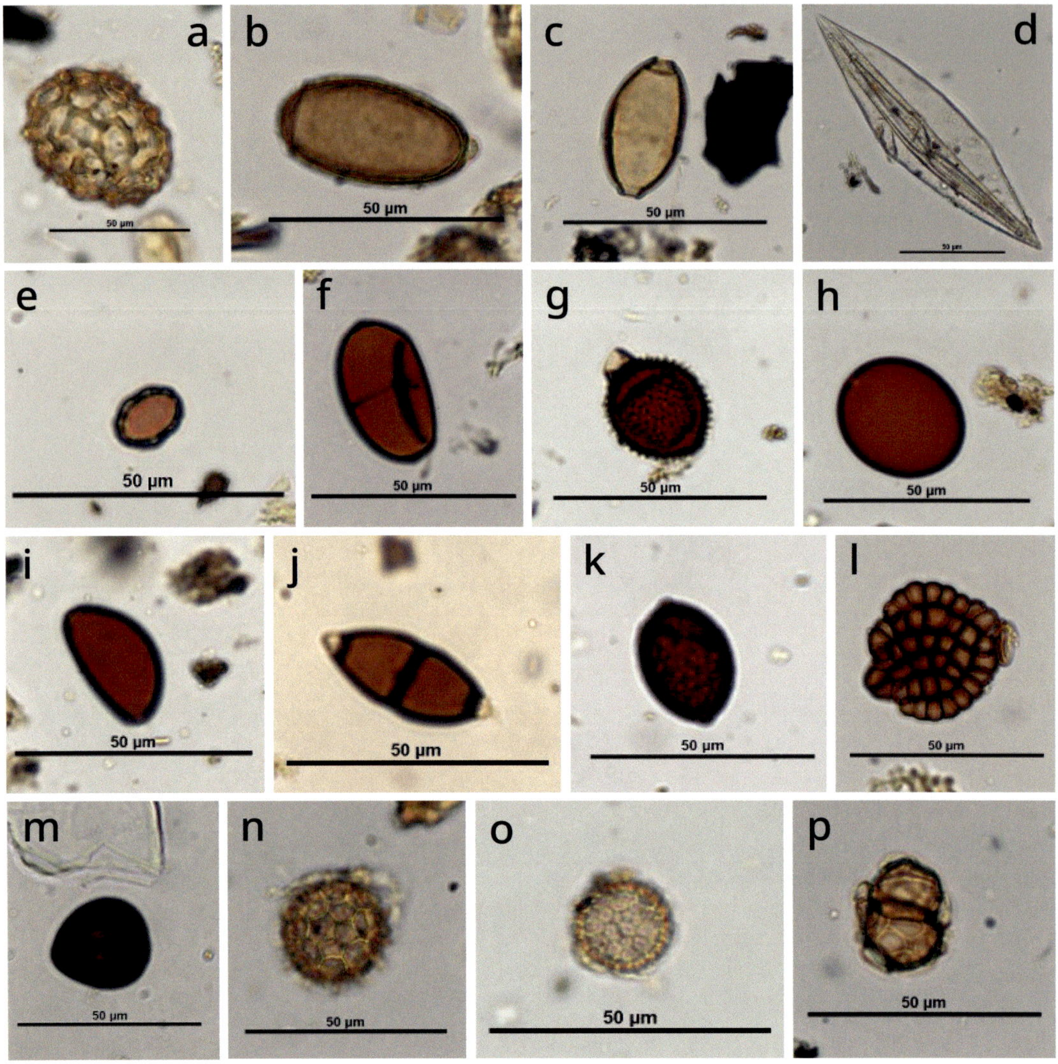

Figure 5. Evidence of selected NPPs from the well finding of Bremen-Kirchhuchting: (a) Ascaris sp.; (b) Dicrocoelium sp.; (c) Trichuris sp.; (d) KIU-235/cf. Spirogyra; (e) HdV-171/Rhytidospora tetraspora; (f) HdV-262/Arnium imitans-type; (g) KIU-266/cf. Apiosordaria; (h) KIU-269/cf. TM-4113/cf. Sordaria; (i) KIU-247/TM-H; (j) KIU-71/Savoryella cf. lignicola; (k) HdV-1/Gelasinospora sp.; (l) Dictyosporium sp.; (m) HdV-461; (n) KIU-211/Tilletia cf. caries; (o) Tilletia sp.; (p) Urocystis sp. (image: M. Wieckowska-Lüth).

Results

All samples are characterised by similar pollen spectra, in which non-tree pollen representatives of heath (9.8-23.9%) and grasslands (25.2-32.7%), cereals (8.8-12.7%) as well as various herbs (21.1-34.3%) were strongly dominant (Fig. 4). Among the high cereal plant proportion, *Triticum*-type was mainly recorded (up to 10.6%), followed by *Secale* (up to 2.4%). Pollen types, which represent the flora of arable farm land and fallow land (6.4-13.3%), are represented by *Convolvulus arvensis*-type, *Agrostemma githago*, *Spergula*, Brassicaeae, *Rumex acetosa*-type, *Lathyrus*-type and *Vicia*-type. Among the representatives of the pollen taxa of ruderal or meadow locations (14.4-21.9%), high proportions of Caryophyllaceae p.p., Liguliflorae, *Matricaria*-type, *Senecio*-type, *Saussurea*-type, *Artemisia*, Chenopodiaceae, *Persicaria maculosa*-type, *Polygonum aviculare*-type and *Ranunculus acris*-type were found. Grazing indicators, such as *Plantago lanceolata*-type, were recorded at comparatively low levels (up to 1%). In addition, pollen from other herbs, such as *Rumex scutatus*-type, *Solanum nigrum*-type, *Rhinanthus*-type, Dipsacaceae indet., Rosaceae indet., Rubiaceae, *Thalictrum*, Apiaceae and *Ballota*-type as well as spores of fern and moss plants from pioneer sites (*Pteridium*, *Anthoceros* and *Riccia*), were noted in lesser amounts.

Among tree (13.7-17.5%) and shrub pollen (1.2-4.5%), *Alnus* is most highly represented (up to 7.3%). But other woody plants, such as *Quercus*, *Corylus*, *Betula*, *Pinus* and *Fagus*, were also regularly recorded. In contrast, taxa such as *Picea*, *Abies*, *Tilia*, *Ulmus*, *Acer*, *Fraxinus*, *Salix*, *Juniperus*, *Sorbus*/*Rubus*-type and *Sambucus nigra*-type appeared only irregularly or isolated. Furthermore, all samples are characterised by very high micro-charcoal levels (80-556 × 10^3 particles/cm^3), whereby the most particles were observed at 34 cm depth.

In addition to the verification of land plants, wetland and swamp plants were also recorded. Among these, cryptogamic spores of Polypodiaceae indet., *Polypodium vulgare*, *Dryopteris*-type, *Thelypteris palustris*, *Equisetum* and *Sphagnum* (up to 4.8%) as well as pollen from herbs of moist to wet locations, such as Cyperaceae, *Filipendula*, *Succisa*, *Valeriana officinalis*-type and *Primula clusiana*-type (up to 16.1%) were represented. The evidence of these taxa was highest in the deepest (66 cm) sample.

Within the NPP-types, eggs of intestinal parasitic worms were recorded (up to 1.4%). While *Trichuris* sp. was consistently found in all spectra, *Dicrocoelium* sp. was only detected in the three lowest samples, whereas *Ascaris* sp. was only found in the upper two samples. The NPP spectra are, in contrast, characterised by very high values of fungal decomposers. Among these, the coprophilous fungal spores, such as HdV-368/*Podospora* sp., HdV-113/*Sporormiella* sp., HdV-171/*Rhytidospora tetraspora*, HdV-262/*Arnium imitans*-type and HdV-261/*Arnium*-type (obligate coprophilous fungal spores: up to 3.9%) and HdV-7A/*Chaetomium* sp., HdV-55A/*Sordaria* sp., HdV-112/*Cercophora* sp., HdV-169/*Apiosordaria verruculosa*, KIU-266/*Apiosordaria* sp., HdV-1/*Gelasinospora* sp. and HdV-172/*Coniochaeta ligniaria* (facultative coprophilous fungal spores: up to 37%) make up a considerable part. In addition, further spores of fungi, which are found on decomposing wood (HdV-498/*Dictyosporium* sp., HdV-263/*Valsaria* sp., KIU-71/*Savoryella* cf. *lignicola*, HdV-44/*Ustulina deusta*, TM-009/cf. *Endophragmiella*) as well as on other dead organic material (HdV-55B/HdV-265, KIU-269/cf. TM-4113/ cf. *Sordaria*, KIU-247/TM-H, HdV-6/*Coniochaeta xylariispora*, HdV-4/*Anthostommella* cf. *fuegiana*, HdV-200), were recorded (up to 4.3%). Overall, the largest percentages of fungal spores from decomposers were found at a depth of 34 cm. All samples also showed spores of smut fungi (up to 11.2%), such as KIU-211/*Tilletia* cf. *caries*, KIU-265/*Tilletia* sp. and *Urocystis*, whereby the uppermost sample (1 cm) included the least amount. Furthermore, fungi spores of both HdV-207/*Glomus* sp. and KIU-238/HdV-461 – both indicators for allochthonous entries – were recorded.

All samples were characterised by the presence of aquatic organisms. Among the green algae components (up to 5.4%), which were highest at a depth of 34 cm, representatives of the taxa *Botryococcus* sp., HdV-314/*Zygnema*-type, HdV-130/*Spirogyra* sp., HdV-214/*Debarya* sp., HdV-303/*Chlamydomonas* sp., HdV-128A/Volvocaceae,

KIU-235/cf. *Spirogyra* and KIU-192 were observed. Moreover, *Rivularia*-type appeared occasionally as a representative of cyanbacteria (0.2%). HdV-181, an unknown probably aquatic organism, was also found to have highest values in the middle samples (up to 1.5%). In addition, testate amoebae were recorded with more or less constant proportions (up to 6.3%) in all spectra.

Discussion

The pollen spectra of all samples reflect a largely open environment. The high evidence of ruderal and meadow herbs with a simultaneous occurrence of fern and moss plants of the pioneer sites mirror a meadow-like environment of a settlement with overused areas. The surrounding landscape was most likely characterised by extensive heath and grassy areas as well as arable farm land and fallow land. The little evidence of plant grazing indicators suggests that probably no pasture land was found in the immediate area of the settlement. The likewise low proportion of tree pollen probably indicates small forest patches in the wider surroundings, whereas the evidence of the wood pollen of alder (*Alnus*) and willow (*Salix*) as well as various herbaceous plants of moist and wet habitats indicate the presence of a watercourse near the settlement. Some trees and bushes, such as birch (*Betula*), hazel (*Corylus*), elder (*Sambucus nigra*-type), and rowan or raspberry/blackberry (*Sorbus*/*Rubus*-type), may have also belonged to the settlement flora.

In light of the high cereal proportion in the deposits of the well shaft, it is also conceivable that this could be the pollen signal of the grain crops that were processed in the settlement. In this context, mainly wheat species were used. In addition, the co-occurrence of relatively high amounts of smut fungus spores (KIU-211/*Tilletia* cf. *caries*, KIU-265/*Tilletia* sp., *Urocystis* sp.) shows that the grain harvest was at least temporarily infested with these pathogens.

The samples from the well filling are also characterised by the presence of fungal spores, which occur on rotting or submerged wood (HdV-498/*Dictyosporium* sp., HdV-263/*Valsaria* sp., KIU-71/*Savoryella* cf. *lignicola*, HdV-44/*Ustulina deusta*, TM-009/cf. *Endophragmiella*). These could be related to the wooden encirclement of the well shaft. It is also possible that the lignin-decomposing fungi appear in the deposits due to wood waste.

Further in this sense is the occurrence of large amounts of microscopic charcoal, which could also have entered the well shaft as settlement refuse. The very high levels of spores of more fungal decomposers (HdV-55B/HdV-265, KIU-269/cf. TM-4113/cf. *Sordaria*, KIU-247/TM-H, HdV-6/*Coniochaeta xylariispora*, HdV-4/*Anthostomella* cf. *fuegiana*) indicate that further organic material must have gotten into the well. In this context, plant material, such as hay or straw, could have possibly been disposed of in the well shaft. The simultaneously attested high proportions of coprophilous fungal spores (HdV-113/*Sporormiella* sp., HdV-171/*Rhytidospora tetraspora*, HdV-262/*Arnium imitans*-type, HdV-261/*Arnium*-type, HdV-7A/*Chaetomium* sp., HdV-55A/*Sordaria* sp., HdV-112/*Cercophora* sp., HdV-169/*Apiosordaria verruculosa*, KIU-266/*Apiosordaria* sp., HdV-1/*Gelasinospora* sp., HdV-172/*Coniochaeta ligniaria*) lead to the assumption that manure or dung were also disposed of in the well. The dispersal and transport of fungal spores is lower than that of pollen, probably partly due to the ground-level location of the fungal fruit body, where wind dispersal is less effective (van

Geel *et al.* 2003). Thus, the signal of coprophilous fungal spores recorded in the well deposits can be actually be interpreted as direct evidence for the presence of manure/dung. The intestinal parasitic eggs (*Trichuris* sp., *Dicrocoelium* sp., *Ascaris* sp.), which likewise occur in the well findings, show that human or animal excrements were eliminated there. Secondarily, their occurrence reveals that the inhabitants of the settlement suffered from parasite infestation. Further NPPs, such as shells of amoebae, green algae, cyanobacteria, and other organisms, which exist under water and eutrophic conditions, indicate that the organic deposits were exposed to the weather over a long time after the abandonment of the well and that a strong eutrophic milieu was established. The sand layers embedded in the humous deposits – these are accompanied by the presence of erosion indicators (HdV-207/*Glomus* sp., HdV-461) – also indicate that the disposal of waste could have occurred in several steps. Thus, it can be assumed that the well shaft had probably been open for some time so that it was additionally filled between the disposal phases by washed and deposited material from the sandy surroundings (Fig. 2)

Conclusion

In summary, it must be assumed that the existing well deposits reflect both the natural pollen precipitation of the vegetation of the settlement and its surroundings shortly before and after the abandonment of the well and the deliberate deposition of organic material. The consistent occurrence of coprophilous fungal and smut fungal spores together with the occurrence of parasitic eggs and the substantial evidence of grass, cereal and arable weed pollen point to a deposition matrix of manure, feces and hay or straw. As a result, the well sediments can be interpreted as a filling of manure or excrements with plant bedding. Moreover, the presence of multiple, embedded sand layers in the deposits demonstrates repeated use. Thus, after it was abandoned, the well served for a long time as a site for waste disposal.

The present study emphasises the promising potential of pollen and particularly NPP analysis for the interpretation of archaeological findings by demonstrating how the well shaft was used secondarily. The additional 'on-site' data also provide valuable information about the living conditions at the Roman Iron Age site. Thus, it was possible to illustrate how waste disposal was regulated at the settlement, that its inhabitants suffered from parasite infestation and that plant processing took place on site.

Acknowledgements

The authors express their sincere thanks to Jan Geidner, who organised the cooperation between the Graduate School "Human Development in Landscapes" and "Landesarchäologie Bremen". We are also grateful to Kálmán Vánky for his help with the identification of smut fungi. Sincere thanks are extended to Matthieu Le Bailly for helping with the parasite egg identification.

References

Andreev, A.A., Tarasov, P.E., Wennrich, V., Raschke, E., Herzschuh, U., Nowaczyk, N.R., Brigham-Grette, J., Mellers, M. 2014. Late Pliocene and Early Pleistocene vegetation history of northeastern Russian Arctic inferred from the Lake El'gygytgyn pollen record. *Climate of the Past* 10, 1017-1039.

Beug, H.-J. 2004. *Leitfaden der Pollenbestimmung für Mitteleuropa und angrenzende Gebiete*. München: Pfeil.

Bischop, D. 2017. Reich an Brunnen. *Archäologie in Deutschland* 5, 2017, 44-45.

Booth, R.K., Lamentowicz, M., Charman, D.J. 2010. Preparation and analysis of testate amoebae in peatland paleoenvironmental studies. Article 2. *Mires and Peat* 7, 1-7.

Bosi, G., Bandini Mazzanti, M., Florenzano, A., Pederzoli, I.A., Rinaldi, R., Torri, P., Mercuri, A.M. 2011. Seeds/fruits, pollen and parasite remains as evidence of site function: piazza Garibaldi – Parma (N Italy) in Roman and Mediaeval times. *Journal of Archaeological Science* 38, 1621-1633.

Brinkkemper, O. and van Haaster, H. 2012. Eggs of intestinal parasites whipworm (Trichuris) and mawworm (Ascaris): Non-pollen palynomorphs in archaeological samples. *Review of Palaeobotany and Palynology* 186, 16-21.

Chichinadze, M. and Kvavadze, E. 2013. Pollen and non-pollen palynomorphs in organic residue from the hoard of ancient Vani (western Georgia). *Journal of Archaeological Science* 40/5, 2237-2253.

Cugny, C., Mazier, F., Galop, D. 2010. Modern and fossil non-pollen palynomorphs from the Basque mountains (western Pyrenees, France): the use of coprophilous fungi to reconstruct pastoral activity. *Vegetation History and Archaeobotany* 19, 391-408.

Dietre, B., Gauthier, É. Gillet, F. 2012. Modern pollen rain and fungal spore assemblages from pasture woodlands around Lake Saint-Point (France). *Review of Palaeobotany and Palynology* 186, 69-89.

Égüez, N., Dal Corso, M., Wieckowska-Lüth, M., Delpino, C., Tarantini, M., Biagetti, S. Under review. Geo-Ethnoarchaeology in Monti Sibillini pastoral rock shelters: dung as indicator for seasonality and intensity use of space. *Archaeological and Anthropological Sciences.*

Florenzano, A., Mercuri, A.M., Pederzoli, A., Torri, P., Bosi, G., Olmi, L., Rinaldi, R., Bandini Mazzanti, M. 2012. The Significance of Intestinal Parasite Remains in Pollen Samples from Medieval Pits in the Piazza Garibaldi of Parma, Emilia Romagna, Northern Italy. *Geoarchaeology: An International Journal* 27, 34-47.

Gelorini, V., Verbeken, A., van Geel, B., Cocquyt, C., Verschuren, D. 2011. Modern non-pollen palynomorphs from East African lake sediments. *Review of Palaeobotany and Palynology* 164, 143-173.

Guarro, J., Gené, J., Stchigel, A.M., José, M. 2012. *Atlas of soil Ascomycetes.* Utrecht: CBA-KNAW Fungal Biodiversity Centre.

Jones, E.B.G., To-anun, C., Suetrong, S., Boonyuen, N. 2016. Mycosphere Essays 12. Progress in the classification of the water-cooling tower ascomycete *Savoryella* and a tribute to John Savory: a review. *Mycosphere* 7/5, 570-581.

Kvavadze, E. and Kakhiani, K. 2010. Palynology of the Paravani burial mound (Early Bronze Age, Georgia). *Vegetation History and Archaeobotany* 19, 469-478.

Le Bailly, M., Leuzinger, U., Schlichtherle, H., Bouchet, F. 2007. «Crise économique» au Néolithique à la transition Pfÿn-Horgen (3400 BC): contribution de la paléoparasitologie. *Anthropozoologica* 42, 175-185.

Miola, A. 2012. Tools for Non-Pollen Palynomorphs (NPPs) analysis: A list of Quaternary NPP types. *Review of Palaeobotany and Palynology* 186, 142-161.

Miola, A., Bondesan, A., Corain, L., Favaretto, S., Mozzi, P., Piovan, S., Sostizzo, I. 2006. Wetlands in the Venetian Po Plain (northeastern Italy) during the Last Glacial Maximum: Interplay between vegetation, hydrology and sedimentary environment. *Review of Palaeobotany and Palynology* 141, 83-102.

Moore, P.D., Webb, J.A., Collison, W.E. 1991. *Pollen Analysis.* Oxford: Blackwell.

Revelles, J., Burjachs, F., van Geel, B. 2016. Pollen and non-pollen palynomorphs from the Early Neolithic settlement of La Draga (Girona, Spain). *Review of Palaeobotany and Palynology* 225, 1-20.

Święta-Musznicka, J., Latałowa, M., Badura, M., Gołembnik, A. 2013. Combined pollen and macrofossil data as a source for reconstructing mosaic patterns of the early medieval urban habitats – a case study from Gdańsk, N. Poland. *Journal of Archaeological Science* 40/1, 637-648.

van Geel, B. and Aptroot, A. 2006. Fossil ascomycetes in Quaternary deposits. *Nova Hedwigia* 82/3-4, 313-329.

van Geel, B., Bos, J.M., Pals, J.P. 1983. Archaeological and palaeoecological aspects of a medieval house terp in a reclaimed raised bog area in North Holland. *Berichten van de Rijksdienst voor het Oudheidkundig Bodemonderzoek* 33, 419-444.

van Geel, B., Buurman, J., Brinkkemper, O., Schelvis, J., Aptroot, A., van Reenen, G., Hakbijl, T. 2003. Environmental reconstruction of a Roman Period settlement site in Uitgeest (The Netherlands), with special reference to coprophilous fungi. *Journal of Archaeological Science* 30/7, 873-883.

Vánky, K. 2013[3]. *Illustrated genera of smut fungi.* St. Paul, Minnesota: APS Press.

Wieckowska-Lüth, M. and Heske, I. 2019. On-site palaeoecological investigations from the Hünenburg hillfort-settlement complex, with special reference to non-pollen palynomorphs, in: Dal Corso, M., Kirleis, W., Kneisel, J., Taylor, N., Wieckowska-Lüth, M., Zanon, M. (eds.), *How's life? Living conditions in Europe in the 2nd and 1st millennia BC.* STPAS 4. Leiden: Sidestone Press, 167-186.

Author addresses

Magdalena Wieckowska-Lüth
PALBOTANA, Labor für Palynologische & Botanische Analysen
Rammseer Weg 27
24113 Molfsee, Germany
wieckowska@palbotana.com

Dieter Bischop
Landesarchäologie Bremen
An der Weide 50a
28195 Bremen, Germany
dieter.bischop@landesarchaeologie.bremen.de

About the authors

The palaeoecologist Magdalena Wieckowska-Lüth worked as a postdoctoral researcher in the framework of the position "Development of Archaeobotanical Methods" at the Graduate School "Human Development in Landscapes", where she concentrated on the analysis of non-pollen palynomorphs. In general, her research interests include vegetation and settlement history, human-environment interactions, climate reconstructions and site characterisation. Geographically, her work covers a wide area – reaching from Northern Mongolia across the Mediterranean, to the northern Central German Upland foothills, the North German lowlands and to Southern Norway and Northwest Russia.

Dieter Bischop studied Pre- and Early History, Classical Archaeology and Ancient History at the Universities of Münster and Perugia. During and after his studies, he worked for various archaeological state offices and the German Archaeological Institute. Since 1998, he has been working for the State Archaeological Office of Bremen as a research assistant for the cities of Bremen and Bremerhaven. In his research, he focuses on the Roman Iron Age and the Middle Ages. In addition, his research interests are concerned with ancient Mediterranean cultures, which is reflected in the framework of various exhibition projects and publications.

Human-Landscape Interconnections

The Döberitzer Heide in the Early Middle Ages (ca. 7th-11th century) as a Space of Action between the Appropriation of Material Wealth and the Destruction of the Basis of Existence

Donat Wehner

Abstract

Interactions between humans and the landscape have been a central topic of archaeology for more than 100 years. While the influence of the environment on human settlement behaviour was emphasised for a long time, recently the active role of humans in the constitution of landscape has increasingly become the centre of discussion. The discourse is characterised, among other things, by references to human-ecological approaches and the concept of the Anthropocene. The case example of the Döberitzer Heide in the Early Middle Ages takes up the debate by not considering landscape as a stage and framework for human action, but rather as in interactive human-landscape space of action. In the interplay, various dynamics between the appropriation of material wealth and the destruction of the basis of existence will be illustrated.

Introduction

Landscape appears in archaeology as a highly dubious term behind which a large scope of ideas and concepts is concealed. To be mentioned, in particular, is the understanding of landscape as a stage, venue and container for human actions, as a part of human-environment relationships, as conceived, mentally perceived and actually experienced space, and recently sometimes as dynamic arrangements and as complex networks of humans, things, animals, nature, techniques, organisations, signs and infrastructures (Meier 2009; Schreg 2017; Wehner 2019). Often, the dependencies of settlement activities on natural factors were and are emphasised in archaeology. An early, prominent

in: Müller, J. and Ricci, A. 2020 (eds.), *Past Societies: Human Development in Landscapes*. Sidestone Press: Leiden, 141-150.

example is represented in a study by Alfred Schlitz (1906) at the beginning of the 20th *c.* in which he draws attention to the coincidence of Linear Pottery settlement and nutrient-rich loess soils (cf. the commentary of Friederich 2003). In this context, adaption to the landscape and not its appropriation, constitution and reproduction is on the scientific agenda. First archaeological perspectives on human-landscape-causal relationships were advocated by supporters of system-theoretical approaches in the 1960s (*e.g.* Binford 1962). In recent years, the discourse in this field of study has been particularly characterised by interdisciplinary, human-ecological approaches in which the interdependency between society, humans and environment are emphasised and analysed in a holistic perspective including all available sources. The debate is fuelled by the concept of the Anthropocene as a geological era which is determined by humans as a decisive geological factor (*e.g.* Edgeworth 2014; Lane 2015; Schmieder 2014; Waters *et al.* 2014).

Material and Methods

Following my dissertation on the Early and High Middle Age Slavic settlement areas of the Havelland and of the northern Zauche area (Wehner 2012), a small subarea will be presented here for which the dependencies and interdependencies between humans and landscapes can be particularly well grasped. Here, we are dealing with an area in the eastern Havelland, which is referred to today as the Döberitzer Heide. Primarily, information on the archaeological sites is available as a data base, as was collected in the dissertation from the local files of the Brandenburg State Office for Conservation and the Archaeological State Museum (BLDAM). Among other things, details on the site types (*e.g.* settlement, depot, tar smoulder, *etc.*), dating as well as an outline of finds and findings are at hand. As a reference, the catalogue numbers (Wehner 2012) are used in the following. Of great importance are also the palynological investigations of Steffen Wolters (2002), who analysed numerous pollen profiles in his dissertation with regard to the vegetation history and in doing so also briefly mentioned questions concerning the development of the climate. In this context, it proves to be favourable that individual sample sections were radiocarbon dated, with which a temporally dynamic view is achieved that can be parallelised with archaeologically recorded upheavals. His specified uncalibrated ^{14}C BP data were calibrated with OxCal 4.1 and the calibration curve IntCal 09 in the ranges of one and two sigma cal AD. Additionally, data on the geomorphology and on the soil types are available, which can be referred to as further natural space factors (Ergenziger *et al.* 1969) (Fig. 1). Furthermore, archaeometric investigations of tar samples can be drawn upon (Baumer and Dietemann 2013).

Methodologically, the contribution falls back on the visualisation of site relations by mappings. This not only facilitates an understanding but is also useful as a means of research in order to correlate and discuss different processes. Intended is an interpretation on the basis of a holistic view of all available sources. The chronological framework is based on absolute data, on the one hand, which are supported by the radiocarbon method, find typology and find analogy, and, on the other hand, the usual relative threefold division in the early, middle and late Slavic period for the areas between the Elbe and the Oder Rivers in the Early Middle Ages. The three time slices cannot be clearly distinguished from one another by absolute data. In general, the early Slavic period in this area is dated in scientific literature from ca. the 7th/8th *c.* until the middle of the 9th *c.* AD, the middle Slavic period from the middle of the 9th *c.* AD until the turn of the millennium, and the late Slavic period from the late 10th *c.* to the middle of the 12th *c.* The Slavic period ends here according to usual interpretation and the High Middle Ages begins with the arrival of German settlers from the West, the so-called Eastern colonisation (see Wehner 2012). The early to middle Slavic period thus correlates roughly with the regional pollen zone 20 according to Steffen Wolters, and the late Slavic period correlates with the regional pollen zone 21 (Wolters 2002, 40-41, 68-72; see fig. 3, right column).

GIS-based models illustrate the landscape change (see Fig. 2). Archaeologically verified settlements and other find sites are represented in the form of geographically located point data; open land, wetlands and forest in the form of area data. The extent of wet and periodically flooded areas is modelled on the basis of the reconstructed groundwater table. This can be adjusted according to changing altitudes of settlement activities in the digital terrain model. Fluctuations can thus be reviewed by means of the pollen analytical findings. Afforestation is assumed for those surfaces for which no archaeological settlement indicators are available and which are not identified as heavily waterlogged lowlands. With the onset of medieval settlements, the forest areas in the models are confined – in relation to open land – to the *Sander* (outwash plain) areas, which were demonstrably not agriculturally used in the respective research area (see Wehner 2012, 43, 61, 97). Larger deviations from the former reality at the borders can certainly to be expected here. The given basic type of forest cover is based on the results of pollen analyses.

Results and Discussion

With regard to vegetational history, the early Slavic period can be corresponded with an oak-beech-hornbeam era (Fig. 1; 2b). According to palynological investigations by Steffen Wolters in association with radiocarbon data, the oak (*Quercus*) maxima and the minima of sunstroke plants and hemerophiles (Helio- and Hemerophytes) can be dated to the first half of the 7th *c.*

The percentage of tree pollen lies over 90% (Wolters 2002, 68, 69, Fig. 21). Thus, the palynological findings exhibit a nearly completely forested area and archaeologically no early Slavic settlement can be verified. Moreover, the considerable portions of water plants (hydrophytes) in the pollen profiles of Weidenkuhle (DWK), Kienfenn (DKF II) and Schwarzes Fenn (DSF) indicate a relatively high-water table (Fig. 3; Wolters 2002, 68 and supplement).

In the late early Slavic and the early middle Slavic period (776-890 cal AD), a strong decrease of oak (*Quercus*) is observable, which is attributed to selective logging. Evidence of willowherb (*Epilobium*) and an increase in birch (*Betula*) are indications of forest clearing (Wolters 2002, 70). This phase could coincide with the founding of the middle Slavic settlements of Dallgow 202, Dallgow 207, Dallgow 208 and Dallgow 210 (Fig. 1a; 2c). Charred construction wood probably of oak was found in the settlement Dallgow 207. The preferred location of the sites in the lower terraces is evidence of a dry phase. The settlement Groß Glienicke 383 is also located relatively low, which existed around ca. 1000 AD so that one may assume that rather dry conditions lasted

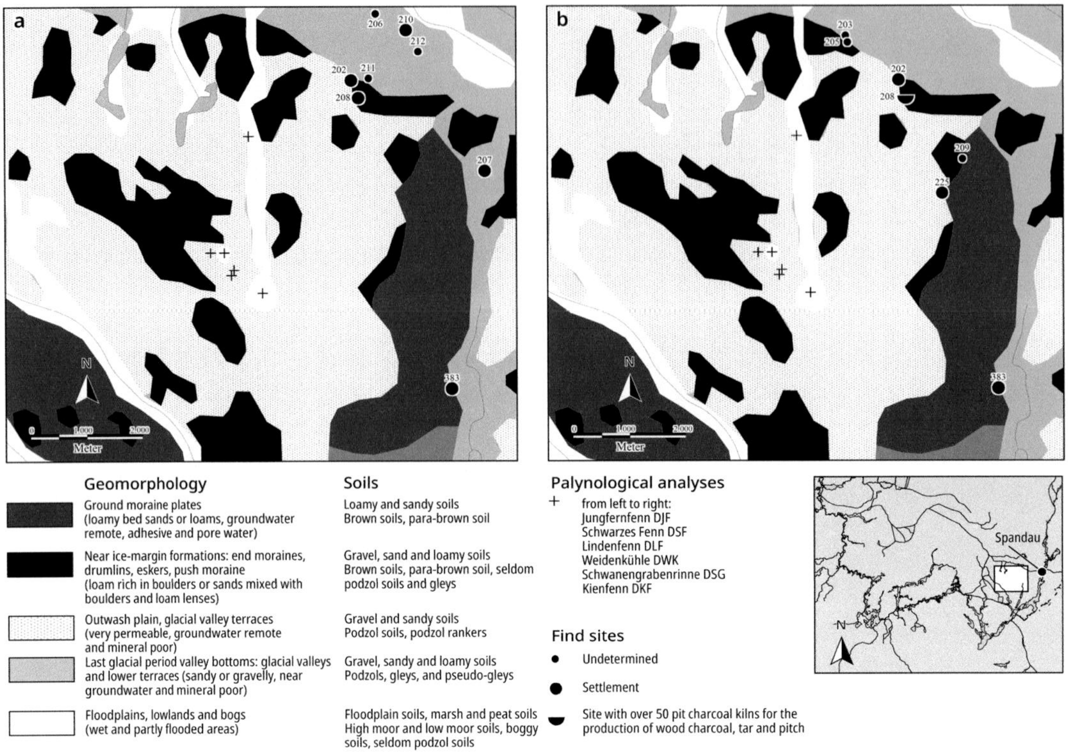

Figure 1. Geomorphology and settlement of the Döberitzer Heide: (a) middle Slavic period; (b) late Slavic period (graphics: D. Wehner; map source geomorphology: Ergenzinger et al. 1969).

into the beginning of the late Slavic period. Assuming that the fields were located not far from the dwellings, then mainly sandy soils of low mineral content and low fertility were available. Agriculture can be indicated by pollen values of grain (cereals *p.p.*), in particular of rye (*Secale cereal*) (Wolters 2002, 70). The cultivation of rye (*Secale cereal*) was advantageous because it was better adapted to a dry climate and sandy soil (cf. Körber-Grohne 1987, 40). A deep storage pit with unspecified grain was archaeologically recorded in the settlement of Groß Glienicke 383. In the settlement of Dallgow 210, a rubbing stone was found for the processing of grain.

In addition, increased values of plantain (*Plantago lanceolata*) and sweet grasses (Poaceae) indicate the emergence of grassland vegetation. Wolters assumes a clearing due to cleared woodlands and wood pasture. He interprets an increasing proportion of oak (*Quercus*) in the pollen spectrum after the logging as a conservation of oak for the purpose of wood pasture with acorn mast in pig farming (Wolters 2002, 71).

In late Slavic times since the turn of the millennium, the water-level rose, possibly triggered by clearings in middle Slavic times (cf. Biermann 2006, 50; Schneeweiß 2003; 28). The lower-lying middle Slavic settlements had to be abandoned. Elevated sites were selected (Fig. 1b; 2d). Due to the spatial proximity, it can be assumed that the settlement Dallgow 207 was shifted ca. 1500 m to the west and continued to exist there in the form of the settlement Döberitz 225. With high probability, the settlement Dallgow 201 "wandered" ca. 1800 m to the west to the sites Dallgow 203 and

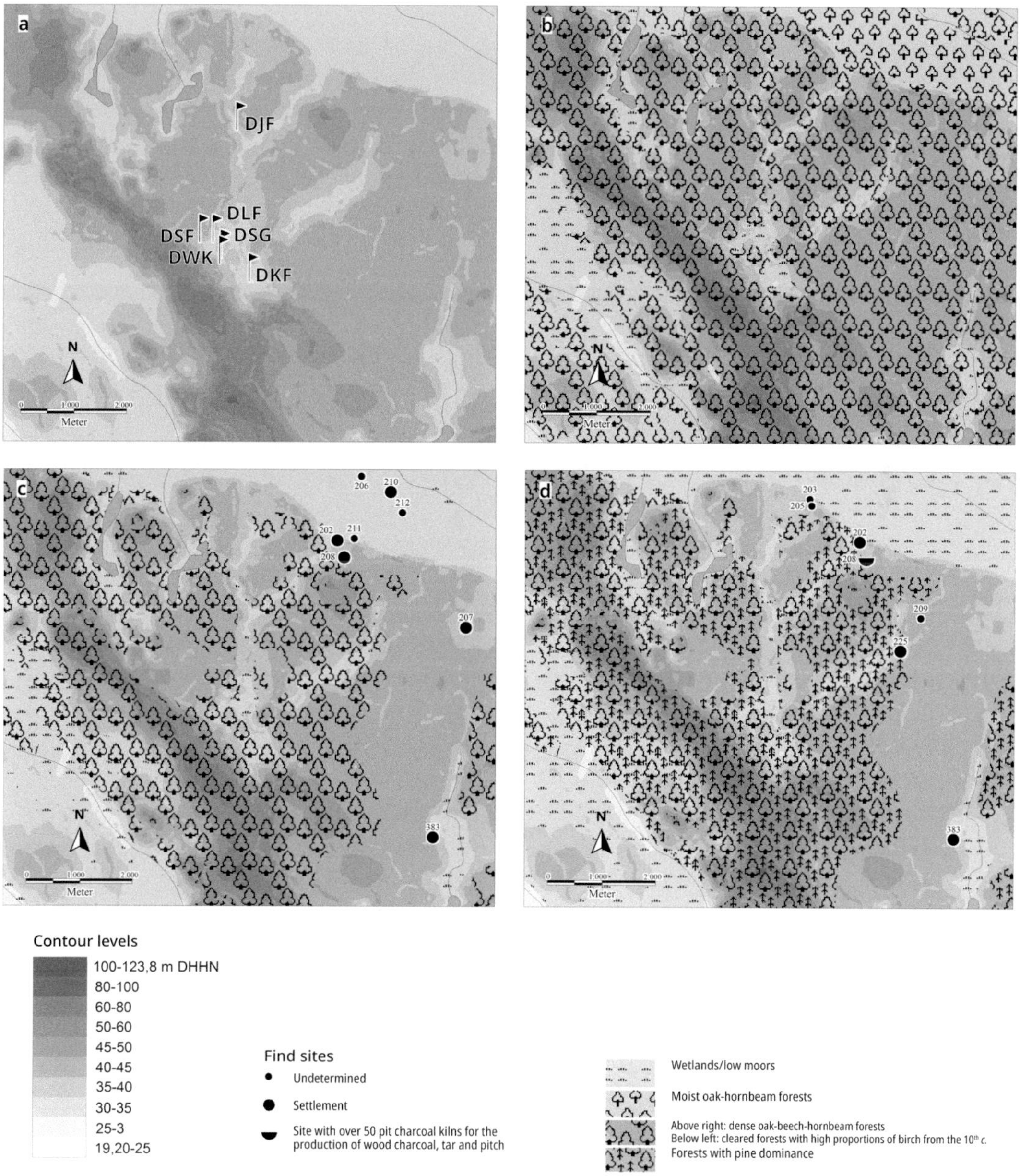

Figure 2. Model of the vegetation and settlement of the Döberitzer Heide: (a) localisation of the pollen profile and the contour plan; (b) early Slavic period; (c) middle Slavic period; (d) late Slavic period (graphics: D. Wehner).

Dallgow 205, which were located close to each other. Due to the high pine (*Pinus*) proportions in the pollen diagram, Wolters assumes pine forests in the surroundings of the settlements and in the pollen analytical findings, a selective logging of oak is reflected once again (Wolters 2002, 72). The logging could be connected with the newly founded late Slavic settlements (Döberitz 225 and most likely Dallgow 203 and

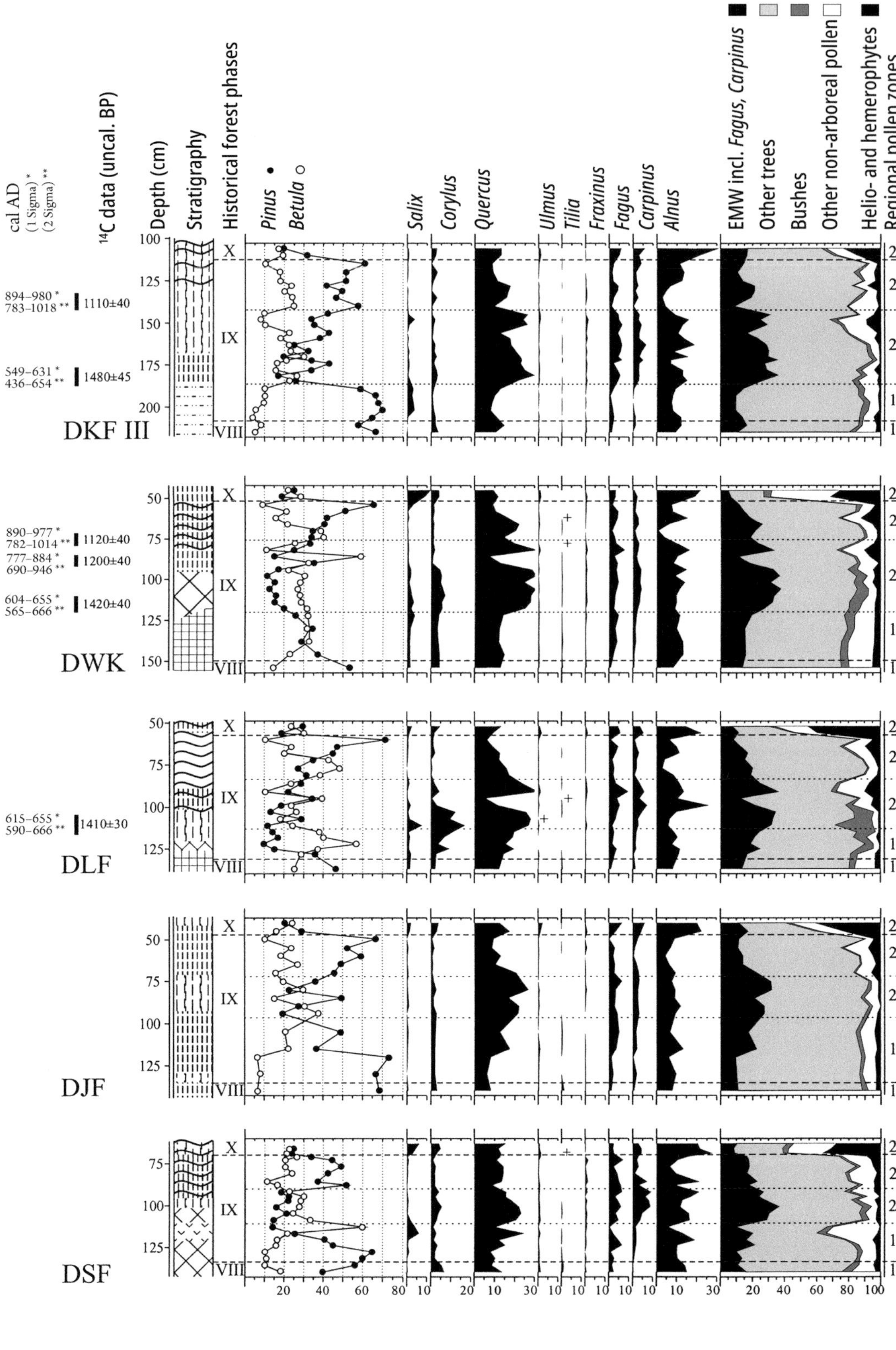

cal AD (1 Sigma)* (2 Sigma)**
14C data (uncal. BP)
Depth (cm)
Stratigraphy
Historical forest phases
Pinus •
Betula ○
Salix
Corylus
Quercus
Ulmus
Tilia
Fraxinus
Fagus
Carpinus
Alnus
EMW incl. Fagus, Carpinus
Other trees
Bushes
Other non-arboreal pollen
Helio- and hemerophytes
Regional pollen zones
894–980 * 783–1018 ** 1110±40
549–631 * 436–654 ** 1480±45
DKF III
890–977 * 782–1014 ** 1120±40
777–884 * 690–946 ** 1200±40
604–655 * 565–666 ** 1420±40
DWK
615–655 * 590–666 ** 1410±30
DLF
DJF
DSF

Figure 3 (opposite page). Selection of diagrams with pollen curves from the area of the Döberitzer Heide (after Wolters 2002, 69 with a supplement of the calibrated ^{14}C data in 1 and 2 Sigma area).

Dallgow 205). These were located on the loam-rich push moraines that were surrounded – island-like – by wet low terraces and the outwash plains. On them was the only possibility to maintain land cultivation, although the crop areas were very limited. The wet meadows, which had developed on the low terraces, were probably used as wet cattle pastures (cf. Fischer and Michaelis 2003, 57).

The settlement Dallgow 202 did not have to be relocated and persisted longer. In close proximity, the largest known charcoal, tar and pitch extraction site of the entire working area with more than 55 pit charcoal piles was created (Biermann *et al.* 2013; Wehner 2012, cat. no. 208). In addition, some storage pits, some long-oval, tub-like recesses with a backfilling heavily interspersed with charcoal, and two pit-houses were documented. These may have been related to the production site or a "worker's settlement" nearby. According to the find material, the place dates from the last third of the 10th to the early 11th *c.* (Biermann *et al.* 2013).

Chemical investigations of 5 tar samples from the pit charcoal piles by Ursula Baumer and Patrick Dietemann (2013) of the Doerner Institute in Munich resulted in a very probable multiple use, whereby both coniferous wood and birch bark tar were attested.

The raw material birch (*Betula*) was sufficiently available from the end of the middle Slavic period to the beginning of the late Slavic period. According to the pollen analytical findings, a strong spread of birch occurred during the 10th *c.* due to the anthropogenic clearing of the forest (Wolters 2002, 40 tab. 7; 8 GrN 25174 and 25177). During the late Slavic period, pine woods dominate, which in turn can be correlated well with the evidence of pine-wood tar (cf. Fig. 2c-d).

Due to the spatial proximity of about 8 km, it is conceivable that the early urban settlement from the so-called Spandau Burgwall or Berlin-Klosterfelde 53 could have been supplied with tar and pitch (cf. Jeute 2007, 68). In addition to the castle-settlement complexes of Brandenburg and Nauen, the site is one of the major central places in the Havelland. An increased demand for tar and pitch, for example, as lubricants, adhesives and sealants and as fuel and remedies (cf. Oettel 1989, 227-235) is therefore obvious. A direct transportation link between the settlement area of Döberitzer Heide and the "Spandau Burgwall" existed in the form of the Spekte stream.

Furthermore, a precious metal depot with coins and silver jewellery from the beginning of the 11th *c.* originates from the settlement Dallgow 202. The treasure was found in 1852 during the digging of stones on a field. The whereabouts of the find are unclear. Little is known about the coins; they probably date between 936 and 1012. Among the pieces of jewellery, a braided bracelet is recorded (Friedel *et al.* 1896, 2).

This indicates that the people living there did not only work on a subsistence-oriented basis. There must have been surplus production, which allowed for some accumulation of wealth in the form of the general silver equivalent. Since no high agricultural yields could be achieved due to limited available croplands and poor soils, it appears likely that the mass production and sale of tar, pitch and charcoal provided a certain amount of wealth.

Conclusion

It can be stated that an area with dense oak-rich forests that existed in early Slavic times was settled by Slavic settlers, who initially operated in a primarily agrarian setting. In late Slavic times, the water table rose, perhaps reinforced by anthropogenic influences. Numerous settlements had to be relocated to higher elevations and the potential amount of land, which would have been available for farming, rapidly decreased in size. The newly developed wet meadows were used as cattle pastures, which probably did not compensate the loss of agricultural land. The stagnation in agriculture was compensated by the installation of a comprehensive pitch and tar production yard. This, in turn, could only have been created by an anthropogenic clearing of the forest in advance and the resulting spread of birch (*Betula*) and later pine (*Pinus*) as raw material for the charging of the pitch and tar smoulder kilns. The silver depot from the settlement Dallgow 202 from the beginning of the 11th *c.* indicates that the locals came to wealth through the commercial operation of the pitch and tar extraction site.

Clearly recognisable are the settlement- and economic-related reactions of the Slavic people to the transformation of the landscape – be it the result of coercion or as seized opportunity – which was consciously or unconsciously self-evoked to a great extent. In conclusion, the case example should not be interpreted as an appeal for the renunciation of human interventions with the environment, but rather as a plea for the active design of multiple interweaving processes as presented by Donna Haraway's (2016) recently introduced Chthulucene concept.

Acknowledgements

My thanks are due to the Brandenburg State Office for the Preservation of Historical Archaeology (BLDAM) for providing me with the archaeological find records and the Graduate School "Human Development in Landscapes" (GSHDL) for the creation of a productive scientific environment and funding. Many thanks are also due to the academic assistant, Lorenz Luick, Institute of Prehistoric and Protohistoric Archaeology, Kiel University, for a review of this contribution.

References

Baumer, U. and Dietemann, P. 2013. Chemische Untersuchungen an Teerproben aus slawenzeitlichen Teermeilergruben von Dallgow 15, in: Biermann, F. (ed.), *Dallgow im Havelland. Vor- und frühgeschichtliche sowie mittelalterliche Besiedlung und slawische Teerproduktion am Fundplatz 15*. Materialien zur Archäologie in Brandenburg 7. Rahden, Westf.: Verlag Marie Leidorf GmbH, 256-258.

Biermann, F. 2006. Siedlung und Landschaft bei den nördlichen Westslawen im späten 9. und 10. Jahrhundert, in: Spieß, K.-H. (ed.), *Landschaften im Mittelalter*. Stuttgart: Steiner, 45-76.

Biermann, F., Blum, O., Semjank, S., Semjank, A., Voigt, H. 2013. Die mittelalterliche Besiedlung und die Teermeilergruben von Dallgow 15, in: Biermann, F. (ed.), *Dallgow im Havelland. Vor- und frühgeschichtliche sowie mittelalterliche Besiedlung und slawische Teerproduktion am Fundplatz 15*. Materialien zur Archäologie in Brandenburg 7. Rahden, Westf.: Verlag Marie Leidorf GmbH, 203-255.

Binford, L. 1962. Archaeology as anthropology. *American Antiquity* 28/2, 217-255.

Edgeworth, M. 2014. Archaeology of the Anthropocene. *Journal of Contemporary Archaeology* 1/1, 73-132.

Ergenzinger, P., Hövermann, J., Jannsen, G. 1969. *Geomorphologie. Historischer Handatlas von Brandenburg und Berlin, Lfg. 28.* Berlin: De Gruyter.

Fischer, U. and Michaelis, D. 2003. Das Naturschutzgebiet "Peenewiesen bei Gützkow", in: Billwitz, K., Michaelis, D., Succow, M. (eds.), *Landschaftsökologische Exkursionen in die Greifswalder Umgebung.* Greifswalder Geogr. Arbeiten 30. Greifswald: Ernst-Moritz-Arndt-Univiversität, 49-59.

Friedel, E., Buchholz, R., Bahrfeldt, E. 1896. *Hervorragende Kunst und Alterthumsgegenstände des Märkischen Provinzialmuseums in Berlin. Die Hacksilberfunde.* Berlin: Merten & Cie.

Friederich, S. 2003. Die erste Verbreitungskarte zur bandkeramischen Kultur, in: Eckert, J., Eisenhauer, U., Zimmermann, A. (eds.), *Archäologische Perspektiven. Analysen und Interpretationen im Wandel. Festschrift J. Lüning.* Stud. honoraria 20. Rahden, Westf.: Leidorf, 27-31.

Haraway, D. 2016. *Staying with the Trouble: Making Kin in the Chthulucene.* Experimental futures: Technological lives, scientific arts, anthropological voices. Durham/London: Duke University Press.

Jeute, G. 2007. *Ländliches Handwerk und Gewerbe im Mittelalter. Untersuchungen zur nichtagrarischen Produktion im westlichen Brandenburg.* Studien zur Archäologie Europas 7. Bonn: Habelt.

Körber-Grohne, U. 1987. *Nutzpflanzen in Deutschland. Kulturgeschichte und Biologie.* Stuttgart: Theiss.

Lane, P.J. 2015. Archaeology in the age of the Anthropocene: A critical assessment of its scope and societal contributions. *Journal of Field Archaeology* 40/5, 1-14.

Meier, Th. 2009. Umweltarchäologie – Landschaftsarchäologie, in: Brather, S., Geuenich, D., Huth, Ch. (eds.), *Historia archaeologica. Festschrift für Heiko Steuer zum 70. Geburtstag.* Ergb. RGA 70. Berlin: De Gruyter, 697-734.

Oettel, G. 1989. Die mittelalterliche Pechsiederei im Südosten der DDR. *Arbeits- u. Forschber. Sächs. Bodendenkmalpflege* 33, 227-287.

Schlitz, A. 1906. *Die Sammlungen des historischen Museums.* Heilbronn: Hist. Verein.

Schmieder, F. 2014. Urgeschichte der Nachmoderne. Zur Archäologie des Anthropozäns. *Forum Interdisziplinäre Begriffsgeschichte* 2/2, 43-48.

Schneeweiß, J. 2003. *Der Werder zwischen Altentreptow-Friedland-Neubrandenburg vom 6. Jahrhundert vor bis zum 13. Jahrhundert n. Chr. Siedlungsarchäologische Untersuchungen einer Kleinlandschaft in Nordostdeutschland.* Universitätsforschungen zur prähistorischen Archäologie 102. Bonn: Habelt.

Schreg, R. 2017. Interaktion und Kommunikation im Raum – Methoden und Modelle der Sozialarchäologie, in: Brather, S. and Dendorfer, J. (eds.), *Grenzen, Räume und Identitäten. Der Oberrhein und seine Nachbarregionen von der Antike bis zum Hochmittelalter.* Symposium Freiburg 2013. Archäologie u. Geschichte 22. Ostfildern: Jan Thorbecke Verlag, 455-492.

Waters, C.N., Zalasiewicz, J., Williams, M., Ellis, M., Snelling, A.M. 2014 (eds.), *A Stratigraphical Basis for the Anthropocene.* Lyell Collection. Special Publ. 395. London: Geological Society Publ. House.

Wehner, D. 2012. *Das Land Stodor. Eine Studie zu Struktur und Wandel der slawenzeitlichen Siedlungsräume im Havelland und in der nördlichen Zauche.* Materialien zur Archäologie in Brandenburg 5. Rahden, Westf.: Leidorf.

Wehner, D. 2019. *Artefakt-Netzwerke im östlichen Mitteleuropa an der Schwelle zum hohen Mittelalter: Zur Quantifizierung, Visualisierung und Beschaffenheit überregionaler Kommunikations- und Austauschbeziehungen.* Universitätsforschungen zur prähistorischen Archäologie 329. Bonn: Habelt.

Wolters, R. 2002. *Vegetationsgeschichtliche Untersuchungen zur spätglazialen und holozänen Landschaftsentwicklung in der Döberitzer Heide (Brandenburg).* Dissertationes Botanicae 366. Berlin/Stuttgart: J. Cramer in der Gebrüder Borntraeger Verlagsbuchhandlung.

Author address

Donat Wehner
Institute of Pre- and Protohistoric Archaeology
Kiel University
Johanna-Mestorf-Straße 2-6
24118 Kiel, Germany
donat.wehner@ufg.uni-kiel.de

About the author

Donat Wehner is an employee at the State Office for Heritage Management and Archaeology of Saxony-Anhalt in Halle (Saale) and a private lecturer of historical archaeology at Kiel University. The focus of his research concentrates on the archaeology of the Western Slavs, medieval and post-medieval archaeology as well as computational archaeology.

Seafaring of the Hansa to the Shetland Islands, Faroe Islands and Iceland

The Maritime-Archaeological Potential of the North Atlantic Islands during the Late Hanseatic Period

Philipp Grassel

Abstract

This contribution provides an overview about late Hanseatic seafaring in the waters of Iceland, the Faroe Islands and Shetland and describes the trade of the Hansa with these islands. Between the 15th and 17th centuries, Bremen and Hamburg were the main Hanseatic traders in the North Atlantic area and important commodities, such as the well-known stockfish or sulphur, were exported. Although there is rich knowledge about historical Hansa trade with the North Atlantic islands as well as late Hanseatic seafaring in this area, archaeological proof of this knowledge has been hardly adduced. This paper illustrates actual archaeological research about the islands for the late Hanseatic period and characterises the potential for maritime-archaeological research, which has rarely been undertaken until now.

Introduction

The Hansa as an economic institution roughly existed between the 13th and the 17th centuries and spanned across almost the whole of Europe (Jahnke 2013, 1-32). The term "late Hanseatic" refers to the time range between the 15th and the 17th centuries and is, in the older academic (especially German) literature, often stigmatised as a period of complete downfall of the Hansa (Dollinger 2012, 433ff.). Younger academic works draw a more sophisticated and less dogmatic picture, and speak of a transition rather than a downfall (Hammel-Kiesow 2008, 96ff.).

in: Müller, J. and Ricci, A. 2020 (eds.), *Past Societies: Human Development in Landscapes*.
Sidestone Press: Leiden, 151-162.

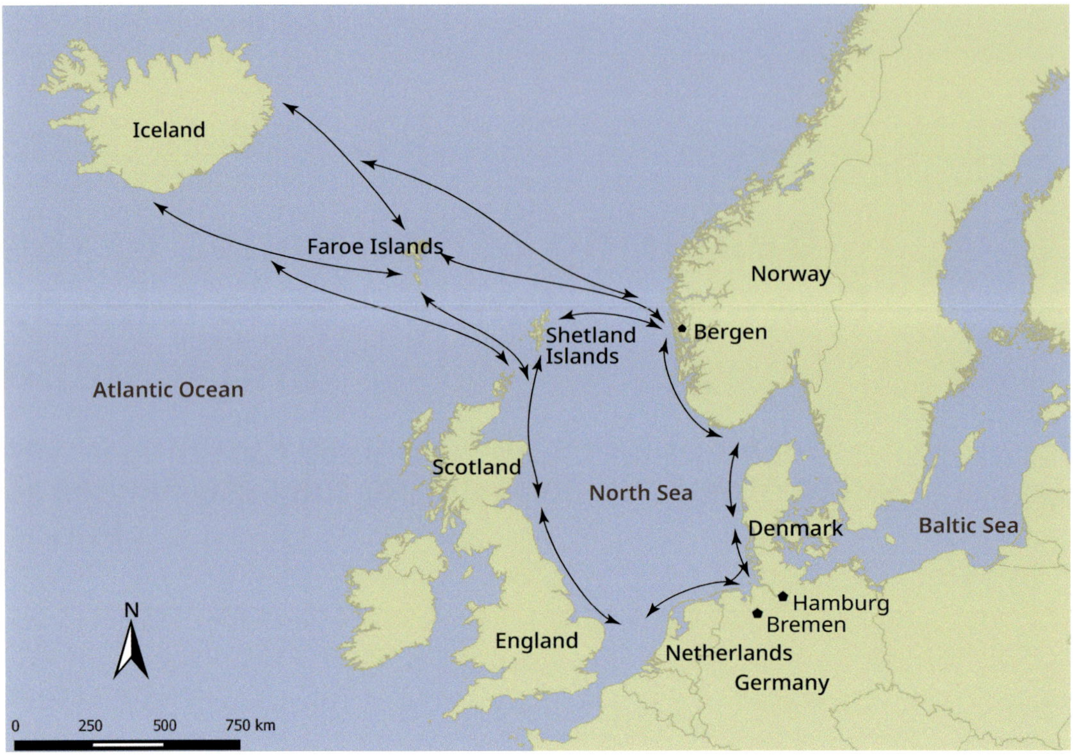

Figure 1. Working area and depiction of the main trading routes to the North Atlantic islands (copyright: created by Philipp Grassel using geographical data provided by OpenStreetMapData (http://openstreetmapdata.com/) (Version April 2017)).

The cities of Hamburg and Bremen were the Hansa members with the largest trading presence on the Shetland Islands, the Faroe Islands and Iceland. Between AD 1400 and 1699, the majority of Hansa merchants and skippers in this area belonged to these cities. Merchants from Lübeck, Danzig (Gdansk) and other Hansa cities also traded in the North Atlantic area, but in much smaller volumes. Non-Hanseatic traders were mainly of Dutch, English or Scottish origin. The 16th century is characterised by the highest amount of Hanseatic activities with the North Atlantic islands. Commodities, such as grain, flour, beer, cloth or metal goods, and luxury products, like spices, were traded for dried or salted fish, wool cloth (the typical vaðmál), gyrfalcons, feathers and sulphur (Grassel 2016, 82f.).

In the 15th and 16th centuries, merchants' regular sea passages normally included one annual voyage. The trading season started in April and finished in August or September (Fig. 1). The number of ships travelling to the Shetland Islands or to Iceland, as well as their home ports, is clearly identifiable. In the middle of the 16th century, 5 ships per year from Bremen and 1 to 2 ships from Hamburg travelled to Shetland on average. Contemporary sources speak of a minimum of 7 ships from Bremen and Hamburg which unloaded cargo in 1560 in Shetland harbours (Friedland 1973, 75). There was a small increase in the number of trading ships from Bremen to Shetland during the 17th century. Equally, the number of permitted voyages per ship was raised from 1 to a maximum of 3 per season (Müller 1975, 120). The number of trading ships from Hamburg was raised up to 6 ships per season in the first half of the 17th century with a maximum of 2 voyages per year and ship.[1] However, compared with Iceland trade, trade with Shetland was rather small. In 1585, for example, 14 ships from Hamburg and 8 ships from Bremen, Lübeck and Danzig (Gdansk) reached Icelandic harbours, and in 1591 as many as 21 ships from Hamburg arrived in Iceland (Hofmeister 2000, 36; Ehrenberg 1899, 19f.). The average number of trading ships sailing annually from Hamburg to Iceland increased between AD 1530 and 1602 from a single-digit number to a two-digit number (Grassel 2017, 69f.). During the 16th century, trade with the Faroe Islands was predominantly controlled by merchants from Hamburg. On average, 1 to 2 ships – maximally 3 ships – sailed annually from Hamburg to the Faroe Islands between AD 1543 and 1593.

There was no clear separation of trade with Shetland, Faroe and Iceland at this time. Contemporaneous sources in Hamburg deliver a good overview of this theme. For example, Hamburg and Oldenburg were the only Hanseatic cities with a regular and officially assured Iceland Travellers Association (German designation: Islandfahrergesellschaft). Because of this organisation, a wide range of documents survived, which include names of merchants, traded goods and their value, the trading period, precise trading areas on the islands, *etc.* There are also many contemporaneous sources about import and export taxes of the islands and the various kinds of lawsuits about them are available in German, Scottish, Danish, Icelandic or Shetland archives.

Specialised ships for certain areas, such as the North Atlantic area, were unknown for Hanseatic seafaring. The merchants and skippers used the same ships which were used for trade with England, the Netherlands and the Baltic area. Sources of detailed measurements for Hanseatic ships are rare, but the most important information about their size is the so-called *Last.*[2] The ships of the merchants, which traded in Iceland, had a size of around 60 *Last* in the 16th century and probably also in the early 17th century.[3] The ships of Shetland traders were smaller and had a size of around 20-40 *Last* in the 16th and 17th centuries.[4] However, the sizes of merchant ships ranged at least from 30-90 *Last* and more.[5] Therefore, the named *Last*-specifications must be seen as average values. Unfortunately, there is a lack of more precise ship measurements or constructional information regarding the number of masts, draught, rigging, *etc.*, in the sources. Names for types of ships, like cog, hulk, nef or krawel, are often traceable in sources of the 15th and 16th centuries, but it is difficult to evaluate what kind of ships are actually described with these appellations. Another problem is the small quantity of wreck finds from the late Hanseatic (and also pre-Hanseatic) periods, which is the

1 An average of 2-4 ships per season went to Shetland in the first half of the 17th century. The reason for the stronger presence of merchants from Hamburg was a complete prohibition of trade for non-Danish merchants with Iceland and the Faroe Islands by King Christian IV in 1602.

2 The German term *Last* (English: load) describes the cargo weight of a ship and is normally converted into metric tonnes using a ratio of 1:2, thus 1 *Last* to 2 tonnes. In contrast, the *Last* used in Bremen, Hamburg and Lübeck (*Kommerzlast* - commercial load) is converted using a ratio of 1:3 (see Alberti 1957, 389).

3 Converted 120 tonnes (ratio 1:2) or 180 tonnes (ratio 1:3).

4 Converted 40-80 tonnes (ratio 1:2) or 60-120 tonnes (ratio 1:3).

5 Converted 60-180 tonnes (ratio 1:2) or 90-270 tonnes (ratio 1:3).

main reason for the currently unsatisfying state of knowledge about medieval and late medieval Hanseatic seafaring and shipbuilding.

Hanseatic ship crews of the 15th and 16th centuries were organised quite similarly to those in later times (Grassel 2015, 175). On average, the number of crew members ranged between 10-20 persons, depending on the ship size, but when the merchant and his entourage are included up to 60 people could travel on a Hanseatic merchant ship (Hofmeister 2000, 43ff.). Often, the number of the persons belonging to the entourage was higher than the number of crew members (Ehrenberg 1899, 22f.).

Archaeology of the Hansa on the North Atlantic islands

The short descriptions above show the high availability of academic knowledge on Hanseatic North Atlantic seafaring and sea trade from the 15th to the 17th century based on contemporaneous historical sources. In contrast, archaeological evidence is very rare. The positions of trading posts on the North Atlantic islands, which were used by Hanseatic merchants, are relatively well-known, but their archaeological evaluation has barely started. One difficulty is that the most of these single trading posts cannot clearly be linked to single Hanseatic merchants. The places were used by different traders, even English and Dutch traders, in different years. There were also no established, fixed harbour structures or larger trading places. The trading posts of the North Atlantic islands were simply organised with single booths, which served as both storage and lodging space for the merchants. The near-shore, shallow water areas of the trading posts complied presumably with only minimal requirements for the safe landing and loading of ships, such as sheltered anchorages to lighten the ships, or shoreline stabilisations such as mooring rings and simple pier constructions. Wide, flat and sandy beach areas were also a landing possibility, but only for smaller ships.

Thus far, the archaeological remains of such landing and loading structures have not been properly surveyed and researched. The situation at the trading posts themselves is similar with only a few having been investigated by archaeological surveys in recent years (Tab. 1).

In turn, only some of these surveys substantiated a late Hanseatic use of the trading posts, for example, Gasír and Gautavík on Iceland, Krambatangi in the Faroe Islands and Brough Head/Pool of Virkie as well as Grutness Voe in Shetland (Grassel 2017, 140-165). But the differentiation and categorisation of Hanseatic finds is still difficult. This is related to the question of how a Hanseatic find is defined and the interpretation of Hanseatic material culture in general. One example is the origin and the dating of Rhenish stoneware from the 15th or 16th centuries found on Iceland and Werra Ware from Lower Saxony found on the Faroe Islands (Mehler 2004, 168; Arge and Mehler 2012, 180-184). The existence of such ceramics cannot simply be taken as evidence for the presence or direct influence of Hanseatic merchants on the islands, as non-Hanseatic intermediary traders are a possible alternative origin of such imported ceramics. Critical discussions of this theme focus on the academic evaluation and are highly relevant (Mehler 2009, 89-108; Müller 2014, 439-542).

Besides the exploration of terrestrial remains, the exploration of maritime and submarine remains of the late Hanseatic period has been established in recent years. The oldest known wreck at Iceland is, for example, the *Melckmeyt*, a Dutch merchant ship

Name	Island	Location	Dating	Reference
Kumbaravogur	Iceland	West Iceland, Northside Snæffelsnes peninsular	1510-1662	Gardiner and Mehler 2013
Gásir	Iceland	North Iceland, Westside Eyafjörður	12th-15th centuries	Gardiner and Mehler 2007
Gautavík	Iceland	East Iceland, Northside Berufjörður	14th-17th centuries	Capelle 1982
Búðasandur/ Maríuhöfn	Iceland	Southwest Iceland, Southside Hvalfjörður	1339-1413	Gardiner and Mehler 2007
Krambatangi	Faroe Islands	Suðuroy, Southside Trongisvágsfjörður	17th century	Arge and Mehler 2012
Tinganes	Faroe Islands	Streymoy, Tórshavn	16th century	Arge and Mehler 2012
Hagrie's Böd/ Gunnister Voe	Shetlands	Mainland, Northside Gunnister Voe	1582-1603	Gardiner and Mehler 2010
Blade of Filbister/ Gluss Voe	Shetlands	Mainland, Westside Gluss Voe	1577-1626	Mehler *et al.* 2012
Papa Stour	Shetlands	Hamna Voe and Culla Voe in Papa Stour	1452 and 1603	Campbell *et al.* 2010
Brough Head/Pool of Virkie	Shetlands	Mainland, Northside Pool of Virkie	17th century	Melton 2004
Grutness Voe	Shetlands	Mainland, Grutness Voe	17th century	Melton 2004

Table 1. List of archaeologically surveyed trading posts at the North Atlantic islands, which were used in the late Hanseatic time. The dating is based on historical sources (table: P. Grassel).

which foundered in 1659 (Grassel and Edvardsson 2020, in press). The situation at the Faroe Islands is quite similar. Here the oldest known wreck, the *Walcheren*, which foundered in 1667, was also of Dutch origin. No other wrecks dated before 1700 have been found thus far in both cases.

In contrast, the oldest known wreck of the Shetland Islands, the *El Gran Grifon*, was a Spanish Armada ship that sunk in 1588 (Grassel 2015, 177f.). Here, 6 other wrecks, which can be dated before 1700, have also been archaeologically researched (Grassel and Edvardsson 2020, in press). The *De Haan* (sunk in 1640), the *Lastdraeger* (sunk in 1653) and the *Kennermerland* (sunk in 1664) were Dutch merchant ships. The *Wrangels Palais* (sunk in 1687) was a Danish navy ship. Two further wrecks include one possible Dutch merchant ship, which probably sank in 1680 and a possible French Navy ship, which sank around 1694 (Wessex Archaeology 2011, 355, 416). Thus, up to this point, only a very low number of wrecks or other maritime archaeological remains at the islands could be clearly dated to the late Hanseatic period. This is astonishing in light of the relatively high frequentation of the North Atlantic islands by Hanseatic merchants and non-Hanseatic traders, such as English, Dutch, Scottish or Scandinavian merchants, as well as the contemporaneous reports of ship losses.

The maritime-archaeological potential of the Hansa at the North Atlantic islands

As mentioned above, the location of trading posts and merchandise and the organisation of trade in the North Atlantic islands during late Hanseatic times are relatively well-known. Contemporaneous sources, such as maps, dept registers, toll registers and

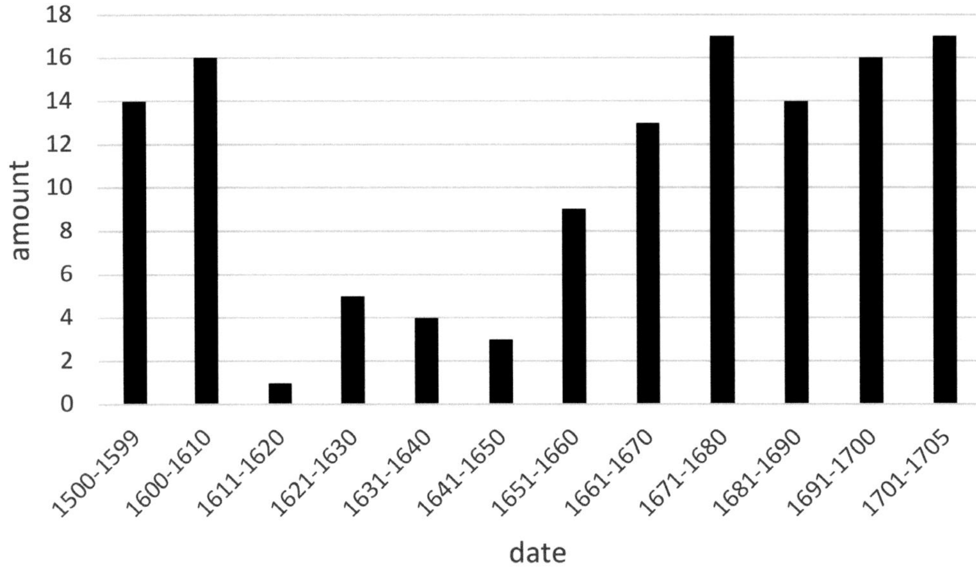

Figure 2. Amount of ship losses in the Shetland Islands between AD 1500 and 1705. A sharp increase of ship losses after 1600 is clearly traceable (diagram: P. Grassel).

court files, enable an extraordinary overview of these terms. The number of trading posts, which were used by Hansa merchants at the Shetland Islands, amounts to at least 21. There were also at least 29 posts on Iceland and 2 at the Faroe Islands. Almost every trading post was located directly near the shore and, as mentioned before, the shallow water areas of the posts were presumably compliant with rather simple but useful possibilities for the safe landing and loading of ships.

To date, marine research about the North Atlantic islands has been primarily focussed on the time after 1600 because of the relatively high number of wrecks and ship losses in this period. This is firstly due to the close integration of the North Atlantic islands into the trading network of, for example, the Hansa and also the growing European powers like England, the Netherlands, France, Denmark and Spain. A second reason is the rise of the whaling and fishing industries in the 17th and early 18th centuries as well as the wider exploitation of the Arctic Sea by European powers. Finally, the North Atlantic region became increasingly connected to war and conflict incidents in early modern times, for example, the English-Dutch trading wars between AD 1581 and 1795, the Eighty Years' War (1568-1648) or the Dutch-French War (1672-1678).

Therefore, there is a high potential to find wrecks of European continental origin from the 16th and later centuries in the bays, sounds and fjords of the North Atlantic islands (Fig. 2). Other types of maritime archaeological remains, such as ballast stone mounds, possible pier structures, *nausts* (boathouses), shipyards or landing places, are also to be expected to be located near shorelines. Especially in Shetland – based on wreck registers, compilations and other sources – over 100 ship losses dated between AD 1500 and 1700 can be mapped around the islands with relatively clear positions (Fig. 3).

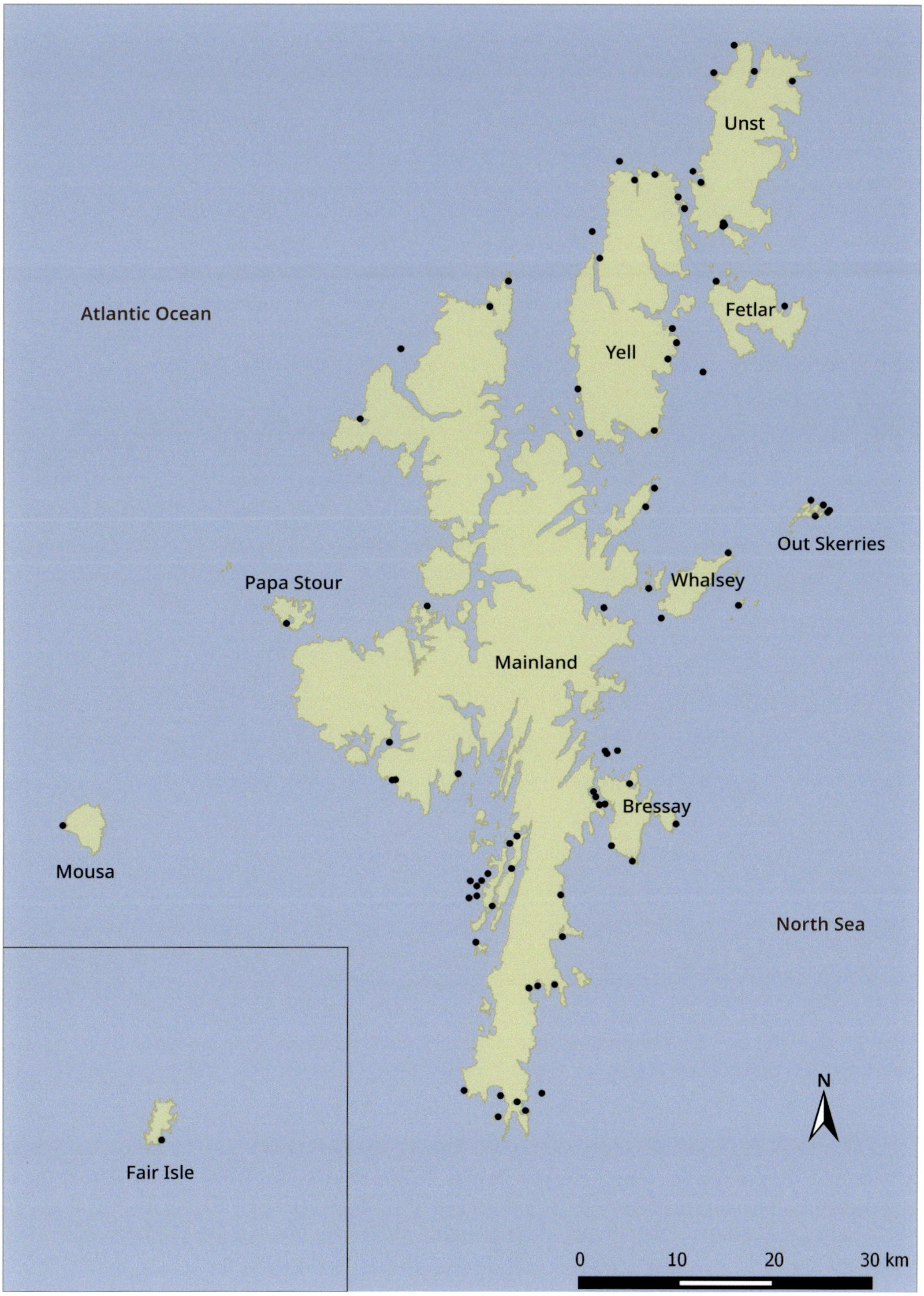

Figure 3. Shetland Islands. Allocable ship losses with relatively clear positions around the islands between AD 1500-1700 (copyright: created by Philipp Grassel using geographical data provided by OpenStreetMapData (http://openstreetmapdata.com/) (Version April 2017)).

Name	Origin	Location	Dating	Reference
unknown	Hamburg	near the islands	1523	Zachariasen 1951
unknown	Mykines	near the islands	ca. 1595	Madsen 1999
unknown	Scottish	Hvalba/Suðuroy	1640	Madsen 1999
Walchern/Walcheren	Dutch	Kvivík/Streymoy	1667	Arge 2007
Koning David	Dutch	Nólsoy	1674	Madsen 1999
unknown	unknown	Tórshavn/Streymoy	1687	Madsen 1999
unknown	Courland	Saltangará/Eysturoy	1687	Madsen 1999
Island	Danish	near the islands	1702	Madsen 1999
Norske Løve	Danish	Lambavík/Eysturoy	1707	Arge 2007

Table 2. List of confirmed ship losses at the Faroe Islands between AD 1523 and 1707. The dating is based on historical sources (table: P. Grassel).

Name	Island	Origin	Location	Dating	Reference
unknown	Iceland	Hamburg	harbour in North Iceland	1529	Baasch 1889
unknown	Iceland	Lübeck	near the island	1538	Hofmeister 2000
unknown	Iceland	Bremen	near the island	1578	Hofmeister 2000
unknown	Faroe Islands	Hamburg	near the islands	1523	Zachariasen 1951
unknown	Shetlands	Braunschweig/ Bremen	near the islands	1469	Hänselmann 1890
unknown	Shetlands	Hamburg	near the islands	1539	Koch 1995
El Gran Grífon	Shetlands	Spain/ Rostock	Stroms Hellier/ Fair Isle	27.09.1588	Grassel 2015
unknown	Shetlands	Danzig	Grutings Voe or Grutness Voe	1591	Friedland 1973
Noahs Arche	Shetlands	Danzig	Burrafirth	01.10.1592	Ballantyne/ Smith 1994
Coninck Davidth	Shetlands	Hamburg	Culswick	1667	Grassel 2015
King Salomon	Shetlands	Hamburg	Burravoe	1680	Grassel 2015
Engel Raphael	Shetlands	Bremen	Vatsetter Ness	30.10.1681	Grassel 2015
Vlieland	Shetlands	Hamburg	near the islands	April 1684	Grassel 2015
St. Anna	Shetlands	Bremen	island in the Dury Voe	October 1685	Grassel 2015

Table 3. List of ship losses of Hanseatic origin at the North Atlantic islands. The spelling of the ship names was adopted from the sources (table: P. Grassel).

Unfortunately, the databases for ship losses during this time period for the Faroe Islands and Iceland are not well-developed thus far.[6] Nevertheless, for Faroe at least 9 ship losses can be confirmed between AD 1523 and 1707 (Tab. 2).

Concerning the Hansa, there are several possible wreck sites. For example, at least 10 wrecks with a Hanseatic origin can be expected at the Shetland Islands for the period

6 Ragnar Edvardsson (University of Iceland) is currently working on this scientific question for Iceland (see Grassel and Edvardsson 2020, in press).

Island	Material	Location	Dating	Additional	Reference
Iceland	ceramic/ stoneware	Rif, Snæfellsnes peninsular	15th – 17th centuries	one ceramic fragment	Mehler 2009
Iceland	glass	Reykjavík	15th – 17th centuries	fragments of cylindrical beakers	Mehler 2000
Faroe Islands	ceramic/ Rheinish stoneware	Tinganes/ Tórshavn	15th – 17th centuries	some ceramic fragments	Arge/Mehler 2012
Shetlands	ceramic/ red-glazed earthenware	Lerwick	late 15th – 18th centuries	around 50 pieces, including one piece of salt-glazed stone ware	Grassel 2017, 268
Shetlands	ceramic/ glass/ metal/ clinker	Scalloway Castle/ Scalloway	late 15th – 18th centuries	lots of finds, including over 900 pieces of ceramic, partly glazed and decorated	Hall/Lindsay 1983
Shetlands	ceramic/ white-glazed red earthenware	North Voe/ Whalsay	late 15th – 18th centuries	well preserved tripod, submarine find	Grassel 2017, 269

Table 4. List of archaeological finds of Hanseatic origin which are directly connected to former late Hanseatic trading posts at the North Atlantic islands (table: P. Grassel).

between the 15th and 17th centuries. Additionally, at least 3 ships of Hanseatic origin were lost at Iceland and 1 ship was lost at the Faroe Islands during the 16th century (Tab. 3).

Because of the close connection of trading posts and their upstream shallow water areas on the islands, the well-known seafaring and maritime trade with the islands during late Hanseatic times, and the high number of ship losses and wreckages between the 15th and 17th centuries, there is an outstanding maritime-archaeological potential for excavations associated with the North Atlantic islands for this period and especially for Hanseatic finds. Until now, there has been only a small number of detectable Hanseatic finds, mostly ceramics, at the North Atlantic islands which are connected to former trading posts (Tab. 4).

There is also a general problem of a limited presence of Hanseatic wreck finds within the entire former Hansa area. This is why maritime-archaeological research projects would be an excellent opportunity to scrutinise source-based knowledge about Hanseatic and non-Hanseatic seafaring in the islands in general, as well as to evaluate Hanseatic shipbuilding of the 15th, 16th and 17th centuries on an archaeological basis.

Structured, long-term archaeological projects for the evaluation, geophysical surveys and assessment of near-shore and offshore underwater anomalies are clearly worthwhile in the islands and some maritime-archaeological research has just begun. For example, a huge number of submarine anomalies have been identified at Iceland which could be interpreted as man-made and further research is already planned here.[7] Similar projects can hopefully be undertaken in the near future, especially for the late Hanseatic period, at the Faroe and Shetland Islands as well. One example for such a project started recently. "Looking in from the Edge (LIFTE) – The Impact of International Commercialisation on North-West Europe's Peripheral Communities 1468-1712: Production, Commerce and Consumption in Orkney and Shetland" is funded by the German DFG and the British AHRC, and scientists from England, Scotland and Germany (including the author) will work together within this project.

7 Many thanks to Ragnar Edvardsson, University of Iceland, for this kind notice.

Acknowledgements

This article is a short overview of the PhD thesis of the author, titled *Late Hanseatic seafaring in the North Atlantic area between the 15th and 17th century. The maritime-archaeological potential of Hanseatic trading posts in the Shetland Islands, Faroe Islands and Iceland based on archaeological and historical sources (Die späthansezeitliche Schifffahrt im Nordatlantik vom 15. Jahrhundert bis zum 17. Jahrhundert. Das maritim-archäologische Potenzial hansischer Handelsplätze auf den Shetland Inseln, den Färöer Inseln und Island anhand archäologischer und historischer Quellen)*, which was successfully finished in November 2017 at Kiel University. I would like to thank the Graduate School "Human Development in Landscapes" and the German Maritime Museum for their support of my research and for the opportunity to receive a PhD.

References

Alberti, H.J. v. 1957. *Mass und Gewicht. Geschichtliche und tabellarische Darstellungen von den Anfängen bis zur Gegenwart.* Berlin: Akademie-Verlag.

Arge, S.V. 2007. Marinarkæologi på Færøerne Fund, forvaltning og udfordringer, in: Hahn-Pedersen, M. (ed.), *Havets kulturarv. De nordiske maritime museers arbejdsmøde i Torshavn.* Esbjerg: Fiskeri- og Søfartsmuseets Forlag, 55-69.

Arge, S.V. and Mehler, N. 2012. Adventures far from home. Hanseatic Trade with the Faroe Islands, in: Harnow, H., Cranstone, D., Belford, P., Madsen-Höst, L. (eds.), *Across the North Sea. Later Historical Archaeology in Britain and Denmark, c. 1500-2000 A.D.* Odense: Syddansk Universitetsforlag, 175-186.

Baasch, E. 1889. *Die Islandfahrt der Deutschen. Namentlich der Hamburger vom 15. bis 17. Jahrhundert.* Hamburg: Herold'sche Buchhandlung.

Ballantyne, J.H. and Smith, B. 1994 (eds.), *Shetland Documents 1580-1611.* Lerwick: Shetland Times.

Campbell, J., Elvestad, E., Gardiner, M., Mehler, N. 2010. *A Report on Preliminary Work on Papa Stour, Shetland.* OITIS Field Report No. 1.

Capelle, T. 1982. *Untersuchungen auf dem mittelalterlichen Handelsplatz Gautavík, Island.* Köln: Rheinland-Verlag.

Dollinger, P. 2012^{6}. *Die Hanse.* Stuttgart: Kröner.

Ehrenberg, R. 1899. Aus der hamburgischen Handelsgeschichte. *Zeitschrift des Vereins für Hamburgische Geschichte* 10, 1-40.

Friedland, K. 1973. Der hansische Shetlandhandel, in: Friedland, K. (ed.), *Stadt und Land. In der Geschichte des Ostseeraums.* Lübeck: Schmidt-Römhild, 66-79.

Gardiner, M. and Mehler, N. 2007. English and Hanseatic Trading and Fishing Sites in Medieval Iceland: Report on Initial Fieldwork. *Germania* 85, 385-427.

Gardiner, M. and Mehler, N. 2010. The Hanseatic trading site at Gunnister Voe, Shetland. *Post-Medieval Archaeology* 44/2, 347-349.

Gardiner, M. and Mehler, N. 2013. On the Verge of Colonialism. English and Hanseatic Trade in the North Atlantic Islands, in: Pope, P.E. and Lewis-Simpson, S. (eds.), *Exploring Atlantic Transitions: Archaeologies of Transience and Permanence in New Found Lands.* Woodbridge: Boydell, 1-14.

Grassel, P. 2015. Late Hanseatic seafaring from Hamburg and Bremen to the North Atlantic Islands. With a marine archaeological excursus in the Shetland Islands. *Skyllis* 15/2, 172-182.

Grassel, P. 2016. Late Hanseatic seafaring from Hamburg and Bremen to Iceland, the Faeroe Islands and Shetland, in: Christ, M., Enzmann, J., Jürgens, F., Steffensen, F., Ulrich, J., Wilkes, F. (eds.), *N.E.R.D. New European Researches and Discoveries in Underwaterarchaeology Conference*. Beiträge der Internationalen Konferenz der Arbeitsgruppe für maritimen und limnischen Archäologie. 21.-23. November 2014 in Kiel. Bonn: Habelt, 82-93.

Grassel, P. 2017. *Die späthansezeitliche Schifffahrt im Nordatlantik vom 15. Jahrhundert bis zum 17. Jahrhundert. Das maritim-archäologische Potenzial hansischer Handelsplätze auf den Shetland Inseln, den Färöer Inseln und Island anhand archäologischer und historischer Quellen.* PhD thesis. Kiel: Universitätsbibliothek Kiel.

Grassel, P. and Edvardsson, R. 2020, in press. The Potential of Underwater Archaeology in the North Atlantic, in: Mehler, N. (ed.), *German voyages to the North Atlantic (c. 1400-1700).* Leiden: in press.

Hänselmann, L. 1890. Braunschweiger und Bremer auf der Islandfahrt. *Hansische Geschichtsblätter* 17/2, 168-172.

Hall, D. and Lindsay, W.J. 1983. Excavations at Scalloway Castle. 1979 and 1980. *Proceedings of the Society of Antiquaries of Scotland* 113, 554-593.

Hammel-Kiesow, R. 2008[4]. *Die Hanse.* München: Beck.

Hofmeister, A.E. 2000. Hansische Kaufleute auf Island im 15. und 16. Jahrhundert, in: Deutschisländische Gesellschaft Bremerhaven und Bremen (ed.), *Kirche-Kaufmann-Kabeljau. 1000 Jahre Bremer Islandfahrt.* Bremen: Staatsarchiv, 33-46.

Jahnke, C. 2013. Die Hanse. Überlegungen zur Entwicklung des Hansebegriffes und der Hanse als Institution resp. Organisation. *Hansische Geschichtsblätter* 131, 1-32.

Koch, C.F. 1995. *Untersuchungen über den Aufenthalt von Isländern in Hamburg für den Zeitraum 1520-1662.* Hamburg: Verl. Verein für Hamburgische Geschichte.

Madsen, H. 1999. *Førøeres hvornår skete det.* Gistrup: Skúvanes.

Mehler, N. 2000. Hohlglas in Island von der Wikingerzeit bis zur frühen Neuzeit. *Offa* 57. Bonn: Habelt, 347-356.

Mehler, N. 2004. Die mittelalterliche Importkeramik Islands, in: Guðmunsson, G. (ed.), *Current Issues in Nordic Archaeology.* Proceedings of the 21st Conference of Nordic Archaeologists, 6.-9. September 2001, Akureyri, Iceland. Reykjavík: Soc. of Icelandic Archaeologists, 167-170.

Mehler, N. 2009. The Perception and Interpretation of Hanseatic Material Culture in the North Atlantic: Problems and Suggestions. *Journal of the North Atlantic*, Special vol. 1, 89-108.

Mehler, N., Coolen, J., Gardiner, M., Elvestad, E. 2012. *Excavation and geomagnetic survey at the Blade of Filbister, Gluss Voe, Northmavine, Shetland.* OITIS Field Report No. 3.

Melton, N.D. 2004. Cod and Ships: Scottish merchant activity in southern Shetland in the 17th century, in: Housley, R.A. and Coles, G. (eds.), *Atlantic Connections and Adaptions. Economics, environments and subsistence in lands bordering the North Atlantic.* Oxford: Oxbow Books, 240-251.

Müller, H. 1975. Untersuchungen zur bremischen Reederei im 17. Jahrhundert. *Bremisches Jahrbuch* 53, 91-142.

Müller, U. 2014. "Archäologie" + "Kultur" = "Hansekultur"? Überlegungen zu einem Begriff, in: Falk, A., Müller, U., Schneider, M. (eds.), *Lübeck und der Hanseraum. Beiträge zu Archäologie und Kulturgeschichte. Festschrift für Manfred Gläser.* Lübeck: Schmidt-Römhild, 439-452.

Wessex Archaeology 2011. *Shipwreck Heritage of Shetland. Desk-based Assessment.* Archaeological Report, July 2011.

Zachariasen, L. 1951. *Føroyar sum rættarsamfelag 1535-1655.* Annales Societatis Scientiarum Færoensis. Supplementum IV. Tórshavn: Foroya Fródskaparfelag.

Author address

Philipp Grassel
Deutsches Schifffahrtsmuseum
Leibniz-Institut für Maritime Geschichte
Hans-Scharoun-Platz 1
27568 Bremerhaven, Germany
grassel@dsm.museum

About the author

Philipp Grassel, born in 1983, studied Pre- and Protohistoric Archaeology, Classical Archaeology and the History of Arts as well as Medieval and Early Modern History at Kiel University between 2004 and 2012. In 2008, he gained a deeper knowledge of Iberian Protohistoric Archaeology during an academic exchange program between the University of Kiel and the Universidad de Cadíz (University of Cadíz) in Spain.

Philipp is a maritime and limnic archaeologist and scientific diver. He is, therefore, a specialist in marine and limnic archaeological research. Although his scientific interests focus on medieval and early modern times in Western and Northern Europe, he is also fascinated by prehistoric sunken landscapes and archaic submarine finds all over the world.

From Salamander to Siren: Landscapes of Identity

Maren C. Biederbick

Abstract

Given that knowledge is power – with the assumption that knowledge provides the attainment of power – it seems pertinent that the rise of complex symbolic scripts in the 15th century would drive interest in their interpretation, since these texts could contain knowledge that would consequently lead to power. The rediscovery of the *Hieroglyphica Horapollonis*[1] in 1419 led European Renaissance humanists to develop new pictorial languages. Several distinct historical developments, such as the aforementioned, induced the rise of devices, a very personalised form of corporate identity.

On the basis of the *Dialogo dell'imprese militari et amorose* of the *symbolorum pater,* Paolo Giovio (1483-1552), from 1574, the PhD project presented here searched for the material presence of the devices beyond their record in books. Applications found on architecture and mobile items established a pictorial complexity between the several co-existing powers that were in play in 16th century Europe. By studying these signs, a clear idea of how these powers interacted with one another could be obtained. The significance of research on these devices lies precisely in linking the historical records with the empirical 'artistic' record, thus providing a multidimensional view of 16th century power politics and the creation of landscapes of identity.

Introduction

In 1504, Francis I. de Valois (1494-1547) was honoured by the release of a medal for his tenth birthday. His mother, Louise de Savoie (1476-1531), had ordered it, because this sort of medal played an important role in the process of constructing identity as well as in communications during the Early Modern Age. On the obverse side of the medal, the portrait of the individual is depicted and, on the

1 This Neoplatonist work from 6th century Alexandria served as the first essential key to an understanding of hieroglyphs (Thissen 1994, 256-258).

in: Müller, J. and Ricci, A. 2020 (eds.), *Past Societies: Human Development in Landscapes*. Sidestone Press: Leiden, pp. 163-180.

reverse side, this person's device appears in a fashion of the tradition that was set by Roman emperors in antiquity.

Identity

Like coats of arms, yet highly individualised, devices were applied on personal belongings and they became a European phenomenon during the 15th and 16th centuries. Like emblems, these combinations of texts and images indulged the courtly lust for riddles and games of de- and encoding during which the proper humanistic education of the court members could be demonstrated, as the single devices often referred to a specific quotation of either contemporary authors or those from Greek and Roman antiquity. Kings and popes, cardinals and dukes as well as humanists and marshals needed to have their own devices with which to adorn their own flags, shields, and garnishes as well as those of their pageants in order to become noticeable in this courtly culture.

Aware of the effects of pictorial power, Francis I. kept this device over his lifetime and after his coronation he decorated every building in his possession with it. In honour of their king, his allegiance did the same. Thus, a 'landscape of salamander' was created, which is the pictorial animal on this device.[2] Spread throughout the French kingdom, the steady presence and numerous recreations of this device over fifty years have provided nearly perfect conditions to study its persistent elements and subtle differences.

The Dialogo dell'imprese

The salamander is one of the most famous and, in France, seemingly ubiquitous devices. It is, however, just one of 139 *imprese*, which are illustrated through woodcuts in the *Dialogo dell'imprese* from 1574 (Rouillé 1574, 28).[3] This book is a centrepiece of emblem literature. Printed in Lyon by Guillaume Rouillé (1518-1589), it contains device texts from three authors: Paolo Giovio, Gabriele Symeoni (1509-1575), and Lodovico Domenichi (1515-1564). Devices – though only of a bipartite motto- and image-structure – influenced many emblems afterwards (Drysdall 2008, 264). Especially, the first work within the compilation, the name giving *Dialogo dell'imprese militari et amorose*, which was written by Giovio in 1551, gave start to a long succession of theoretical discussions about these signs (Russell 1985, 25). Accordingly, following generations of emblem authors referred to him as the *symbolorum pater.* Analogous to this tribute, Paolo Giovio can be equated with the 'father of emblems', Andrea Alciat (1492-1550), whose work influenced European culture for three centuries (Scholz 2002, 22-23).

Research objectives

Given that Giovio's manuscript about the devices dates, in many cases, after the death of the respective device owners, and given, in addition, that his dialog was only first published and illustrated after his own death, one of the objectives was to compare

---

2 Charged with the belief of having talismanic properties, the device-animal has served not only as a nickname for this king but also as his *pars pro toto* (Lippincott 1990, 55; Caldwell 2004, 9-10).

3 For the French translation of this work, Rouillé used the title *Dialogue des devises* (Rouillé 1559b), which is why I will use "impresa" and "device" here as synonyms, though they are not identical, as an impresa is a far more developed concept.

Figure 1. Castello Aragonese on Ischia. Residence of Vittoria Colonna, who was praised in her device to weather her enemies like the unbowed rock has broken the waves (copyright: Kiel University library (signature: Cb 6371). Photo and picture copyright: M.-C. Biederbick).

a) the published work with its manuscript and first sketches (Giovio 1551; Symeoni 1556), and b) the fictional with the material records of these devices.

A second objective was to trace the iconological development, which led to the choice of a certain device. This included an evaluation of the socio-cultural background of each device-owner.

Given here that the devices mentioned in the book from 1574 were spread over Europe from Hungary to Britain, from Spain to Switzerland, from sacral to mundane nobility, from (fore)father to son, from young lover to widow, and from humanist to soldier, a third objective emerged: to examine group(s) of the device owners for social and geographic likenesses since the late 14th century.

Landscapes

Examining the landscape-scenery within the devices, meaningful results were attained. In the case of the sign of Vittoria Colonna (1490-1547), the rock of the Castel Aragonese on Ischia was identified (Fig. 1).

In most of the cases, however, the other 'landscape' of devices has proven to be more interesting. In this, the term here includes more than the biogeographic scenery. "Landscape" is a figure of speech for a system (Jackson 1989, 177; Schlögel 2003, 68-69, 291). As such, it served in this study to be suitable for each of the three research aspects, the spatial, social and symbolic turn. Humans develop a plurality of spaces. There are as many spaces as we can define artefacts, subjects, media, and actors (Cosgrove 1984, 13). Yet, space cannot be told, but only selectively visualised (Schlögel 2003, 49). Therefore, for each device an atlas was set up, where in Warburgian manner the multivariate examples from different media were collected (Warnke 1999, 127). Unlike the work *Mnemosyne* by Warburg, however, these mood boards are meant to point out the constancies and archetypes for each symbol. This is where the iconographic elements of each device become apparent. Furthermore, the social net of the delimited timeframe was georeferenced. Finally, the applications of devices *in situ* were localised.

Point of departure, material and methods

Research on devices is a minor part of the relatively young field of emblem studies (Della Latta 2008, 230). Whereas devices only consist of a motto and a picture, emblems have a tripartite structure (Heckscher and Wirth 1967). The third part being a poem. At first, they aroused the interest of philologists and only later that of art historians interested in applied arts (Russell 1985).

As applied arts was assigned a secondary position during the institutionalisation of art history, the semiotic meanings of the devices were lost. However, during the 19th and the early 20th century, these signs gradually became an object of interest for scholars again (Springer 1860; Warburg 1905; Giehlow 1915; Volkmann 1923). A modern edition of the *Dialogo dell'imprese* as early as 1863 stands as a landmark for this evolution (Daelli 1863). In the 1930s, single case studies attracted iconologists (Wind 1937; Wittkower 1937/38). The compilation of bibliographies of the diverse books – among them the printed editions of Giovio and Symeoni – started soon afterwards (Green 1870; Praz 1947; Landwehr 1976; Adams *et al.* 1999). In 1967, the first explicit index of emblems based on early modern emblem books was published, in which the devices of Giovio and Symeoni are sometimes referred to (Henkel and Schöne 1967). A commented edition of the Giovio text with footnotes about creational circumstances of the mentioned devices was collated (Doglio 1978). In the early 1980s, the drawings of the two manuscripts of *Dialogo dell' imprese* in Florence and Como were compared (Nova 1985). The manuscript of Como was also transcribed in these years (Penco 1984). The culture of *imprese* dialogs as well as the connection between devices and identities, mainly for the devices of editing houses, universities and their members in Italy, including a few of the devices in the *Dialogo dell'imprese*, was then examined (Bregoli-Russo 1990; Arbizzoni 2002). Research about outstanding personalities of history, such as Francis I de Valois, has thrown light on him as a Maecenas for art and on the icons symbolising him (*i.e.* Leqoc 1987; Fourrier and Parot 2010). The same can be said about the Medici and Gonzaga, who repetitively come into the focus of research institutions in Florence and Mantua (*i.e.* Ames-Lewis 1979; Malacarne and Signorini 1996). In fact, since devices were highly personalised and associated with single individuals, who, at first glance, used them as ornaments, devices as a courtly phenomenon have so far been the best researched by historians (*i.e.* Pastoureau 1981; Hablot 2001; Slanička 2002; Paravicini 2011). With the emancipation of applied arts as a research subject in art history, single case studies on one item or one monument, on which devices are displayed, come into focus (Maffei 2004).

In general, there is the ambition to achieve 1) a complete digitalisation of the existing emblem and device books, and to create 2) databases, as these books are the key for an understanding of the secular iconography in Europe of a period lasting longer than over 300 years. For the *Dialogo dell'imprese*, the first step was accomplished by research institutions in 2006 and in 2011 (Rouillé 1574). The second step – an interlinkable database – does not exist yet.

Organising information – Transforming text and images into catalogue charts

Given this panorama, the *Dialogo dell'imprese* was transformed into a catalogue. So far, indexes have presented the mottos with their reference, picture content, and meaning (Henkel and Schöne 1967). Indexes specialised on devices also included a section about the respective owners (Duer 1988; Daly and Duer 1993; Tung 2006). The latter also supplied information about further whereabouts of the same sign throughout device books of other authors.

The research presented here started to combine the information of these precedent works, including the comments about the historical backgrounds that Doglio had furnished. In addition, the new handbook adds the precise quotes of the motto-references as well as written and pictorial sources, which gave the inspiration for the *pictura* of a sign. These icon-references on the mood boards then continue with the examples of the respective device found in applications.

Furthermore, the new handbook provides information about the historic inventor of a device and its whereabouts in other editions of Giovio and Symeoni. Moreover, it contrasts the exact text excerpts of the 1574 edition with the two remaining manuscripts: the anonymous one in Como and the 1556 sketch from Symeoni (Codex Ashburnam 1372). Device per device, it also supplies the first German translation of the 1574 edition. In addition, the identity of the respective device-owner is given more precisely, adding to his title, his proper name and life-data. Finally, each catalogue number contains an explanation about the speciality of the device and ends with an abbreviated bibliography.

Rendering text and visual impressions calculable – Setting up a database

In a second step, an Access-database was set up.[4] It includes the information for each catalogue number, but also the referential images, the text quotations and the explanation.

Furthermore, it has variables for the geographic and situational location of the device applications as well as for the intentional location of the device use mentioned in the 1574 edition. For every object, it has precise and relational dating with regard to a) 1559 (which is the year of the first publication of the 1574 woodcuts (Rouillé 1559a)), b) the birth of the bearer, c) the death of the bearer, and d) the invention of the device. In addition, it has variables for the specific motto and picture sources

4 See "*Die Entstehung von Landschaften durch Markenzeichen in der frühen Neuzeit*"; http://www.jma.uni-kiel.de/en/research-projects/data-exchange-platform [13.10.2019].

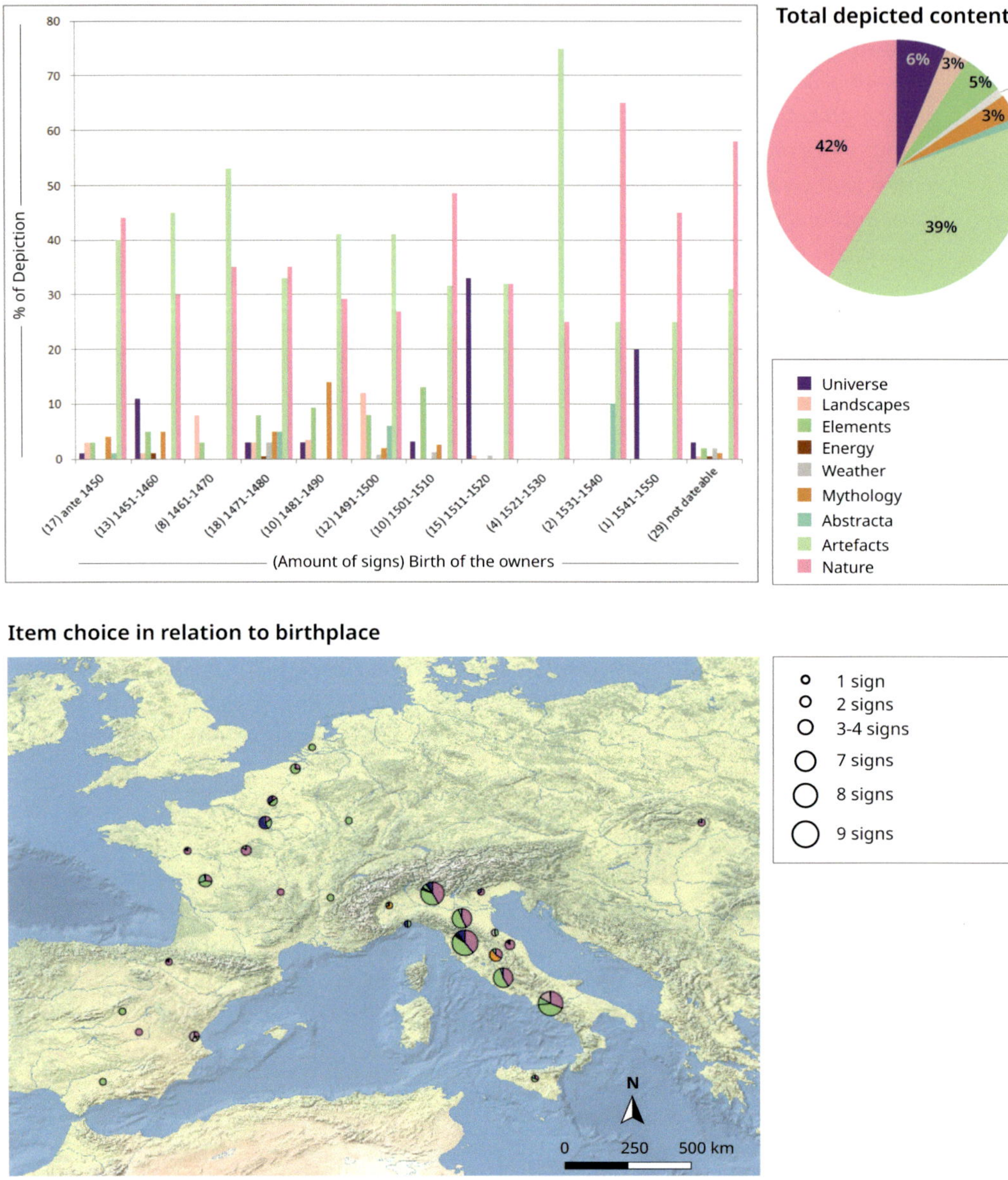

Figure 2. Results of the quantitative analysis of the pictorial components of the 139 illustrated devices of the 1574 Dialogo edition in reference to the time and place of the owners' birth. Visualisation via QGIS-results for the Giovio / Symeoni devices (© M.-C. Biederbick 2014).

for authors and their works, as well as general information, for example, if they were derived from antiquity or not.

In contrast to the catalogue, the database contains further charts for systemisation. It indicates the language of the motto and whether or not applications were found with both the mottos and pictures or with just one of either. With regard to the picture description of the 139 woodcuts of the *Dialogo*, the semiotic contents, for instance for the salamander device, were not only labelled from species to larger category: salamander <

amphibian < animal < nature, which is defined as the sum of zoology and botany, but also valued according to the percentage of the space and meaning its depiction takes in the visual composition. For the salamander, the score is 70%, as alongside the animal we find a crown < jewellery < artefact: 20% and fire < (alchemic) element: 10% in that device (Rouillé 1574, 28). Similar generalisations were done for the device-owners' dates of birth in year < decade < quarter of a century < first or second half of a century < century and for their birthplaces in towns and regions.

Quantitative analysis of device compositions

Given this panorama, an analysis of the devices on a larger scale was rendered possible. By examining the total of 139 illustrations from the 1574 edition, it can be stated that a device consists of one to three different pictorial items of meaning. If the contribution rate of each of the items in a device, such as the results of the above-mentioned salamander (nature: 70, artefact 20, element 10), is then combined with the percentages associated with 'nature', 'artefacts', 'elements' and further scores for the rest of the 139 devices, we obtain final values for a total of nine different categories identified as picture content. When these values are summed up and then once again assigned percentages, this analysis provides the following results: 'universe' has a score of 6%, 'landscapes' 3%, 'elements' 5%, 'energy' less than 1%, 'weather' 1%, 'mythology' 3%, 'abstracts' 1%, 'artefacts' 39%, and 'nature' 42% (Fig. 2).

Device composition classification according to temporal phases (decades)

These scores become more interesting when examined for diverse temporal phases (decades).[5] When grouping devices over a total period of one hundred years from 1450-1550 into the birth-decades of their owners, a variety in depiction is only given for the period of a decade, if Giovio and Symeoni provided more than one example. This is the case for devices of people born from 1451-1460 and from 1471-1510. For the ones from the 1461-1470 decade, besides the main categories of "nature" and "artefacts", "landscapes" and "elements" were the categories that were most favoured, instead of just a variety, whereas owners from the decade 1511-1520 grew so fond of the "universe" category that this even overruled the categories "nature" and "artefacts" (Fig. 2).

Devices according to geographic influence

Further results were obtained by adapting the data set via QGIS to the birth-regions of the owners. First, colouring these regions in relation to the birth-decades depicts European history, which in this epoch was on the threshold of modern centrally organised states. The colour changes between decades demonstrate how, at first, the owners belonged to the different courts and *signorie* throughout the countryside (from today's point of view) and then show a switch to regions, which today include the capitals of France, Spain and Italy (Biederbick 2014, 159). Second, linking the classificatory statistics to geographic parameters illustrates that there are no significant differences throughout Europe in the selection of the depiction of "nature" and "artefacts", in

---

5 The following analyses were based on the assumptions that the owners of the devices no. 4 and no. 11 are Lorenzo il Magnifico (1449-1492) and Charles V (1500-1558).

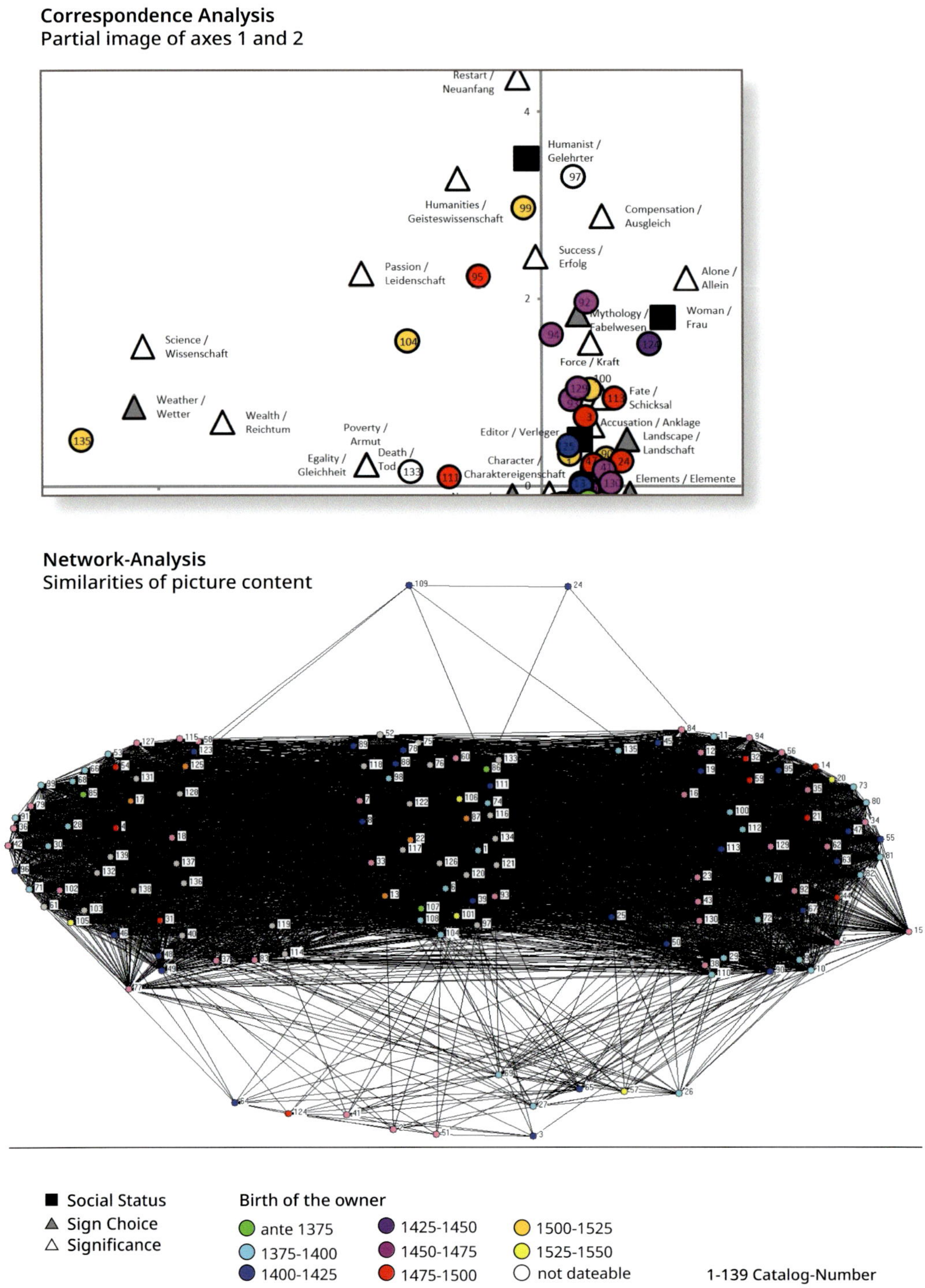

Figure 3. Results of the correspondence analysis in CAPCA 2.2 regarding the relation between the social status of a device-owner, the pictorial content of his or her device, and its meaning, as well as results of the network analysis in UciNet calculating similarities of the pictorial compositions, which was visualised with Netdraw. Each time, the dataset was coloured according to the birth date of the device-owner (© M.-C. Biederbick 2014).

general. While in fact, there are slight preferences concerning the less represented other categories: Owners from regions today belonging to the Netherlands, Northern France and Northern Italy favoured the "universe", while owners from Spain and Southern Italy preferred "landscapes". Curiously, "mythology" occurs only in icons from people of mountain scenery (Fig. 2).

Preferences and expectation of social roles – Correspondence analysis of sign choice and personal status

Via CAPCA 2.2, the correspondences of the 139 devices as objects were analysed among the three variable-types: "social role of the owner", "picture-classification", and "interpreted significance of the sign". A central knot-accumulation is visualised on the three first axes.[6] Among these results are the close corresponding pairs of the social role of "wives" and the significance of "luck"; of "military personal" and "vengeance"; and of "humanists" and "humanities" (Fig. 3).

The latter is accompanied by another signification: "success". Both are well separated from the significance-significance pair "science" and "wealth", while the depiction "weather" is attached. The significance "passion" results to be at mid-distance between "humanities" and "science". In close proximity are three more variables: the depiction "mythology", the social role of a "woman [not being wife]", and the signification "alone". The most repellent significances are "friendship" and "marriage-right". Adding to this visualisation, the objects coloured per birth of the owners in quarter centuries from 1375 till 1550 show no teleological development, as the colours sprinkle over the variable-set (Greenacre 2007). Yet, the 26 objects from the owners born between 1500-1525, followed by the 29 from people born between 1475-1500, and the 35 from 1450-1475 spread most equally distributed across the total variable set. This aspect of more centre-focused other century-quarters is due to their lack of a sufficient number of objects in order to potentially represent a similar variety.

Similarities among signs and alliances among their owners – Network analysis

When inserting UciNet with the data in percentage of depicted items of the above-mentioned nine different categories in net-work-similarity, in general, the category "abstracts" is grouped with "artefacts" and "nature", although being at the other end of the scale in the statistics. Again, "mythology" obtains a special position. Now, when considering the 139 devices, device no. 104, for example, scores the highest both in a similarity- and a betweeness-network. This device has already been categorised as outstanding by its unique vertical shape, which is due to its function as a title-page for the second author (Fig. 4).

The depicted contents of this device include universe (11%), landscapes (0%), elements (0%), energy (0%), weather (12%), mythology (25%), abstracts (0%), artefacts (17%) and nature (35%). Being the strongest in the network, and having a relatively high score for "mythology", this device's structure explains the above noticed, special position of the category "mythology".

---

6 Only 5/9 variables of social roles, 17/49 of significances, and 2/9 of depictions lay gradually distinct from the centre.

Figure 4. Device and the author mark of Gabriele Symeoni (Rouillé 1574, 168) (copyright: Kiel University library (signature: Cb 6371)).

For an interpretation of the UciNet-output, the data was categorised in a second step according to "time" (Fig. 3), and in a third in "birth-regions", in order to examine if the tripartite shape of the network-cluster corresponds to either one of the respective motives – different time spans or specific regions. Having obtained no clear results, it is suspected that the three accumulations refer to the representation of the nine categories, in which the percentages form two strong opponents and a group of the beautiful rest.

The network of the real agents within this cultural system, that of the owners of these devices, was also analysed. On the one hand, genealogical tables were drawn and filled with the devices. Hereby, a better overview of this "landscape" was obtained, and especially, how a theme of a device was maintained over generations in a family and, at the same time, was altered slightly by its individual members, as in the case of the diamond ring of the de' Medici (Fig. 5).

On the other hand, such a mind map of family bonds was calculated on a larger scale. Therefore, the relationship between two device owners was expressed in numbers. The highest score was given for the closest relation, for example for fathers and sons, the second highest for grandparents and grandchildren, or between siblings, the third for uncles and nephews, and so on. A similar rating was done for alliances: the highest between husband and wife, the second highest for parents-in-law, *etc.* A third rating concerns rivals and enemies. With respect to their geographic territory within Europe and the time span in which each generation lived, the position of all device-owners mentioned was then calculated with UciNet and visualised with Netdraw. The resulting net demonstrates the complexity of cultural exchange across Europe (Fig. 6).

It underlines that family ties do not automatically mean fair affairs between two agents. In fact, the higher the social status of a family the more often cousins developed lethal hatred for each other. Geographical distance increased these sentiments, which we also find reflected in their respective devices.

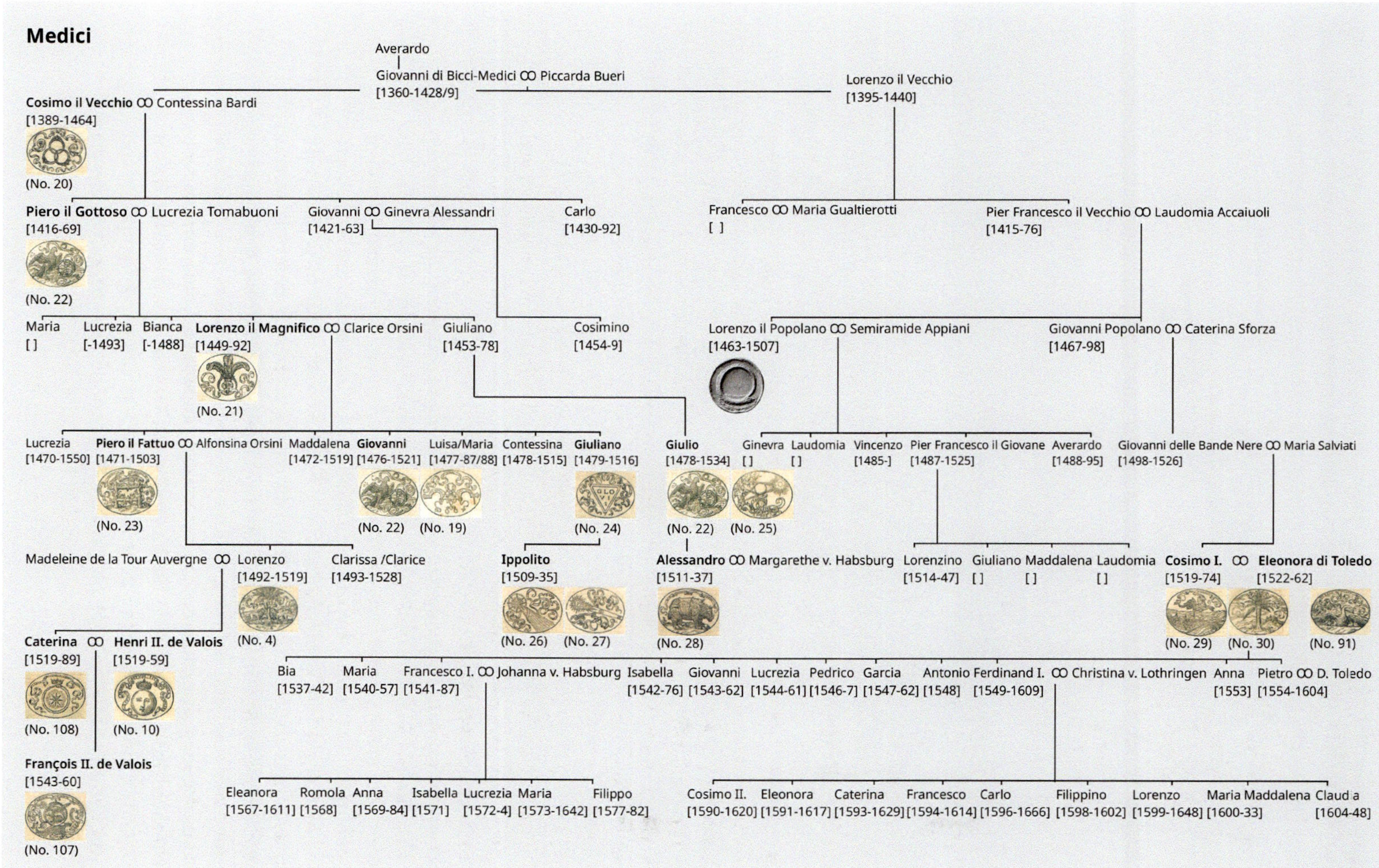

Figure 5. Genealogical table of the de' Medici with their devices as given in the 1574 Dialogo edition, showing consistencies and variations of identities signs within a family (© M.-C. Biederbick 2017 and T. Pape 2020; cf. Cecchi 1980; Schreiber 1994; Acidini Luchinat and Scalini 1998. Medalreverse of Lorenzo il Popolano di Pierfrancesco de' Medici by N. Spinelli, ø 38mm; Firenze, Museo Nazionale del Bargello, Inv.-No. 6042; cf. Hill 1930/1984).

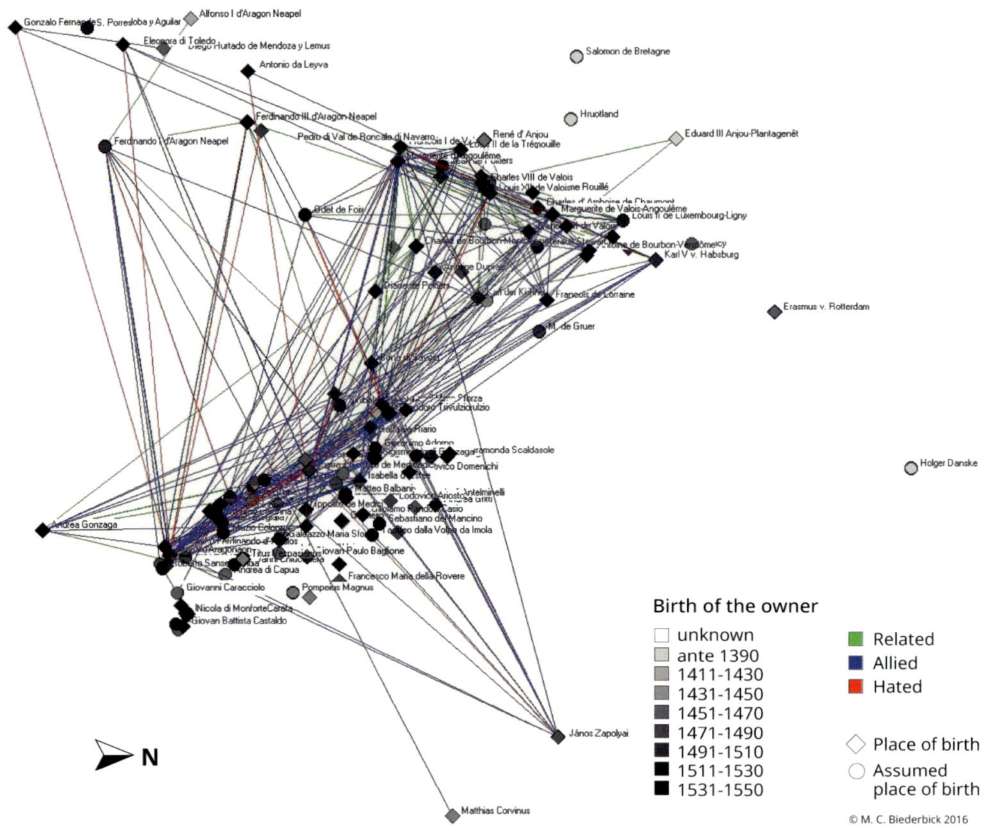

Figure 6. Results of a network analysis in UciNet calculating personal relationships of the device owners among each other. Georeferenced visualisation with Netdraw according to the birthplaces of the device owners (© M.-C. Biederbick 2016).

Aura-Testing – Field Work

No object-research should be conducted without having experienced the *aura* of the original (Benjamin 1972). For some devices, the material evidence of their use has been conserved in museums and libraries. Their applications on monuments have been broadly published. For others, hypothetical applications on certain places throughout Southern Europe were assumed, according to the course of life of their owners. Their existence was testified alongside the road during a research excursion to sites with significant examples. In order to understand similar social roles, representative samples were compared and contrasted with each other: 1) Francis I and Charles V for device use by king and emperor; 2) the Gonzaga, Medici and the Sforza as families of Northern Italian *signorie*; 3) the Colonna and Aragona as a Southern Italian comparison. As a further contrast to these secular sovereigns of city governments and martial arts, 4) the use that the pope and cardinals made of devices was studied as were

5) the devices of humanists as well as 6) devices of women to conclude the picture.[7] Inspecting, for example, Palestrina, the provenience of the Colonna, there is but a little genius in conjunction with the canting arms applied on the monuments of this noble family. In the *Dialogo*, the column is accompanied with a siren (Rouillé 1574, 149). In the 15th century, the Colonna had to flee the outreach of Alexander IV (1431-1503) and found political asylum in Naples. Mythology asserts that a siren is the powerful protector of the city. Since then, we find the image of Partenope as the strong "siren", master of storms, in the device of the family. The powerful symbol was installed with the Colonna back into their old territory in the 16th century (Cioci 2013).

Thereby, it must be concluded that the establishment of a visual reign through landmarks of own possessions with the proper identity symbol was not only a strategy of King Francis I but also of this Southern Italian noble family.

Discussion of Results

The applied methods – statistics, geo-referencing, correspondence- and network-analysis – are innovative in art-historical analysis. On a macro-inspection, they have verified the influence of landscape on the item choice, as well as the impact of the social role of the bearers. However, these methods cannot replace iconographical analysis and iconological interpretation (Biederbick 2016, 156). Here, field work and the registration of collected data in the catalogue with its picture-atlas were essential. This work has enabled the application of the Morelli method to distinguish repetitive patterns and trifling clues. Although they are secondary in composition, they are highly indicative because they are unlikely to be imitated. For this micro-inspection, an insight more profound than the glimpse cast on the salamander and the siren can be gained by some exemplary results of this research, which have already been published (Biederbick 2017a and b).

Conclusion

During a transition period that placed a stronger focus on the works of mankind in detriment to works of religious nature, a new focus on human achievements encouraged a desire to display one's own individuality. For the European elite, displaying the coat of arms of their ancestors proved to be no longer sufficient, because its rules had grown so stiff over previous decades that it tolerated no personal modifications. In contrast, the use of devices stated their social distinction and expressed their aims.

However, by micro-inspection this research could prove that often the devices, which were supposedly 'individually' created, are actually a combination of copied mottos or icons, which fall back on traditions and conventions. These were unconsciously set by earlier famous device-bearers. Their signs became symbols for their specific social statuses. Furthermore, the iconological analysis revealed that the higher the social status the more likely the chosen sign originates from an order or votive action of

7 Caterina de Medici (1519-1589), Diane de Poitiers (1500-1566), Blanche de Savoie (1336-1387), Isabella d'Este (1474-1539), Eleonora di Toledo (1522-1562), Vittoria Colonna, and Maria d'Aragona (1503-1568) mirror perfectly the roles of wife, widow or just lady, and are all intermingled in the above-named families.

a respected ancestor. Moreover, the three authors – Giovio, Symeoni, and Domenichi – referred to traditional knowledge and exploited it for connotations, which reinforced the syllogisms that took place between a chosen sign and its owner. In the common perception, this had a strong impact on his or her identity. The *Dialogo* neither truly presents how a person wanted to be interpreted nor does it display an average picture of his or her device. The authors applied them rather as mnemotechnic supplies for their personal, sometime very satirical view on history, or for didactic scopes. Concerning the posthumous illustrations, it is testified that not the more prestigious visualisation was depicted, but the more common representations of everyday items were displayed to a larger public. In addition, the woodcuts sometimes turn towards a complete artificialised representation, a fashion of the mid-16th century, while for their sketches a more realistic depiction had been favoured.

In total, the reconstruction of the cultural and socio-political landscape to which these devices refer to has testified how these devices represent the power of their owners in European culture. It was proven how landscape not only had an influence on mentality but was also transformed into the scenery of a stage, where device owners applied their signs. Devices served as instruments to communicate and legitimise proper aims. On a three-dimensional scale of device application, different mental maps revealed hot spots and their shift in time.

To sum up, by looking closely at the *Dialogo dell'imprese* in a symbolic turn, a guide about secular iconology of the Renaissance was assembled. In a social turn, a prosopographic register of different members of the society, and in a spatial turn a cartography of these devices as fundamental mechanisms of power in proto-authoritarian states were accomplished.

Acknowledgements

I would like to thank my supervisors, Ulrich Kuder and Ingrid Höpel, as well as many cooperating private and public research institutions throughout Great Britain, Spain, France, Italy, the Vatican, Switzerland, and Germany, my international colleagues and friends, and last but not least my family, who encouraged and advised me adding their critical remarks on the road. I am also very grateful to the GSHDL for making this research possible.

References

Primary Sources

Not-printed

Giovio, P. 1551. *Dialogo dell'imprese militari et amorose*. Manuscript. Como: Società Storica Comense.

Symeoni, G. 1556. *Discours Francois, Toscan, et Latin sur la cognaissance des esprits et desseings des hommes, suivant un Dialogue Italien i, parfaict des Devises amoureuses et militaires de Monsieur Paul Iovio*. Manuscript. Lyons: Biblioteca Medicea Laurenziana Firenze; Codex Ashburnam 1376.

Printed

Rouillé, G. 1559a (ed.), *Dialogo dell'Imprese Militari et Amorose di Monsignor Giovio Vescovo di Nocera; Con un Ragionamento di Messer Lodovico Domenichi, nel medesimo soggetto. Con la tavola*. Lyons.

Rouillé, G. 1559b (ed.), *Dialogue des devises d'armes et d'amour du S. Paolo Giovio, avec un discours de M. Loys Dominique sur le mesme sujet, traduit de l'italien par le S. Vasquin Philieul auquel avons adiousté les Devises héroïques et Morales du Seigneur Gabriel Symeon*. Lyons.

Rouillé, G. 1574 (ed.), *Dialogo dell'imprese militari et amorose di Monsignor Giouio Vescovo di Nocera; Et del S. Gabriel Symeoni Fiorentino. Con vn ragionamento di M. Lodovico Domenichi, nel medesimo soggetto. Con la Tauola*. Lyons.

[Online]. Glasgow: University. Stirling Maxwell Centre. Signature: SM 520. Available at: http://www.italianemblems.arts.gla.ac.uk/book.php?book-id=sm_0520 [Accessed: 3 December 2017].

[Online]. Pisa: Scuola Normale Superiore / Istituto Nazionale di Studi sul Rinascimento. Biblioteca Virtuale On-line. Available at: http://bivio.filosofia.sns.it/bvWorkEditions.php?workFileName=Giovio_Imprese_militari.xml&authorSign=GiovioPaolo&titleSign=DialogoDellImprese [Accessed: 3 December 2017].

[Online]. Kiel: University Library. Signature: Cb 6371. Available at: http://dibiki.ub.uni-kiel.de/viewer/resolver?urn=urn:nbn:de:gbv:8:2-651072 [Accessed: 3 December 2017].

Secondary Sources

Acidini Luchinat, C. and Scalini, M. 1998. *Die Pracht der Medici. Florenz und Europa*. Munich: Prestel.

Adams, A., Rawles, S., Saunders, A. 1999. *A Bibliography of French Emblem Books of the Sixteenth and Seventeenth Centuries*. Travaux d' Humanisme et Renaissance 331. Genève: Droz.

Ames-Lewis, F. 1979. Early Medician Devices. *Journal of the Warburg and Courtauld Institutes* 42, 122-143.

Arbizzoni, G. 2002. *'Un nodo di parole e di cose'. Storia e fortuna delle imprese*. Studi e saggi 26. Rome: Salerno Editrice.

Benjamin, W. 1972. Das Kunstwerk im Zeitalter seiner technischen Reproduzierbarkeit, in: Benjamin, W., *Gesammelte Schriften 1*. Frankfurt: Suhrkamp 1972, 471-508.

Biederbick, M.-C. 2014. Imprints of Loyalty and Corporate Identity in Early Modern Landscapes: A New Handbook on Paolo Giovio's and Gabriele Symeoni's Devices, Lyon 1574 – Die Entstehung von Landschaften durch Markenzeichen in der frühen Neuzeit – Neues Handbuch zu Paolo Giovios und Gabriele Symeonis Impresen, Lyon 1574, in: Müller, J. (ed.), *Exploring Landscapes: The Reconstruction of Social Space – Landschaft erforschen: Sozialen Raum rekonstruieren*. Bonn: Habelt, 158-159.

Biederbick, M.-C. 2016. 'Lapillum in pede' – Die Kraniche im Heiligen-Geist-Hospital in Wismar. Ein Anwendungsversuch der Korrespondenz-Analyse in der Kunstgeschichte, in: Höpel, I. and Larsson, L.O. (eds.), *Emblematik im Ostseeraum – Emblematics around the Baltic*. Beiträge zur 10. Internationalen Tagung der Society for Emblem Studies an der Christian-Albrechts-Universität zu Kiel, 28 July-1 August 2014. Mundus Symbolicus 3. Kiel: Ludwig, 151-167.

Biederbick, M.-C. 2017a. Tradition and Empirical Observation – Nature in Giovio's and Symeoni's Dialogo dell'imprese from 1574, in: Enenkel, K.A.E. and Smith, P.J. (eds.), *Emblems and the Natural World. Intersections*. Interdisciplinary Studies in Early Modern Culture 50. Leiden: Brill, 271-318.

Biederbick, M.-C. 2017b. Von Cosimo il Vecchio zu Cosimo I. – Herrscher-Inszenierung der Medici durch Impresen-Anbringung im öffentlichen und privaten Raum, in: Fouquet, G., Hirschbiegl, J., Rabeler, S. (eds.), *Konflikt und Ausgleich. Möglichkeiten der Aushandlung in Städten der Vormoderne*. Zweites Atelier des Akademieprojekts ‚Residenzstädte im Alten Reich', Kiel, 14 September 2016. Mitteilungen der Residenzen-Kommission, Neue Folge: Stadt und Hof. Special edition 2. Kiel: Fotosatz Nord, 33-69.

Bregoli-Russo, M. 1990. *L'Impresa come ritratto del Rinascimento*. Valutazioni 22. Naples: Loffredo.

Caldwell, D. 2004. *The Sixteenth-Century Italian Impresa in Theory and Practice*. New York: AMS Press.

Cecchi, A. 1980. *Palazzo Vecchio e i Medici. Guida storica*. Florence: Studio per Ed. Scelte.

Cioci, F. 2013. *Il Castello di Pofi*. Pofi nella storia 4. Pofi.

Cosgrove, D.E. 1984. *Social Formation and Symbolic Landscapes*. London: Croom Helm.

Daelli, G. 1863 (ed.), *Ragionamento sulle imprese di Monsignor Paolo Giovio, ovvero Dialogo sopra i motti e disegni d'arme e d'amore che comunemente chiamano imprese. Con il ritratto dell'autore. Con Proemio, note, le varianti delle principali edizioni, e l'indice dei nomi propri e delle cose notabili*. Milan.

Daly, P.M. and Duer, L.T. 1993 (eds.), The Heroical Devises of M. Claudius Paradin [and] The Purtratures or Emblems of Gabriel Simeon, A Florentine (London: William Kearney, 1591), in: Daly, P.M. (ed.), *Index Emblematicus. The English Emblem Tradition 2*, P. S. (Paradin), P. S. (Simeoni), Willet, Combe. Toronto: Univ. of Toronto Press, 3-244.

Della Latta, A. 2008. Dar forma alle imprese: epica, parole e immagini per gli scudi del Cinquecento, in: Bolzoni, L. and Volterrani, S. (eds.), *Con parola brieve e con figura. Emblemi e imprese fra antico e modern*. Pisa: Ed. della Scuola Normale, 229-254.

Doglio, M.L. 1978 (ed.), *Giovio, Paolo – Dialogo dell'imprese militari et amorose. Centro studi "Europa delle Corti"*. Biblioteca del Cinquecento 4. Rome: Bulzoni.

Drysdall, D.L. 2008. Devices as 'Emblems' before 1531. Emblematica. *An Interdisciplinary Journal for Emblem Studies* 16, 253-269.

Duer, L.T. 1988 (ed.), Paolo Giovio. The Worthy Tract of Paulus Jovius, translated by Samuel Daniel, London (1585), in: Daly, P.M. (ed.), *Index Emblematicus. The English Emblem Tradition 1*. Jan van der Noot. A Theatre for Worldings – Paolo Giovio. The Worthy Tract of Paulus Jovius – Lodovico Domenichi. Certain Noble Devises both Militarie and Amorous – Geffrey Whitney. A Choice of Emblemes. Toronto: Univ. of Toronto Press, 34-77.

Fourrier, T. and Parot, F. 2010. Qu'est-ce que à Chambord? Etude du décor sculpté et nouvelles interpretations, in: *Comprendre Chambord à travers de son décor sculpté*. Mémoires de la Société des Sciences & Lettres de Loir-et-Cher 65. Blois, 21-55.

Giehlow, K. 1915. *Die Hieroglyphenkunde des Humanismus. Besonders der Ehrenpforte Kaiser Maximilian I*. Jahrbuch der kunsthistorischen Sammlungen des allerhöchsten Kaiserhauses 32/1. Wien: Halm & Goldmann.

Green, H. 1870. *Shakespeare and the Emblem Writers. An Exposition of their Similarities of Thought and Expression*; preceded by a View of Emblem-Literature down to A.D. 1616. London: Trübner.

Greenacre, M. 2007[2]. *Correspondence analysis*. London: Chapman & Hall.

Hablot, L. 2001. *La Devise, mise en signe du prince, mise en scene du pouvoir: Les devises et l'emblématique des princes en France et en Europe à la fin du Moyen Age. Devisier*. PhD thesis, University of Poitiers, Typoscript. Poitiers.

Hablot, L. 2006. La devise, un nouvel emblème pour les princes du XVe siècle, in: Taburet-Delahaye, É. (ed.), *La création artistique en France autour de 1400*. Actes du colloques international. École du Louvre – Musée des Beaux-Arts de Dijon – Université de Bourgogne. 7-10 July 2004. Rencontres de l'école du Louvre 19. Paris: Documentation Française, 177-192.

Heckscher, W.S. and Wirth, K.-A. 1967. Emblem – Emblembuch, in: Heydenreich, L.H. and Wirth, K.-A. (eds.), *Reallexikon zur deutschen Kunstgeschichte* 5. Stuttgart: Druckenmüller, 86-228.

Henkel, A. and Schöne, A. 1967 (eds.), *Emblemata. Handbuch zur Sinnbildkunst des XVI. und XVII. Jahrhunderts*. Stuttgart: Metzler.

Hill, G.F. 1930/1984. *A Corpus of Italian Medals of the Renaissance before Cellini*. Florence: Scelte.

Jackson, P. 1989. *Maps of Meaning. An Introduction to Cultural Geography*. Cambridge: Routledge.

Landwehr, J. 1976. *French, Italian, Spanish and Portuguese Books of Devices and Emblems 1534-1827. A Bibliography*. Bibliotheca Emblematica 6. Utrecht: Dekker & Gumbert.

Lecoq, A.-M. 1987. *François Ier imaginaire. Symbolique et politique à l'aube de la Renaissance française*. Paris: Macula.

Lippincott, K. 1990. The Genesis and Significance of the Fifteenth-century Italian Impresa, in: Anglo, S. (ed.), Chivalry in the Renaissance. Woodbridge: Boydell, 49-76.

Maffei, S. 2008. "Iucundissimi emblemi di pitture". Le imprese del Museo di Paolo Giovio a Como, in: Bolzoni, L. and Volterrani, S. (eds.), *Con parola brieve e con figura. Emblemi e imprese fra antico e modern*. Pisa: Ed. della Scuola Normale, 135-183.

Malacarne, G. and Signorini, R. 1996. *Monete e medaglie di Mantova e dei Gonzaga dal XII-XIX secolo. Stemmi imprese e motti gonzaghesche*. Milan: Electa.

Nova, A. 1985. Dialogo dell'imprese: la storia editoriale e le immagini, in: *Atti del Convegno Paolo Giovio. Il rinascimento e la memoria*, Como 3-5 June 1983, Raccolta Storica, Pubblicata dalla Società Storica Comense 17. Como: Presso la Società a Villa Gallia, 73-92.

Paravicini, W. 2011[3]. Die ritterlich-höfische Kultur des Mittelalters. Enzyklopädie Deutscher Geschichte 32. Munich: Oldenbourg Wissenschaftsverlag.

Pastoureau, M. 1981. Aux origines de l'emblème: La crise de l'héraldique européenne aux XVe et XVIe siècles, in: Jones-Davies, M.-T. (ed.), *Emblèmes et Devises au Temps de la Renaissance*. Paris: Touzot, 129-140.

Penco, M. 1984. Dialogo de l'imprese militari e amorose. Di Monsignor Paulo Iovio vescovo di Nocera al Magnanimo signore Cosmo de' Medici Duca di Fiorenza interlocutori: detto Mon.re Jovio e M. Ludovico Domenichi, in: Travi, E. and Penco, M. (eds.), *PAULII IOVII. Opera, 9, Dialogi et descriptiones*. Rome: Istituto poligrafico e zecca dello Stato, 427-443.

Praz, M. 1947. *Studies in Seventeenth-Century Imagery 2: A Bibliography of Emblem Books*. Studies of the Warburg Institute. London: Univ. of London.

Russell, D. 1985. *The Emblem and the Device in France*. French Forum Monographs 59. Lexington: French Forum Publ.

Schlögel. K. 2003. *Im Raume lesen wir die Zeit. Über Zivilisationsgeschichte und Geopolitik.* Munich: Hanser.

Scholz, B.F. 2002. *Emblem und Emblempoetik: Historische und systematische Studien.* Allgemeine Literaturwissenschaft – Wuppertaler Schriften 3. Berlin: Erich Schmidt.

Schreiber, H. 1994. *Florenz. Eine Stadt und ihre Menschen.* Munich: List.

Slanička, S. 2002. *Krieg der Zeichen: Die visuelle Politik Johanns ohne Furcht und der armagnakisch-burgundische Bürgerkrieg.* Veröffentlichung des Max-Planck-Instituts für Geschichte 182. Göttingen: Vandenhoeck und Ruprecht.

Springer, A. 1860. *Ikonographische Studien.* Mittheilungen der k. u. k. Central-Commission zur Erforschung und Erhaltung der Baudenkmale 59. Vienna: Kaiserlich-Königlichen Hof- und Staatsdruckerei.

Thissen, H.-J. 1994. Horapollonis Hieroglyphica. Prolegomena, in: Minas-Nerpel, M. and Zeidler, J. (eds.), *Aspekte spätägyptischer Kultur. Festschrift für Erich Winter zum 65. Geburtstag.* Aegyptiaca Treverensia 7. Mainz: Zabern, 255-263.

Tung, M. 2006. *Impresa Index to the Collections of Paradin, Giovio, Simeoni, Pittoni, Ruscelli, Contile, Camilli, Capaccio, Bargagli and Typotius.* AMS Studies in the Emblem 21. New York: AMS Press.

Volkmann, L. 1923. *Bilderschriften der Renaissance.* Leipzig: Hiersemann.

Warburg, A. 1905. Delle imprese amorose nelle più antiche incisioni fiorentine. *Rivista d'arte* 3, 1-14.

Warnke, M. 1999. Aby Warburg (1866-1929), in: Dilly, H. (ed.), *Altmeister moderner Kunstgeschichte.* Berlin: Reimer, 116-130.

Wind, E. 1937. Aenigma Termini. *Journal of the Warburg Institute* 1, 66-69.

Wittkower, R. 1937/38. Chance, Time and Virtue. *Journal of the Warburg and Courtauld Institutes* 1, 313-321.

Author address

Maren C. Biederbick
QSIT GmbH
Käthe-Paulus-Straße 8
85092 Kösching, Germany
maren.biederbick@q-sit.de

About the author

Maren C. Biederbick (*1980) studied Art History, European Ethnology, Roman Philology, and Early Modern History at the universities of Kiel (Germany) and Florence (Italy). She passed her Magister exam in 2008 and received her PhD in 2017 with the predicate "*magna cum laude*". From 2017 until 2019, she worked as a curator trainee and project manager at the German Museum for the History of Medicine in Ingolstadt (Germany). She has been a member of the Society for Emblem Studies since 2011, of the international research project Mundus Emblematicus since 2015 and a member of the Gesellschaft für die Geschichte der Wissenschaft, der Medizin und der Technik since 2017. Currently, she is working at QSIT GmbH.

Warscapes: Managing Space on the Western Front, 1914-1918

Christoph Nübel

Abstract

It is quite common to call the First World War a 'machine war' or a 'total war'. Both concepts highlight structural dynamics of warfare between 1914-1918 but hardly take geography or landscapes into account. Nevertheless, war might just as well be seen as a large-scale spatial encounter. This paper aims to show that the spaces of World War One were man-made and highly dynamic.

Firstly, it is assumed that a spatial analysis of the First World War needs to specify the relevant concepts. It is deficient just to make space a catchy label without developing a concise notion of space. Instead, it is necessary to identify particular physical or mental spaces which shall become the objects of research.

Secondly, by applying this assumption, this paper will elaborate on three categories of warscapes and ask how the German soldiers grappled with these spaces on the Western Front. The *environment* posed an enduring threat to the soldiers. Weather and ground conditions affected their living situation and forced them to develop ingenious techniques of trench building. The conditions of the *terrain* were under constant change: novel tactics were developed which permanently produced new spatial structures. At the same time, the soldiers had to learn about the microstructures of the front zone in order to stay orientated and to deal with the terrain during battle. Thus, a constant training of cognition and moves was necessary. The soldiers were well aware of the *landscapes*. While conceiving the destroyed countryside, they reflected on the war. Interestingly enough, they were able to make sense of all the chaos and destruction. Some welcomed the war as an opportunity to master nature, others complained about the devastation. In very different ways, landscapes served as a medium to come to terms with the war experiences. These three spatial studies show how the soldiers struggled to adapt to the warscapes of the Western Front.

in: Müller, J. and Ricci, A. 2020 (eds.), *Past Societies: Human Development in Landscapes*.
Sidestone Press: Leiden, 181-190.

Introduction

This paper focuses on the everyday life of German soldiers and considers how they conceived space and how they learned to adjust to the dangerous warscapes of the Western Front. It is inspired by Henri Lefebvre's dictum that

> *'every society* [...] *produces* [...] *its own space'*
> (Lefebvre 1991, 31).

Thus, space is not to be conceived as a given entity, but as man-made and highly dynamic. The conflict witnessed the production of various spaces. They are referred to as 'warscapes' here. Thus, fundamental experiences of the war were intrinsically spatial (Nübel 2014b). Warscapes became a prominent feature of the soldiers' war experiences and served as a sounding board for interpretations and conceptions of the war both during and after the conflict. As will become apparent, the war zone proved to be an unfamiliar space fundamentally at odds with civilian life. Here, spatial adaptation was a highly demanding process which occasionally ended in failure on behalf of individual soldiers. This is why images of warscapes often dealt with war's distressing nature and its calamities, together with notions of heroism, which have been conventionally more heavily emphasised in historical research.

In order to avoid getting lost in the concept of space as a vast and indeterminate historical category, it is necessary to identify specific spaces for research. Here, warscapes are understood through three distinct elements which at the same time form the structure of this paper: 1) The *environment* provided the basis for the soldiers' living conditions as affected by weather and ground conditions, 2) the conditions of the *terrain* were under constant change: novel tactics were developed which produced new and reversible spatial structures, and 3) soldiers were aware of the *landscape* as well. While beholding the obliterated countryside, they concomitantly contemplated the war. In very different ways, landscapes served as a medium to come to terms with their experiences of war. These three spaces are chosen here because they had a decisive influence on everyday life of the soldiers. As environment and terrain affected their conditions of survival, landscapes presented the visible life-space and mirrored their efforts to make sense of the war. The warscapes demonstrate that the war constantly created and profoundly transformed space, which made the problem of adjusting to space a perpetual challenge.

Environment: Fighting nature

In April 1916, Heinrich Röder, serving in the German Landsturm reserve forces, wrote that "the bad weather bothers us most". The situation had almost become unbearable

> *'because the body breaks down because it is wet and cold every day'*
> (20.4.1916, Röder 1916).

To the modern reader, it may be surprising that Röder's major source of concern was not the enemy's weapons, but instead environmental factors. Indeed, in their letters and diaries, soldiers' pens spilled more ink writing about the weather than the danger posed by bullets and shells. Soldiers were only directly involved in fighting for a comparably short amount of time. For example, in 1916 the Prussian 186th Infantry Regiment spent 32 days in heavy combat and several weeks on dangerous battlefields; however, much more time was spent either resting, on the march or in 'cushy sectors' (Pfeffer 1926, 276-277). Obviously, coping with the weather was a daily demand and was thus considered as the most notorious feature of wartime experience.

Two factors had an impact on the environmental conditions of the war. The natural geography and climate of the battlefield were remoulded and its harshness exacerbated by modern warfare. Subsequently, the military established more stringent regulations regarding the shape and construction of trenches, together with inspections and reports on trench conditions. Further indicative of the professionalisation of military environment management, authorities began to issue detailed regulations for trench building which relied on experience gained during the war. With the help of geologists, complex drainage systems with pumps and seepage pits were installed. The work of these scientists and engineers was conceived as an essential part of the war effort and thus labelled "water combating" (VII. Armeekorps 1915).

The purpose of fortified positions in the First World War was twofold: they strengthened the defence of a tactical position and enhanced the living conditions of the troops. The equilibrium between these two uses became increasingly fragile during the conflict due to its evolution into a war of attrition. The radicalisation of warfare manifested itself on the battlefield, as military necessities overshadowed concerns about living conditions. German regulations on trench building concentrated on the military value of the positions and showed how to construct strongpoints or wire entanglements. As the "*Allgemeines über Stellungsbau*" manual explicitly highlighted in 1918, "bearable conditions of life" in the trenches were only of secondary importance (Ludendorff 1922, 596). Instructions such as these illustrate the increasing exhaustion and decline of the German army towards the end of the war.

Terrain: Spacing trench warfare

The great firepower of modern weapons, tactical innovations and the extensive possibilities of field reconnaissance that came into existence around 1900 forced armies to consider the importance of the terrain. In 1913, the Prussian manual on terrain instruction stated that

> *'the impact of the terrain is steadily growing on every kind of military activity in the field'* (Leitfaden 1913, 1).

At this time, it was almost a truism that cover was of supreme importance during battle, although military training conferred greater honour on the offensive spirit over the necessity for seeking cover. The heavy losses, which all belligerents suffered during the battles in Belgium and France in 1914, proved the dangerousness of this preference. These bloody lessons and the interplay of technology and tactics made positional warfare the defining characteristic of warfare in the west.

Writing about the "battle landscape" ("*Schlachtenlandschaft*") in 1917, Heinrich Luz highlighted its "frontality". Everything seemed to be organised and directed to-

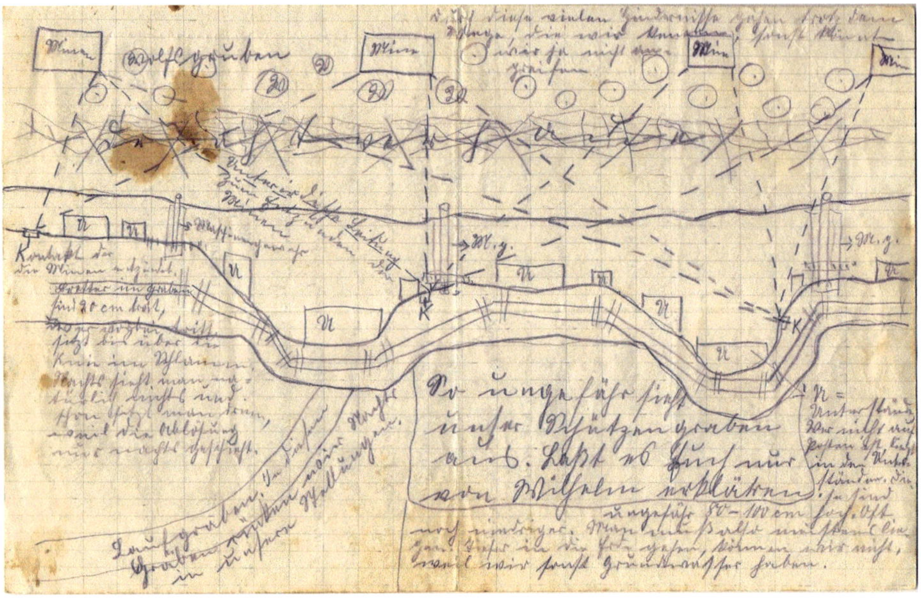

Figure 1. Private Carl Spiegelberg, Sketch, 7.2.1915 (Württembergische Landesbibliothek, Schüling Collection No. 4).

wards the enemy (Luz 1917, 19-20). Hence, in describing the spatiality of the front line, soldiers developed a specific language with 'left', 'right', 'ahead' and 'behind' being the pertinent terms. Trench warfare also had its own microstructure that was of utmost importance for soldiers. Single houses, trees or even bodies could serve as landmarks. They were anchor points for orientation and formed a reference grid. The terrain's properties became famous amongst soldiers, who then named these characteristic features. In naming and therefore engaging with the warscapes, a "soldiers' geography" emerged. Landmarks were labelled "Blood Lake" ("*Blutteich*") or "Devil's Mill" ("*Teufelsmühle*") (Liller Kriegszeitung 1916).

Writing to his parents in February 1915, Private Carl Spiegelberg tried to give them an overview of the spatiality of trench warfare (Fig. 1).

His sketch is a perfect example of the overwhelming complexity of the terrain. It contained communication and fire trenches, dugouts, wire entanglements, machine guns and much more. Finally, the complexity of his sketch necessitated him to add a remark advising his parents to ask somebody familiar with these issues for detailed explanation. Nonetheless, orientation proved problematic not only because it was common for units to be redeployed after spending several weeks in an area but also because the terrain itself was constantly transformed by shelling, mining and demolition. Moreover, changing tactics generated new forms of space.

Given the relentlessly changing terrain, armies' ability to adapt became a critical issue during the war. In November 1916, the German Supreme Army Command ("*Oberste Heeresleitung*", OHL) stated that *'development is in a state of permanent flux. Every day brings something new. Thus, we have to learn and relearn quickly in order to develop and apply new tools according to new circumstances'* (OHL 1916).

The OHL began to issue a range of new manuals, which aimed to turn soldiers into masters of the terrain. The increasing necessity of camouflage is one example in this respect (Nübel 2015).

The consequences of the ever-increasing spatial complexity of the terrain became clearly visible during operations. In early 1916, the 3rd battalion of the Bavarian 15th Infantry Regiment was ordered to conduct an attack on a 300-metre-wide stretch of French lines close to the village of Neuville-Saint-Vaast, situated in Artois between Arras and Vimy. A few days after the assault of 23 January, the battalion sent a detailed report to the regiment (15. bayerisches Infanterie-Regiment 1916). The central issue raised in the report was that attacks were not conducted all of a sudden, but instead carefully and individually prepared. The preparations described in this report took one week. By taking account of the superior importance of the terrain, the battalion was evidently trained in effective space management of the front-line microcosm.

First of all, they had to learn the composition of French positions in order to be able to interpret and implement their new stratagems; a problem solved by photographic aerial reconnaissance. The implementation of this spatial knowledge was increasingly efficient with the Bavarians building a special training site ("Übungswerk") several kilometres behind the front line. Here, they implemented all the spatial knowledge they had acquired, as this site was an exact copy of the French positions. It contained all trenches, dugouts and even craters that could be found on the real battlefield. In this surrounding, the battalion had good conditions to practise for the actual attack. During their seven days of training, small combat groups internalised the spatiality of the war zone. Thus, they were not only able to study the sequence of the attack but to practise their sense of orientation in order to avoid getting lost in the labyrinth of the enemy trench system.

Fighting commenced on a Sunday at 7:20 a.m. Mines were detonated, whilst artillery and machine guns fired at the French positions which, at the same time, were attacked by 540 German soldiers. After vigorous fighting, the battalion took 250 metres of the French trenches. As a consequence of this assault, 35 German and 100 French soldiers perished, 89 Frenchmen were taken prisoner and several hundred combatants were wounded on both sides (15. bayerisches Infanterie-Regiment 1916; Pages d'histoire 1916, 39). This outcome was seen as a success by the German officials. Obviously, the spatial training had reached its goal.

Landscape: Understanding devastation

Fighting at the Somme in 1916 and witnessing its immense artillery barrage, Ernst Jünger stated that

> *'this landscape is unforgettable for those who have seen it. A short while ago there were meadows and woods in this area. Of them, nothing, really not anything can be seen any more.* [...] *Every millimetre of the soil is ploughed up again and again.* [...] *In short, everything was made a desert'* (28.8.1916, Jünger 2010, 176-177).

These remarks show that war ravaged landscapes into wasteland, as they were transformed into an alien sphere where their former pastoral characteristics were extirpated. This made it even harder for soldiers to come to terms with the war. Struggling with the environment and learning about the terrain were indeed crucial for survival, but managing the landscape was equally vital. In 1913, philosopher Georg Simmel wrote that landscapes only came into existence through the mind. Humans conceived landscapes as "whole beings" as they always attributed meaning to them. According to Simmel, imagining and describing landscapes could be understood as a process of "sensemaking" (Simmel 1957, 141-152). Thus, soldiers' representations of their environments provided information about experiences of war and about the ways the soldiers tried to come to terms with the alienness surrounding them.

During the First World War, soldiers were living in a rapidly changing landscape. The dynamics of landscapes were understood as one of the most characteristic and disturbing features of the war, as landscapes were typically perceived as a stable entity which could possibly be altered over years, not within days. Soldiers were not silent while witnessing the destructive impact of the war on landscapes, as research has often suggested. The destroyed landscapes were not beyond their comprehension, as a wealth of descriptive accounts shows. Instead, they paid attention to them in order to give meaning to the war. Many soldiers perceived the front line as a zone of violence where destruction was commonplace. Eight months after his experience at the Somme, Jünger wrote that the "total alteration of the landscape" had become a "natural phenomenon" to him (27.4.1917, Jünger 2010, 243). Such changes give meaning to the term "shifting baselines" (Papworth *et al.* 2009). This term stems from ecological research and describes the phenomenon that man is barely aware of changes because the reference points with which he compares the transition are also in flux. Through this mode of thought, destroyed landscapes could even be understood as normal and not as alien. Thus, they became a less confusing feature of everyday life in wartime, for which the sometimes dry and laconic contemporary landscape descriptions often found in letters, diaries and even publications provide proof.

Many notions on landscapes shared the idea that mankind was the creator of the devastation. The making of war-torn landscapes could be interpreted as proof of either national superiority, the reckless ambitions of foes, or ruinous modernity. But there were other ways of interpreting the landscape, in which human responsibility for the developments hardly played a role. By naturalising landscape, destructive human agency was obscured. Such interpretations often referred to shell craters, certainly the most noticeable feature of the front line. A way to make the surroundings on the battlefield conceivable was to compare them with volcanoes. In 1914, Private Ernst Hiller likened the explosions of shells to volcanic eruptions, whereas others saw the combat zone as a mere "lava field" where "fire gullets ('*Feuerschlünde*') sprayed iron" (7.10.1914, Hiller 1914). These likenesses were in part created due to the increased public interest in volcanoes at the time of the First World War as a result of the spectacular eruptions of Mount Pelée in 1902 and Vesuvius in 1906, which were reported on as global media events. Moreover, the story of the destruction of Pompeii in 79 AD was widely known. Referring to Roman antiquity, the artilleryman Adolf Spemann described the battlefield of the Somme in 1916 as a "desert-like rubble ('*Trümmerwüste*') compared to which Pompeii is well preserved" (5.10.1916, Spemann 1916). The volcano was used as an interpretative pattern to understand and describe the power of modern warfare. When this analogy was used in troops' letters home, it was a striking metaphor to elucidate the remoteness and alienness of life in the war zone to loved ones at home.

But the meaning of war-torn landscapes was not restricted to desolation; it was also about beauty and hope. Many soldiers described the landscape as "impressive" (1.5.1916, Laue 1916) and concluded that it had a

> *'tremendously romantic appeal never seen before'* (5.2.1916, Spemann 1916).

It was an aesthetic environment that emerged during modern warfare. What is striking about these remarks is that they required a certain distance from direct combat. During fighting and mortal danger, soldiers were unlikely to have been so philosophical, but seen from the rear or when the guns fell silent, a more contemplative appreciation of the battlefield was possible. In such cases, aesthetic ideas were shared among soldiers.

A certain degree of a consoling aestheticism could be found in nature as well. Serving outdoors, the soldiers were deeply connected with the seasons and showed attentiveness for nature. They were keenly observant of the cyclic nature of time in order to make sense of the war. As spring saw the blossoming of vegetation, hopes were cherished that the war would soon come to an end or at least that trench life would become more bearable. Soldiers, such as the famous artist Otto Dix or the ordinary soldier Albrecht Ritz, drew sketches of gaping shell craters in a war-torn landscape with a variety of vegetation sprouting again, thus alluding to the strength of nature's regenerative power over the destructiveness of mankind (Nübel 2014a, 397). These images showed that war did not obliterate the cycle of life. Obviously, this was a way to come to terms with the horror of death caused by modern weaponry.

Conclusion

The history of the First World War is mirrored in the spaces of 1914-1918. They incessantly changed, and, in doing, so they proved that attritional warfare involved dynamism and radicalisation. Germany progressively lacked sufficient resources to cope with the spatial realities of the war, a fact that put increasingly high pressure on the army and made service difficult and dangerous for the soldiers. The environment, terrain and landscapes played a significant role in wartime experiences. They were utilised here as specific spatial examples which showed that managing warscapes was a highly challenging and complicated, yet indispensable, process.

In highlighting the close interrelations between man and space, the three warscape features chosen here had shared characteristics. Clearly, space was moulded and given meaning by human ideas and actions, but space in turn forced soldiers to adapt – thereby forming new experiences of war. Building infrastructure, military training and picturing the unfamiliar could be conceived as ways to cope with the danger and alienness of the war zone. These particular qualities engendered various interpretations and descriptions of warscapes and thus there were rather different ways and stories about coping with the challenges they posed in everyday life. In this respect, a broad spectrum of war images arose, which could not be described merely as heroic or nationalistic, because they pointed at the hardships of trench life and the formidable challenges of war.

Acknowledgements

I would like to thank the Graduate School "Human Development in Landscapes" for freely allowing me to conduct studies on the First World War in a truly academic fashion. This paper presents an extract of the results of my research which is published as Nübel 2014a.

References

15. bayerisches Infanterie-Regiment. 1916. *Combat Report,* 23.1.1916. Bayerisches Hauptstaatsarchiv/IV, HS 3181.

Hiller, E. 1914. *Papers.* Württembergische Landesbibliothek, Hiller Papers.

Jünger, E. 2010. Kriegstagebuch 1914-1918, in: Kiesel, H. (ed.), *Kriegstagebuch 1914-1918.* Stuttgart: Klett-Cotta, 176-177.

Laue, F. 1916. *Papers.* Württembergische Landesbibliothek, Schüling Collection No. 27.

Lefebvre, H. 1991. *The Production of Space.* Oxford, UK/Cambridge, MA: Blackwell.

Leitfaden für den Unterricht in der Feldkunde, im Aufnehmen und Planzeichnen auf den Königlichen Kriegsschulen. 1913[15]. Berlin: Mittler.

Liller Kriegszeitung 1916: *Liller Kriegszeitung* No. 37, 18.11.1916.

Ludendorff, E. 1922[4] (ed.), *Urkunden der Obersten Heeresleitung über ihre Tätigkeit 1916/18.* Berlin: Mittler.

Luz, W.A. 1917. Schlachtenlandschaft, in: *Flandrische Erde in Stimmungen und Bildern von Soldaten der 4. Armee.* Stuttgart: Deutsche Verlags-Anstalt 1917, 18-22.

Nübel, C. 2014a. *Durchhalten und Überleben an der Westfront. Raum und Körper im Ersten Weltkrieg.* Paderborn: Schöningh.

Nübel, C. 2014b. Raum in der Militärgeschichte und Gewaltgeschichte. Probleme, Ergebnisse und neue Felder der Forschung. *Militärgeschichtliche Zeitschrift* 73, 285-307.

Nübel, C. 2015. Modern warfare: camouflage tactics ('Tarnung') in the German army during the First World War. *First World War Studies* 6/2, 113-132.

OHL. 1916. *Oberste Heeresleitung, Report,* 22.11.1916. Hauptstaatsarchiv Stuttgart, M 34 Bü 130.

Pages d'histoire. 1916. Pages d'histoire – 1914-1916, vol. 18. Paris/Nancy.

Papworth, S.K., Rist, J., Coad, L., Milner-Gulland, E.J. 2009. Evidence for shifting baseline syndrome in conservation. *Conservation Letters* 2, 93-100.

Pfeffer, G. 1926 (ed.), *Geschichte des Infanterie-Regiments 186.* Oldenburg: Stalling.

Röder, H. 1916. *Papers.* Württembergische Landesbibliothek, Schüling Collection No. 136.

VII. Armeekorps. 1915. *VII. Armeekorps, Manual,* 12.1.1915, Bundesarchiv PH 14/241.

Simmel, G. 1957. *Brücke und Tür.* Stuttgart: Koehler.

Spemann, A. 1916. *Papers.* Hauptstaatsarchiv Stuttgart, M660/041.

Author address

Christoph Nübel
Zentrum für Militärgeschichte und Sozialwissenschaften der Bundeswehr/
Center for Military History and Social Sciences of the German Armed Forces
Zeppelinstrasse 127/128
14471 Potsdam, Germany
christoph1nuebel@bundeswehr.org

About the author

From 2008 to 2011, Christoph Nübel wrote his doctoral thesis at Kiel University. From 2011 to 2016 he was a research associate in 19th century European history at the History Department of Humboldt-Universität zu Berlin. Since 2016, he has been conducting research on contemporary military history at the Center for Military History and Social Sciences of the German Armed Forces. In 2012, he received the Werner Hahlweg prize for his PhD thesis. Nübel's research interests focus on military history, spatiality, security and memory studies.

Ethics in the Practice of Archaeology and the Making of Heritage: Understanding beyond the Material

Artur Ribeiro and Gustav Wollentz

Abstract

One of the most popular current trends in archaeology and heritage studies is New Materialisms. This trend has shifted the attention of scholars from a human and subject centred perspective of reality, to one focusing on objects in-themselves and the complex networks in which these objects navigate. Despite the interesting research that New Materialisms has generated, this trend has done little to engage in political and ethical critique, largely due to two central tenets of New Materialisms: that of distributed agency and essentialism.

With regards to agency, according to New Materialisms, it is argued that agency is distributed across a network of both humans and non-human objects, all mutually affecting each other. As pointed out by some critics, this conception of agency leads to problems concerning how we can ascertain responsibility, especially in sensitive contexts such as war contexts or political corruption. The risk of essentialism, on the other hand, is that it may recognise objects in-themselves, such as monuments, as containing within themselves aspects like beauty and inspiration, that in turn make them 'heritage'. However, recognising heritage as inherent hides the (seldom innocent) negotiation that makes heritage 'heritage'. This negotiation includes silences that are not valued as heritage and it is often built upon unequal power relations.

The aim of this paper is to demonstrate through the Gazimestan monument in Kosovo that both the idea of distributed agency and essentialism obscure complex problems when it comes to recognising responsibility for how heritage is recognised and managed in post-war environments. Rather than distributed agency and essentialism, this paper argues for the acceptance of heritage as a meaning-making process, where value associated with heritage is constantly negotiated.

in: Müller, J. and Ricci, A. 2020 (eds.), *Past Societies: Human Development in Landscapes*.
Sidestone Press: Leiden, 191-202.

Introduction

One of the most interesting trends that has come out of archaeology and heritage studies in recent years is New Materialisms (Witmore 2014). This trend embraces a wide variety of ideas, such as Bruno Latour's actor-network-theory (Webmoor and Witmore 2008; Witmore 2007), ontologies of objects (Olsen 2013; Olsen *et al.* 2012), assemblage theory (Fowler and Harris 2015; Harris 2017), speculative realism (Edgeworth 2016), and the vitalism of Jane Bennett (Crellin 2017). Despite vast differences separating individual ideas, there are certain fundamental common premises that underlie most of them. Furthermore, there is also a common animosity against the ideas developed under the rubric "postprocessual archaeology" (Alberti *et al.* 2013; Olsen 2012). According to the New Materialisms, postprocessual research is overly anthropocentric; it places the human at the centre of the universe, in a world of representations, dominated by significance created by the human subject. This perception has led postprocessual scholars to ignore the material world in which human subjects operate – it has favoured worldviews instead of the actual world.

Against this, New Materialisms advocate seeing the world in light of three ontological principles – reality is composed of things in themselves, these things are intricately connected to one another, and things are actors in their own right (Witmore 2014). Thus, rather than seeing the human as the sole initiator of actions, as the subject that acts towards passive objects, New Materialisms believe that action emerges from the interaction between humans and non-human objects. Furthermore, New Materialisms recognise that it is not only humans who are imbued with the capacity to act but that non-human objects are also imbued with "vibrancy" and energy of their own (Alberti *et al.* 2013, 16). What does this all entail in terms of heritage studies and archaeological practice? This varies from author to author, but there seems to be a general consensus that the best route is to adopt approaches that highlight the relationship between humans and objects (Watts 2013) with many archaeologists favouring Latour's actor-network-theory (Latour 1999; Latour 2005) or Hodder's entanglement theory (Hodder 2012). Both of these approaches are fully committed to the three ontological principles described above, but especially the principle that states that action starts not from human intention but rather from the relation between humans and objects. In Latour, this has been termed the '*principle of symmetry*', that is to say, human and objects are both agents in equal measure (or *actants* as Latour prefers to call them). Perceiving society in this manner allows us to bypass the subject-object dichotomy that, according to Latour, prevents us from understanding the nature of social collectives (Latour 1999).

The New Materialisms have given rise to some very interesting research (*e.g.* Fowler 2013; Whitridge 2004) and despite their general popularity, many archaeologists remain sceptical as to their widespread applicability. The aim of this paper is to highlight the shortcomings of New Materialisms with research cases involving nuanced ethical issues, and how the New Materialisms have misunderstood agency theory by ignoring responsibility. This will be exemplified by looking at the process of "making heritage" in the context of the Gazimestan monument in Kosovo, which we will touch upon later. The reason why we focus on the making of heritage is that it puts ideas of responsibility and essentialism to the forefront, which gains heightened resonance with regards to difficult heritage such as the Gazimestan monument.

It is important to note that we do not claim to cover all attitudes and perspectives among the New Materialisms in this short chapter. Instead, we are focusing on a specific trend which takes its main influence from Bruno Latour. Thus, we do not argue that all supporters of the New Materialisms fall into the traps of essentialism outlined here. Rather than an overarching critique of the New Materialisms, it is an attempt to highlight shortcomings in order to navigate ways forward.

Responsibility and Essentialism

Amidst the several issues surrounding the New Materialisms, there are two which we would like to highlight: first, the New Materialisms have done little to engage with ethical and political critique (Appadurai 2015, 222); and second, New Materialisms seem to involve a return to essentialism, *i.e.,* that objects have essential qualities to them, which are not imposed on them by human actors. Both of these concerns have dire consequences when it comes to understanding the role of ethics in archaeology and heritage studies.

To use Latour's classic example: when it comes to gun violence, it is important to think beyond whether the problem lies exclusively with humans or guns but to think of both humans and guns as responsible for gun violence. A gun becomes a different object in the hands of a person and accordingly, a human is also different the moment he or she has a gun. Ultimately, this means that to understand gun violence, rather than thinking of the human actor (the subject) and the gun (the object) as independent, we have to think in terms of hybrid actors composed of relations between humans + guns. Latour goes on to argue that when we recognise social reality in these terms it becomes possible to understand why responsibility needs to be shared among the various agents involved in gun violence (Latour 1999, 180).

While logically attractive, this type of reasoning involves some serious consequences regarding the role of ethics and ultimately, what it means to be an agent in society. The concept of agency is one that has been discussed in philosophy for centuries and central to this discussion is the idea that an agent has "freedom to choose otherwise". What does this mean? This means that agents have to be aware that they are acting purposefully, that is, with an aim in mind. Without being aware of these purposes, it is impossible to choose not to act (Ribeiro 2016). Returning to Latour's gun example, in many situations where gun violence occurs (*e.g.* such as in the USA), it is assumed that humans are in a position in which they can choose not to shoot a gun. The same, however, cannot be said of guns. This is why we must assume, in the case of gun violence, that it is humans who are responsible for gun violence (*e.g.* criminals, gun manufacturers, members of gun associations, gun lobbyists, *etc.*). Latour's principle of symmetry promotes the ontological equalisation of all objects, human and non-human, yet ignores the historical processes that lead to real-world asymmetries that not only separate humans from objects, but also humans from other humans. Thus, regardless of how effective actor-network theory might seem at face-value, its method of analysis automatically precludes it from recognising the asymmetrical differences between, for example, school shooters in the US, who act out of their own volition, and child soldiers in Africa, who are coerced into wars not of their own choosing.

Prima facie, it seems that what we are arguing is that humans have to deal with responsibility, unlike inert objects (*e.g.* guns), because humans are agents, but this is not entirely correct. Following Friedrich Hegel's work on ethics and freedom, it must be understood that humans can be considered agents because of the ethical role humans have placed upon themselves (Pippin 2008). In other words, humans do not have responsibility because they have agency, they have agency because they have responsibility. When viewed under this light, we are able to understand why agency must be socio-historically contextualised.

Following this logic, it becomes clear why the New Materialisms have had a difficult time in engaging in political and ethical critique – it is because they lack any explanation of how responsibility and the power that comes with responsibility comes into play in past and modern societies. As argued by Slavoj Žižek, according to the New Materialisms the Holocaust can be conceived as a network in which the Nazis, the trains, the gas ovens, and the Jews are all agents (Žižek 2014, footnote 8). This is what Latour wants us to see as "symmetry" among agents.

The second issue raised by New Materialism concerns its implicit essentialism. In archaeology and heritage studies, this has been expressed by a desire to "re-member things" (Olsen 2003). As stated earlier, New Materialists wish to overcome the inherent bias that the humanities and the social sciences put on human beings and shift toward approaches that see reality as comprised of networks of humans and objects. Accordingly, the New Materialisms believe that objects are irreducible to human representations of them, that is, it is not about "things-for-us" but "things-in-themselves". Where do the problems lie in essentialism?

It seems uncontroversial to state that granite has some inherent properties to it, like its grainy texture and the presence of feldspar and quartz. These elements are essential to granite. However, it is much harder to argue that granite is, in its essence, monumental or beautiful. It becomes even harder to find essential qualities in things like social institutions, such as democracy for instance. When faced with things like democracy, a concept that is continuously contested (Gallie 1955-1956), New Materialists are pushed into a corner. Either democracy has to be perceived as nothing but an illusion that has no material properties, which would automatically make the New Materialisms irrelevant to any political type of discussion, or they have to argue that democracy involves some inherent and essential material elements. This latter argument is difficult to pull off because what might be democratic in one country might be considered undemocratic in another. Although democracy can manifest materially (such as voting through locales, voting cards, *etc.*), and can even manifest in the form of a network, democracy is at the same time irreducible to these manifestations and networks. Indeed, it is possible, albeit difficult, to imagine a democratic system that leaves no tangible traces, for instance if voting is caste verbally or through bodily movement (such as raising your hand) instead of through voting cards. How does one then identify the essential qualities of democracy? Like the problems associated to agency, the problems associated to essentialism puts the New Materialisms in a position where it becomes even harder for it to make any substantial contributions to political or ethical critique.

We would like to pose the following basic, but nonetheless fundamental question: what is it that makes heritage "heritage"? If we venture to when the so-called Authorized Heritage Discourse (AHD) (Smith 2006) was first established in the Western world during the 19th century, heritage was approached as found *within* specific sites and thus based on perceived eternal values residing somewhere inside of their very own materiality, waiting to be retrieved by the heritage expert (see Fredheim and Khalaf 2016 for an excellent discussion of heritage values). Usually, these inherent values were based on perceived age, monumentality, or beauty (Sørensen 2013). Even though heritage practice is still, more often than not, functioning within the premise inherited from AHD (Högberg 2012), there has been considerable criticism directed towards AHD (*i.e.* Lowenthal 1985; Smith 2006; Kisić 2016), which has been influencing more recent legislations and frameworks (for example, Council of Europe 2005). Within these approaches, heritage is a never-finalised, meaning-making process carried on through embodied engagements and is, therefore, both inherently dissonant and inherently intangible (Smith 2006; Kisić 2016). It follows that heritage is not found within material culture. Instead, it is continuously produced through human interactions. Heritage is *creating* values but it is not a *created* value.

Such an argument does not sit well with the New Materialisms, but why is this the case? When Laurajane Smith provokingly argued that

> *'Stonehenge, for instance, is basically a collection of rocks in a field'*
> (Smith 2006, 3),

the statement led to attacks from some proponents of New Materialisms (Solli 2011, 45; Olsen *et al.* 2012, 201; Pétursdóttir 2013; Olsen and Witmore 2015, 193). Instead, it was (re)enforced that Stonehenge is in fact heritage based on its own *inherent values*. Whether these values are of inherent "stoniness" (Solli 2011, 45) or of inherent "difference" (Olsen *et al.* 2012, 201) seemed to be less clear. It would be easy to argue that proponents of the New Materialisms lashed out against what they perceived to be a disregard of the materiality of Stonehenge, and in so doing, ventured to essentialism. But to say that heritage is not inherent is not the same as saying that materiality does not matter (see also Carman 2009; Jones 2010; 2016; Holtorf, 2013; 2017). This can be illustrated through a thought experiment which takes the argument to its logical conclusion: to say that heritage is inherent would inevitably mean that Stonehenge would still be "heritage" even if no humans existed. Nonetheless, a dog in a post-human world would just as gladly pee against the stones of Stonehenge as it would pee against any other stone it may come across.

It is also within this argument that essentialism and ethics can be regarded as two sides of the same coin. To see heritage as "inherent" *naturalises* the processes which serve to make heritage "heritage". If these processes are seen as natural and self-given, they are not only disregarded, but they are also *legitimised.* To build upon the work of Michel-Rolph Trouillot (1995), such an approach carries silences which serve to hide the (often unequal) power-relations informing and shaping heritage. Nowhere else is this more apparent than concerning post-war heritage, simply because in no other environment is it more ethically vital to *not* muddy the issue of responsibility. Therefore, we would like to illustrate the argument through the Gazimestan monument in Kosovo, where one of the authors (GW) has conducted fieldwork.

Figure 1. The Gazimestan monument (photo: G. Wollentz).

Ethics in the context of the Gazimestan monument

The Gazimestan monument (Fig. 1) was built in 1953 on order from the Serbian government, on the field of Kosovo, in remembrance of the 1389 battle of Kosovo Field where a coalition of Christian forces fought against the Ottoman Empire.

There is no space here to go into any details concerning the battle and its history (see instead Emmert 1990; Vucinich and Emmert 1991; Malcolm 1998, 140; Ćirković 2004, 77-119; Rexha 2009). What is significant for the argument is that the battle became highly mythologised in Serbia, especially during the 19th century struggle for Serbian independence from the Ottoman Empire. Additionally, the myth was employed by Slobodan Milošević during and preceding the breakup of Yugoslavia, emphasised by a famous speech by Milošević held at the Gazimestan monument on the 28th of June (so-called Vidovdan) 1989, on the 600th anniversary of the battle.

Annual gatherings at the Gazimestan monument are still occurring on Vidovdan, and they often include groups of Serbian nationalists proclaiming anti-Albanian propaganda (see Duijzings 2000, 176-202; 2005; Bieber 2002; Popović 2007; Djokić 2009; Čolović 2011; Wollentz 2019).[1] At the time of writing this chapter, approximately 20 years have passed since the 1998-1999 war between Kosovo and Serbia, and Serbia has

1 With this we do not argue that every Serbian participating at the Gazimestan monument on Vidovdan is a nationalist. Instead, Serbians may participate on Vidovdan for a wide array of reasons.

yet to recognise the independence of Kosovo, which was adopted on February 17th, 2008. Therefore, the Gazimestan monument plays a role within a dormant, but not resolved, conflict.

When interviewing the local population living close to the monument, who are mostly Kosovo Albanians, it was investigated how responsibility was framed surrounding the Gazimestan monument. The Gazimestan monument is often made meaningful (or denied meaning) by the local population based on actions of individuals, such as the actions of Slobodan Milošević; *i.e.,* based on the intentions perceived to lie *behind* the monument, not within the monument. This does not mean that the monument is inevitably bound to the perceived intentions of specific actors. On the contrary, I noted how individuals employed time in order to position the monument within various temporalities. While the perceived "pastness" of material culture is based upon multiple factors, such as material clues, including use-wear, the expectations of the audience and a plausible narrative linking past and present (Holtorf 2013; 2017), individuals may play an active role in temporally positioning heritage, which fundamentally affects how responsibility is being framed. Let us provide two examples among the people interviewed.

A male Kosovo Albanian taxi driver in his mid-thirties living in Obilić/Kastriot stated that the Gazimestan monument was constructed in 1989 by Slobodan Milošević. When it is mentioned to him that this is not the case, he did not seem interested to learn more. The off-the-cuff argument that only deep engagement is significant when analysing the different emotional responses to heritage is a common bias within heritage studies. However, shallow and banal engagement with heritage can in certain instances be more meaningful than deep engagement (Smith and Campbell 2015). To not *want* to feel anything, to *reject engagement,* is also meaningfully constituted. Acknowledging the agency of individuals also demands acknowledging other forms engagement with heritage than simply the ones connected to deep commitment and/or emotion. A few questions later on in the interview, the man was asked whether the monument should be left as it is, prompting him to remark that it should be destroyed "because it was of Milošević, and he is a criminal".[2] Here we can see how the temporal positioning of the monument to 1989 strongly affected his views on responsibility. The fact that Slobodan Milošević was only 12 years old when the monument was constructed does not stop the interviewee from calling the monument Milošević's. Following his reasoning, the monument should be destroyed because it is Milošević's monument who was acting with criminal intentions, and who should be held responsible for those actions.

A radically different example came from a director of a kindergarten in her mid-sixties, who is Kosovo Albanian and lives in Pristina. She argued, in contrast, that the Gazimestan monument was "hundreds of years old" and that it did not bother her since it had been there for such a long time. Consequently, temporally positioning the heritage into a distant and irrelevant past made the issue of responsibility irrelevant. This refers to a temporal positioning which is aimed at *gaining* distance to the past, and thus locating it as part of "history" *instead* of "heritage". Drawing on the work of Sharon Macdonald (2006, 22; 2009), there is a distinct difference between concep-

2 It is important to keep in mind that a large majority of the people of the Kosovo Albanian population, who were interviewed, expressed no wish to see the monument destroyed.

tualising the past as part of history, on the one hand, and conceptualising it, on the other hand, as part of heritage. This is because heritage is fundamentally concerned with finding continuity with the past, constituting a sense of belonging (Ashworth *et al.* 2007, 1). Within the interview presented above, the opposite is at play. Later in the interview when she states that "it doesn't matter who won or who lost. It is just a remembrance", the woman cuts away all possible ideas of continuity or relevance, and instead expresses a desire to let the monument simply be left standing in the landscape within an opened rift into an irrelevant and long-gone past. Analysed within the context of Vidovdan, with Serbians travelling to the monument every year on the 28th of June due to the monument's perceived significance and role for the present, often in order to make future claims on the soil of Kosovo opposed to the Kosovo Albanians, the production of *irrelevance* may be the strongest counter-statement possible.

Within a post-war environment, a recognition of where responsibility is placed for war crimes is vital in order for people to achieve a sense of truth and justice (Viejo Rose 2011). Therefore, to "blame" a war on a monument (such as the Gazimestan monument) or a myth (such as the myth of the Kosovo Battle), and in such a way attribute agency to these elements, can be ethically precarious. Instead of attributing agency or inherent values to such elements, this example provides an illustration of the necessity to recognise responsibility as a prerequisite for agency, and how individuals may acquire agency through various strategies of engaging with material culture, including forms of challenging its very significance, relevance and status as heritage. In other words: no heritage can be regarded as "natural" or "self-given". Thus, we argue that nothing is inherently heritage even though everything carries the potential to become or stop becoming heritage through (un)meaning-making processes and, with that, responsibility arises.

Acknowledgements

We would like to thank the Graduate School "Human Development in Landscapes" for their support. For the conducted fieldwork, GW would like to thank Edona Rugova, Dea Luma and Marko Barišić for their essential help as translators in many of the interviews and through exciting discussions. Further thanks are due to Cornelius Holtorf, Antonia Davidovic, Johannes Müller, Milot Berisha, Boban Todorović, Enver Rexha, Haxhi Methmetaj and all the anonymous interview partners.

References

Alberti, B., Jones, A.M., Pollard, J. 2013. *Archaeology after interpretation: returning materials to archaeological theory.* Walnut Creek, CA: Left Coast Press.

Appadurai, A. 2015. Mediants, materiality, normativity. *Public Culture* 27, 221-237.

Ashworth, G.J., Graham, G., Tunbridge, J.E. 2007. *Pluralising pasts: heritage, identity and place in multicultural societies*. London: Pluto Press.

Bieber, F. 2002. Nationalist Mobilization and Stories of Serb Suffering: The Kosovo myth from 600th anniversary to the present. *Rethinking History* 6/1, 95-110.

Carman, J. 2009. Where the Value Lies: The Importance of Materiality to the Immaterial Aspects of Heritage, in: Smith, L. and Waterton, E. (eds.), *Taking Archaeology out of Heritage.* Newcastle upon Tyne: Cambridge Scholars Publishing, 192-208.

Ćirković, S.M. 2004. The Serbs. Malden, MA: Blackwell.

Čolović, I. 2011. The Balkans: The Terror of Culture: Essays in Political Anthropology. Baden-Baden: Nomos Verlagsgesellschaft.

Council of Europe 2005. Council of Europe Framework Convention on the Value of Cultural Heritage for Society. https://rm.coe.int/1680083746 [07.02.2018].

Crellin, R.J. 2017. Changing Assemblages: Vibrant Matter in Burial Assemblages. *Cambridge Archaeological Journal* 27, 111-125.

Djokić, D. 2009. Whose Myth? Which Nation? The Serbian Kosovo Myth Revisited, in: Bak, J., Jarnut, J., Monnet, P., Schneidmueller, B. (eds.), *Uses and Abuses of the Middle Ages: 19th-21st Century.* Munich: Wilhelm Fink Verlag, 215-233.

Duijzings, G. 2000. *Religion and the politics of identity in Kosovo*. London: Hurst.

Duijzings, G. 2005. New myths are needed: reconciliation in Kosovo as an intellectual challenge. *Studia Historica Nitriensia* 12, 263-267.

Edgeworth, M. 2016. Grounded objects. Archaeology and speculative realism. *Archaeological Dialogues* 23, 93-113.

Emmert, T. 1990. *Serbian Golgotha: Kosovo, 1389.* Boulder: East European Monographs.

Fowler, C. and Harris, O. 2015. Enduring relations: Exploring a paradox of new materialism. *Journal of Material Culture*, 1-22.

Fredheim, L.H. and Khalaf, M. 2016. The significance of values: heritage value typologies re-examined. *International Journal of Heritage Studies* 22/6, 466-481.

Gallie, W.B. 1955-1956. Essentially Contested Concepts. *Proceedings of the Aristotelian Society* 56, 167-198.

Harris, O.J.T. 2017. Assemblages and Scale in Archaeology. *Cambridge Archaeological Journal* 27, 127-139.

Hodder, I. 2012. *Entangled: an archaeology of the relationships between humans and things.* Malden, MA: Wiley-Blackwell.

Högberg, A. 2012. The Voice of the Authorized Heritage Discourse: A critical analysis of signs at ancient monuments in Skåne, southern Sweden. *Current Swedish Archaeology* 20, 131-167.

Holtorf, C. 2013. On Pastness: A Reconsideration of Materiality in Archaeological Object Authenticity. *Anthropological Quarterly* 86/2, 427-443.

Holtorf, C. 2017. Perceiving the Past: From Age Value to Pastness. *International Journal of Cultural Property* 24, 497-515.

Jones, S. 2010. Negotiating Authentic Objects and Authentic Selves: Beyond the Deconstruction of Authenticity. *Journal of Material Culture* 15/2, 181-203.

Jones, S. 2016. Unlocking Essences and Exploring Networks: Experiencing Authenticity in Heritage Education Settings, in: Van Boxtel, C., Grever, M., Klein, S. (eds.), *Sensitive Pasts: Questioning Heritage in Education.* New York/Oxford: Berghahn Books, 130-152.

Kisić, V. 2016. *Governing Heritage Dissonance: Promises and Realities of Selected Cultural Policies.* European Cultural Foundation. Belgrade: Vizartis

Latour, B. 1999. *Pandora's hope: essays on the reality of science studies.* Cambridge, MA/ London: Harvard University Press.

Latour, B. 2005. *Reassembling the social: an introduction to actor-network-theory*. Oxford: Oxford University Press.

Lowenthal, D. 1985. The Past is a Foreign Country. Cambridge: Cambridge University Press.

Macdonald, S. 2006. Undesirable Heritage: Fascist Material Culture and Historical Consciousness in Nuremberg. *International Journal of Heritage Studies* 12/1, 9-28.

Macdonald, S. 2009. *Difficult Heritage: Negotiating the Nazi Past in Nuremberg and Beyond*. Abingdon: Routledge.

Malcolm, N. 1998. *Kosovo: a short history*. London: Macmillan.

Olsen, B. 2003. Material culture after text: re-membering things. *Norwegian Archaeological Review* 36, 87-104.

Olsen, B. 2012. After interpretation: Remembering archaeology. *Current Swedish Archaeology* 20, 11-34.

Olsen, B. 2013. *In defense of things: archaeology and the ontology of objects*. Lanham, MD/Plymouth: AltaMira Press.

Olsen, B. and Witmore, C. 2015. Archaeology, symmetry, and the ontology of things: A response to critics. *Archaeological Dialogues* 22/2, 187-197.

Olsen, B., Shanke, M., Webmore, T., Witmore, C. 2012. *Archaeology: the discipline of things*. Berkeley, CA: University of California Press.

Pétursdóttir, Þ. 2013. Concrete matters: Ruins of modernity and the things called heritage. *Journal of Social Archaeology* 13/1, 31-53.

Pippin, R.B. 2008. *Hegel's practical philosophy: rational agency as ethical life*. Cambridge/New York: Cambridge University Press.

Popović, M.V. 2007 [1976]. Vidovdan i casni krst. Biblioteka XX Vek. Belgrade: Čigoja štampa.

Rexha, E. 2009. *Historiografia Serbe Per Kosoven (XIII-XIX)*. Prishtine.

Ribeiro, A. 2016. Against object agency. A counterreaction to Sørensen's 'Hammers and Nails'. *Archaeological Dialogues* 23, 229-235.

Smith, L. 2006. *Uses of heritage*. Abington: Routledge.

Smith, L. and Campbell, G. 2015. The elephant in the room: Heritage, affect and emotion, in: Logan, W., Nic Craith, M., Kockel, U. (eds.), *A companion to heritage studies*. Malden, MA: Wiley-Blackwell, 443-460.

Sørensen, T.F. 2013. We Have Never Been Latourian: Archaeological Ethics and the Posthuman Condition. *Norwegian Archaeological Review* 46/1, 1-18.

Solli, B. 2011. Some Reflections on Heritage and Archaeology in the Anthropocene. *Norwegian Archaeological Review* 44/1, 40-54.

Trouillot, M.R. 1995. *Silencing the past: power and the production of history*. Boston, MA: Beacon Press.

Viejo-Rose, D. 2011. *Reconstructing Spain: Cultural Heritage and Memory after Civil War*. Brighton: Sussex Academic Press.

Vucinich, W. and Emmert, T. 1991 (eds.), *Kosovo: Legacy of a Medieval Battle*. Minneapolis, MN: University of Minnesota Press.

Watts, C.M. 2013. *Relational archaeologies: humans, animals, things*. London/New York: Routledge.

Webmoor, T. and Witmore, C.L. 2008. Things are us! A commentary on human/things relations under the banner of a 'social' archaeology. *Norwegian Archaeological Review* 41, 53-70.

Whitridge, P. 2004. Whales, Harpoons, and Other Actors: Actor-Network-Theory and Hunter-Gatherer Archaeology, in: Crothers, G.M. (ed.), *Hunters and Gatherers in Theory and Archaeology.* Carbondale, IL: Southern Illinois University, 445-474.

Witmore, C.L. 2007. Symmetrical archaeology: excerpts of a manifesto. *World Archaeology* 39, 546-562.

Witmore, C.L. 2014. Archaeology and the new materialisms. *Journal of Contemporary Archaeology* 1, 203-246.

Wollentz, G. 2019. Conflicted memorials and the need to look forward. The interplay between remembering and forgetting in Mostar and on the Kosovo Field, in: Sørensen, M.L.S., Viejo-Rose, D., Filippucci, P. (eds.), *Memorials in the Aftermath of Armed Conflict: From History to Heritage.* London: Palgrave Macmillan, 159-182.

Žižek, S. 2014. *Absolute Recoil: Towards a New Foundation of Dialectical Materialism.* London/New York: Verso.

Author addresses

Artur Ribeiro
Research Fellow
CRC 1266: Scales of Transformation –
Human-Environmental Interaction
in Prehistoric and Archaic Societies
Kiel University
Leibnizstr. 3, R. 136
24118 Kiel, Germany
aribeiro@gshdl.uni-kiel.de

Gustav Wollentz
Project Leader / Research Assistant
Nordic Centre of Heritage Learning and Creativity
Arkivvägen 1, 831 31 Östersund, Sweden
gustav.wollentz@nckultur.org

About the authors

Artur Ribeiro is an archaeologist who obtained his BA degree in archaeology at the University of Lisbon, his MA at University College London, and his PhD at the Graduate School "Human Development in Landscapes", Kiel University, Germany. He worked for many years as a contract archaeologist in Portugal and Ireland, having excavated prehistoric, Roman, and modern sites. Currently, he is working as a Research Fellow at Kiel University on the impact of climate events on prehistoric societies on the Iberian Peninsula. He has also produced extensive work on archaeological theory with a particular emphasis on the relation of historical understanding and archaeological interpretation, the concept of intentionality and teleology in archaeology, and the importance and role of posthumanist approaches in archaeological practice.

Gustav Wollentz defended his PhD in the summer of 2018 at the Graduate School "Human Development in Landscapes", Kiel University, Germany, focusing on the relationship between difficult heritage and temporalities, which involved fieldwork in Mostar and in Kosovo. He received his Bachelor's and his Master's degree in Archaeology from Linnaeus University in Sweden. He was previously (2012-2013) involved in the research project 'One hundred thousand years back and forth: Archaeology meets Radioactive waste', led by Cornelius Holtorf and Anders Högberg at Linnaeus University, studying future perspectives within heritage management. In 2014, he was involved in a project at Kalmar County Museum, focusing on how heritage can be used as a resource in conflict resolution. He is a member of the team involved with the research on the ringfort Sandby borg, on Öland, Sweden. In 2018 and in 2019, he was hired within the AHRC-funded "Heritage Futures" research programme to co-author a chapter on "Toxic heritage". He is currently working as a project leader / research assistant at the Nordic Centre of Heritage Learning and Creativity.

Publications in the Series of the Kiel Graduate School "Human Development in Landscapes"

Band 1
Kiel Graduate School "Human Development in Landscapes", Workshop and Session Organizers (eds.)
Landscapes and Human Development: The Contribution of European Archaeology
Proceedings of the International Workshop "Socio-Environmental Dynamics over the last 12,000 Years: The Creation of Landscapes (1st-4th April 2009)"
Universitätsforschungen zur prähistorischen Archäologie 191 (Bonn 2010)
307 p., numerous illustrations
ISBN 978-3-7749-3709-3

Band 2
Jutta Kneisel/Wiebke Kirleis/Marta Dal Corso/Nicole Taylor/Verena Tiedtke (eds.)
Collapse or Continuity? Environment and Development of Bronze Age Human Landscapes
Proceedings of the International Workshop "Socio-Environmental Dynamics over the last 12,000 Years: The Creation of Landscapes II (14th -18th March 2011)" in Kiel, Volume 1
[Human Development in Landscapes, Graduate School at the University of Kiel]
Universitätsforschungen zur prähistorischen Archäologie 205 (Bonn 2012)
279 p., numerous partially coloured illustrations
ISBN 978-3-7749-3763-5

Band 3
Martin Furholt/Martin Hinz/Doris Mischke (eds.)
"As time goes by?" Monumentality, Landscapes and the Temporal Perspective
Proceedings of the International Workshop "Socio-Environmental Dynamics over the last 12,000 Years: The Creation of Landscapes II (14th -18th March 2011)" in Kiel, Volume 2
[Human Development in Landscapes, Graduate School at the University of Kiel]
Universitätsforschungen zur prähistorischen Archäologie 206 (Bonn 2012)
263 p., numerous partially coloured illustrations
ISBN 978-3-7749-3764-2

Band 4
Robert Hofmann/Fevzi-Kemal Moetz/Johannes Müller (eds.)
Tells: Social and Environmental Space
Proceedings of the International Workshop "Socio-Environmental Dynamics over the last 12,000 Years: The Creation of Landscapes II (14th -18th March 2011)" in Kiel, Volume 3
[Human Development in Landscapes, Graduate School at the University of Kiel]
Universitätsforschungen zur prähistorischen Archäologie 207 (Bonn 2012)
233 p., numerous partially coloured illustrations
ISBN 978-3-7749-3765-9

Band 5
Fevzi-Kemal Moetz
Sesshaftwerdung – Aspekte der Niederlassung im Neolithikum in Obermesopotamien
Universitätsforschungen zur prähistorischen Archäologie 244 (Bonn 2014)
327 p., numerous partially coloured illustrations, 47 tables
ISBN 978-3-7749-3873-1

Band 6
Jutta Kneisel/Marta Dal Corso/Wiebke Kirleis/Heiko Scholz/Nicole Taylor/Verena Tiedtke (eds.)
The Third Food Revolution? Setting the Bronze Age Table: Common Trends in Economic and Subsistence Strategies in Bronze Age Europe
Proceedings of the International Workshop "Socio-Environmental Dynamics over the last 12,000 Years: The Creation of Landscapes III (15th -18th April 2013)" in Kiel
Universitätsforschungen zur prähistorischen Archäologie 283 (Bonn 2015)
288 p., numerous partially coloured illustrations
ISBN 978-3-7749-4003-1

Band 7
Nicole Taylor
Burning Questions – Identity and Late Bronze Age / Early Iron Age Cremation Cemeteries
Universitätsforschungen zur prähistorischen Archäologie 286 (Bonn 2016)
172 p., numerous illustrations
ISBN 978-3-7749-4029-1

Band 8
Ralph Großmann
Das dialektische Verhältnis von Schnurkeramik and Glockenbecher zwischen Rhein und Saale
Universitätsforschungen zur prähistorischen Archäologie 287 (Bonn 2016)
280 p., numerous partially coloured illustrations
ISBN 978-3-7749-4035-2

Band 9
Martin Furholt/Ralph Großmann/Marzena Szmyt (eds.)
Transitional Landscapes? The 3rd Millennium BC in Europe
Proceedings of the International Workshop "Socio-Environmental Dynamics over the last 12,000 Years: The Creation of Landscapes III (15th -18th April 2013)" in Kiel
Universitätsforschungen zur prähistorischen Archäologie 292 (Bonn 2016)
230 p., numerous partially coloured illustrations
ISBN 978-3-7749-4061-1

Band 10
Monica De Cet
Long-term Social Development on a Mediterranean Island: Menorca between 1600 BCE and 1900 CE
Universitätsforschungen zur prähistorischen Archäologie 303 (Bonn 2017)
240 p., numerous partially coloured illustrations
ISBN 978-3-7749-4113-7

Band 11
Svend Hansen/Johannes Müller (eds.)
Rebellion and Inequality in Archaeology
Proceedings of the Kiel Workshops "Archaeology of Rebellion" (2014) and "Social Inequality as a Topic in Archaeology" (2015)
Universitätsforschungen zur prähistorischen Archäologie 308 (Bonn 2017)
332 p., numerous partially coloured illustrations
ISBN 978-3-7749-4132-8

Band 12
Marta Dal Corso
Environmental History and Development of the Human Landscape in a Northeastern Italian Lowland During the Bronze Age: a Multidisciplinary Case-Study
Universitätsforschungen zur prähistorischen Archäologie 312 (Bonn 2018)
232 p., numerous partially coloured illustrations
ISBN 978-3-7749-4151-9

Band 13
Stefanie Bergemann
Zauschwitz (Landkreis Leipzig): Siedlungen und Gräber eines neolithischen Fundplatzes
Universitätsforschungen zur prähistorischen Archäologie 314 (Bonn 2018)
436 p., numerous partially coloured illustrations
ISBN 978-3-7749-4155-7

Band 14
Artur Ribeiro
Archaeology and the Historical Understanding
Universitätsforschungen zur prähistorischen Archäologie 318 (Bonn 2018)
192 p., coloured illustrations
ISBN 978-3-7749-4168-7

Band 15
Maria Gelabert Oliver
Landscape Distribution of Talaiotic Monuments as Markers of Social Space
Universitätsforschungen zur prähistorischen Archäologie 323 (Bonn 2018)
253 p., numerous partially coloured illustrations
ISBN 978-3-7749-4190-8

Band 16
Gianpiero Di Maida
Marks on the Rocks
Universitätsforschungen zur Prähistorischen Archäologie 343 (Bonn 2020)
352 p., numerous partially coloured illustrations and a catalogue
ISBN 978-3-7749-4238-7